## Letter

*Randy does not "love" Cindy. Randy hates Cindy.*

*Randy hates Cindy's face makeup.*

*Randy hates Cindy's lipstick.*

*Randy hates Cindy's blond hair.*

*Randy hates Cindy's ugly toes—they're the ugliest toes he's ever seen.*

*Randy hates all of Cindy's 5 or 6 perfumes.*

The list went on and on, to the agonizing limits of human endurance. With growing fascination, the police read this note that Cindy Roth had written to herself shortly before her death. This, then, was the truth about her marriage to her "Prince Charming," Randy Roth. But it was only the first of the many damning discoveries about the monster behind Roth's mask of moral rectitude and marital perfection . . . as bit by bit what happened to all his other wives and their children came to the surface . . . and the police and prosecuting attorney had to find a daring and innovative way to prove to a jury what they knew to be true, and convict a killer who had come so close to never being caught.

# FATAL CHARM

## The Shocking True Story of Serial Wife Killer Randy Roth

# CARLTON SMITH

AN ONYX BOOK

ONYX

Published by the Penguin Group
Penguin Books USA Inc., 375 Hudson Street,
New York, New York 10014, U.S.A.
Penguin Books Ltd, 27 Wrights Lane,
London W8 5TZ, England
Penguin Books Australia Ltd, Ringwood,
Victoria, Australia
Penguin Books Canada Ltd, 10 Alcorn Avenue,
Toronto, Ontario, Canada M4V 3B2
Penguin Books (N.Z.) Ltd, 182–190 Wairau Road,
Auckland 10, New Zealand

Penguin Books Ltd, Registered Offices:
Harmondsworth, Middlesex, England

First published by Onyx, an imprint of New American Library, a division of
Penguin Books USA Inc.

First Printing, July, 1993

10  9  8  7  6  5  4  3  2  1

 REGISTERED TRADEMARK—MARCA REGISTRADA

Printed in the United States of America

# CONTENTS

Acknowledgments  *ix*

## THE LAKE

1 The Hottest Day of the Year *3*
2 Roth *8*
3 Too Calm *14*
4 Randy's Story *18*
5 A Probable Accident *24*
6 "Why Wouldn't I Be?" *28*
7 "Something's Wrong" *35*
8 Mary Jo *38*
9 Free Fall *43*
10 "Get It All . . ." *46*
11 Lori *51*
12 The Interview *60*

**13** Donna #2      *68*

**14** Going to the Prosecutors      *75*

**15** Brenneman      *80*

**16** "I Know Things about the Man"      *84*

# THE LOVER

**17** The Badlands      *91*

**18** Billy Jack      *99*

**19** "He Was Very Serious"      *108*

**20** Semper Fi      *116*

**21** Busted      *129*

**22** Donna #1      *137*

**23** Davy      *140*

**24** Debbie and Tim      *147*

**25** "Throw Your Mother in the Slammer"      *151*

**26** Jan and Jalina      *162*

**27** "Randy Has Many Very Good Qualities"      *172*

**28** Trick or Treat      *176*

**29** Beacon Rock      *179*

**30** Aftermath      *188*

**31** "I Don't Want to Tell You Anything . . ."      *199*

**32** The Big Spender      *205*

**33** Misty Meadows      *210*

**34** For the Birds                                   220

**35** Burgled                                         230

**36** Hot August Nights                               235

**37** The Swamp                                       244

**38** Randy Is Not Like Us                            251

**39** "I Had a Damn Good Idea"                        256

**40** The Case                                        263

**41** Woodinville                                     270

**42** A Message from Cindy                            276

# THE TRIAL

**43** Nothing There                                   281

**44** For the Defense                                 286

**45** The Whole Truth, Nothing But . . .              294

**46** "A Bad, Bad Time for Anybody"                   300

**47** "I Was Very Glad"                               303

**48** Band-Aids                                       319

**49** Badly Damaged                                   323

**50** "Sick to My Stomach"                            331

**51** On the Cross                                    339

**52** "Isn't It True, Mr. Roth . . ."                 351

**53** No Blueberry Pie                                359

**54** How Say You?                                    365

**55** Extreme Cruelty                                 368

Epilogue                                               371

# ACKNOWLEDGMENTS

The contents of this book were drawn primarily from police and court files relating to the investigation, arrest, trial and conviction of Randolph G. Roth in 1991 and 1992. Well over three thousand pages of investigative reports and over six thousand pages of trial transcripts were consulted, along with several thousand additional pages in pretrial briefings and memoranda. All of this written material was supplemented by numerous interviews of many of the principals in the case.

The author wishes to express his gratitude to the individuals who assisted in the preparation of this manuscript. Special thanks go to Ms. Marilyn Brenneman of the King County Prosecutor's Office, who frequently and generously provided both her recollections and her legal insights; to Dawn Nelson of the Prosecutor's Office, who provided invaluable assistance in tracking down various documents; to Detectives Susan Peters and Randy Mullinax of the King County Police Department, who patiently submitted to many interviews and explained much that might have otherwise been inexplicable; to the Seattle law firm of Davis Wright Tremaine, who provided legal representation at a critical juncture; to Tammy Swift of the *Bismarck Daily Tribune* for her help in North Dakota, and to the Glen Ullin Historical Society, for their local history of the Roth family and other pioneers; to Helga Kahr, who provided valuable legal background on the rules of evidence; to Judge William Downing, for the same; to George Cody for his own insights within the confines of the attorney-client privilege; to my editor, Michaela Hamilton of NAL/Dutton, for her steadfast support; and most of all, to Official Court Reporter Jean Majury, without whose kind and generous assistance this book could not have been written.

A final note on style: wherever possible, I have used the actual words spoken by the participants, either as reflected in tape recorded interviews conducted by the police, in trial transcripts where applicable, or in words specifically recollected by those involved. Where the substance and the flow of dialog was available but not the exact wording, the material is paraphrased in the form of conversation but without quote marks to indicate that these were words substantially similar to what was actually said.

# ROTH FAMILY

### Gordon Roth m. Isabelle Messer, Dec. 9, 1954

**Randy Roth, born Dec. 26, 1954**

**David Roth, born 1957**
serving life in prison for
murder

**Three Roth
daughters**

**Randy Roth m. Donna Sanchez, July 4, 1975**
Greg Roth, born Aug. 30, 1977
Divorced, Feb., 1980

**Randy Roth m. Janis Miranda Roth, March, 1981**
Janis dies in fall, Nov. 27, 1981
Jalina Miranda, child from Jan's earlier marriage

**Randy Roth m. Donna Clift, May 1985**
Divorced, September 1985
Brittany, Donna's child from earlier marriage

**Randy Roth m. Cynthia Baumgartner, Aug. 3, 1990**
Cynthia drowns, July 23, 1991
Tyson Baumgartner
Rylie Baumgartner
Cynthia's children from earlier marriage

# THE LAKE

# 1

# The Hottest Day of the Year

It had been the hottest day of the year, and as the long afternoon drew on toward evening, the two boys sat on the beach and peered out across the lake, arguing idly. Tyson Baumgartner, eleven, thought he could see the rubber raft; his brother Rylie, nine, was certain he couldn't. "I think I see them," Tyson said. "Where?" said Rylie, doubting it.

The lake was Lake Sammamish, one of the Seattle area's most popular recreation spots, and on a day as hot as July 23, 1991, when the temperature was nearly one hundred, the water was filled with motorboats churning endlessly up and down, some towing skiers, others heading into or away from shore. With all the waves and the boat traffic, the low-riding, small gray inflatable was easy to overlook.

"Yep," said Tyson, "that's them. But I don't see Mom."

"She's probably lying in the bottom, sunbathing," Rylie said.

The two brothers watched as the raft picked its way through the boat traffic. A shirtless man in dark glasses was rowing steadily but not with any particular

3

haste. As the tiny craft neared the roped-off swimming area, the rower turned around so he was facing the beach and began to push the raft in toward the shore with the two plastic oars. It took longer, but the rower didn't seem to mind. The boys saw that the raft was pointed toward the south end of the swimming area. They walked over to meet it as it neared the shore. Yep, it was Randy all right.

"Keep your raft twenty-five yards away from the swimming area," a lifeguard boomed through a bull-horn, but the man kept on rowing. When the lifeguard called out again, the rower looked up, puzzled, as if to say, *Who, me?* Then the raft reached the beach, and the man in the sunglasses got out and started pulling the craft up on the sand, ignoring the two boys.

Tyson and Rylie looked down into the well of the raft and saw their mother. She was lying in about four inches of water. Her blond hair hung in wet, unruly, tangled strands across her face. Her eyes were vacant. Her face and upper torso were blue. She wasn't breathing. She lay completely still. She wasn't sun-bathing.

The man in the sunglasses turned to Tyson and spoke quietly.

"Go get the lifeguard," he said. "Ask him for help. But don't make a commotion."

There were probably three or four hundred people on the beach that day, and so ordinary was the landing of the rubber raft only a few paid any attention. The nearest lifeguard barely gave the raft a glance as it came ashore. Now, as Michael McFadden's eyes ha-bitually scanned the roped-off swimming area for swimmers in trouble, he gave little notice to the two boys calling up to him in his elevated seat. They wanted help with something, but McFadden wasn't sure with what, exactly.

"I can't leave the chair right now," McFadden said.

"Go up to the lifeguard shack, they can help you there." Then, out of the corner of his eye, McFadden caught a glimpse of something strange about the raft thirty yards away.

"Eighty-eight! Eighty-eight!" McFadden screamed, calling the lifeguards' emergency signal. He jumped down onto the sand and went into a sprint, nearly knocking over a couple of people as he ran. Another lifeguard, hearing McFadden's alarm, raised her megaphone: "Clear the water! Clear the water!" she shouted. The urgency of the shout froze everyone for an instant. Then there was chaos as everyone tried to get out of the water at the same time.

McFadden was nineteen years old. Lifeguarding was just a summer job, something to earn a bit to help out for college in the fall. Now as he looked down into the gray inflatable boat, he knew he was going to have to try to save a life. McFadden had never seen anyone look as bad as the woman lying motionless in the bottom of the raft. He gave little notice to the short man wearing sunglasses who was standing idly next to him.

"Give me some help," McFadden said, and then together the sunglasses man and someone else, McFadden never knew who it was, helped him lift the inert weight of the blond woman out of the raft and onto the sand. The woman was in imminent danger of death, if not already dead, McFadden realized. *This is it,* he thought. *When they're blue like that, that means they're cyanotic—no oxygen.*

"What happened?" McFadden asked the man with the sunglasses while he checked the victim for breathing and a pulse. He couldn't find either.

"She was underwater," the man said. "She swallowed some water." McFadden tilted the woman's head back, checked her airway, pinched her nostrils shut and began blowing air down her throat.

"How long was she under?" he asked between

breaths. "Ten minutes," the man offered. After two breaths the woman threw up. The fluid was reddish and sticky. McFadden thought perhaps it might be blood. A crowd started gathering. *Oh God, I'm going to have to save this woman's life,* McFadden thought.

"I'm a paramedic, let me help," came the voice of a nearby woman. McFadden gladly gave up his place at the dying woman's mouth to Patti Schultz. Schultz pinched the woman's nostrils shut and took over the breathing while McFadden started vigorous compressions on the dying woman's chest, trying to get her heart started again. The man with the sunglasses squatted quietly on his heels at her feet, watching their efforts impassively.

In between breaths; Schultz puffed questions. "How long was she under?" she asked. *Breath.*

The man in the sunglasses shook his head. "I don't know."

"Was it five minutes?" *Breath.*

"I don't know."

"Was it ten?" *Breath.*

"Twenty?" *Breath.* The man just kept shaking his head. McFadden and Schultz stripped away the top of the woman's black, red and yellow bathing suit. Schultz saw that her stomach was distended; she'd obviously swallowed a large amount of water. Every few seconds more water came up, so she and McFadden kept rolling the woman over onto her side to empty the fluid. Sand stuck to her face.

Sirens sounded in the distance. Schultz kept breathing and McFadden kept pushing. There was no response from the woman. *Breath, push, breath, push.* The man in the sunglasses watched them without expression or comment. A rescue van braked to a stop a short distance away. Uniformed paramedics ran up with resuscitation equipment. McFadden and Schultz stood back to let them in. One of the uniformed rescuers shoved a stainless steel tube down the dying woman's throat and coupled it to the breathing equipment. He started an intravenous line. He administered a heart stimulant. He monitored his instruments. He thrust a defibrillator paddle under the woman, laid its mate on her chest, and gave the woman's heart a jolt. Again. Again. A fourth time. Nothing. No breathing, no pulse.

As he worked, he too noticed the man in the sunglasses squatting placidly at the woman's feet.

"Who are you?" the new paramedic asked.

"I'm her husband," the man told him.

# 2 | Roth

Tyson and Rylie Baumgartner stood among the gawkers, watching people pound on their mother and roll her about on the sand as the efforts to save her life grew increasingly frantic and violent. Lifeguard Kelli Crowell saw them standing at the edge of the crowd, clearly upset. Someone was holding up beach blankets to conceal the lifesaving effort from the rubberneckers.

"Are you okay?" asked Crowell, not knowing who they were.

"That's our mom," said Tyson, nodding at the activity. Crowell took them by their hands.

"Oh, I'm so sorry," Crowell said. "Come with me. You don't need to stand here and watch this. You come with me and we're gonna go up to the guard shack." As they went to the lifeguard office, Crowell asked Tyson and Rylie for their names and ages. The two boys looked alike, neat and clean, sturdily built, with light brown hair. They could have been anyone's idea of normal, healthy, happy kids, except for the fact that they had just been watching their mother die.

"Is there anyone I can call for you? Your dad?"

"That's our dad down there," Tyson told Crowell. Tyson was obviously referring to the man in the sunglasses. Crowell was flabbergasted. She thought the man squatting at the drowned woman's feet was probably a stranger, someone who found the woman floating in the lake and had done the responsible thing by rowing her into shore. The man sitting by the woman seemed so remote, so uninvolved with what was going on.

"What's your dad's name?" Crowell asked.

"Randy," Tyson told her. "Randy Roth."

Crowell pictured the man she'd seen next to the dying woman. He was short, maybe five eight or so, but very well-built, quite muscular actually, and attractive. His weight might have been around one hundred sixty to one hundred seventy pounds. He looked like he was in his mid-thirties or so. He had dark hair, not overlong, and a thick, neatly trimmed mustache. He was shirtless and wearing shorts and rubber beach sandals, along with the sunglasses. The most noticeable thing about the man was his utter lack of demonstrativeness while his wife's life was ebbing away. He had said nothing, showed no signs of agitation or anxiety. Crowell now saw him in a different light. She guessed the man was in severe shock.

Actually, Tyson continued, Randy was really their stepfather. Their own father had died years before, and their mother married Randy only a year ago. After the marriage, Randy and their mother bought a new house, in a new neighborhood, and they had all moved in together, along with Randy's son Greg. Now they were worried Randy might lose track of them and go to the hospital without them, stranding them at the beach. Crowell told the boys she would tell their stepfather where they were if they promised to stay at the lifeguard office. The boys said they would, so Crowell set off to talk with Randy Roth.

* * *

While Crowell was walking back down the beach, Randy Roth suddenly stood up and walked over to his raft. Several people in the crowd of onlookers saw him remove several soaking wet plastic tote bags and empty a considerable amount of water from the bottom of the craft. Then he opened the raft's air valves. The paramedics continued to call out to each other and back to their base on their radio.

Police arrived. Motorcycle officers pushed the crowd back, and another officer produced a notebook and started assembling the facts. He noticed the dark-haired man with a mustache deflating the raft. Because the man was only a few feet from the lifesaving work, the police officer told him to get out of the way.

"I'm her husband," Randy said, pressing on the raft's air chambers to force the deflation.

"You're her *husband?*"

Officer Randall G. Cox was taken aback. Until that moment, Cox had assumed no one present knew who the woman was. He'd been trying to figure out a way to identify her. Now this. It was weird; whoever this guy was, he sure wasn't acting like anybody involved. "I'm her husband," Randy repeated.

Cox covered his surprise by pressing the man for the details. Like the victim's name. "Cindy," Randy said. "Well, Cynthia. Roth."

Randy wasn't looking directly at Cox. He continued pushing the air out of the raft. Cox got Randy's own name, address and phone number.

"What boat were you in?"

"This one," Randy said as he pushed the last of the air out. His actions were beginning to bother Cox. "Maybe you shouldn't be deflating it," Cox suggested.

"Well, I have to get ready to go."

"Tell me what happened," said Cox.

"Well, we were paddling around the lake," Randy said, finally looking directly at Cox. "We were swimming around out there. And she got a cramp in her leg. She was hanging on the side of the raft. And then a boat went by and swamped us. That was when the raft flipped over. I heard her choke, like she swallowed some water. I turned the raft over and I found her floating face down. I tried to get her back into the raft, and I did. And then I just paddled in, to get help.''

Randy's tone made it all sound so matter-of-fact. He might as well have been talking about an everyday event. "Where are you going to take her?'' he asked.

Overlake Hospital, Cox told him. "We'll give you an escort,'' Cox said.

"No, that's okay,'' Randy said. "I've been there before.'' He began rolling the raft up.

One of the onlookers in the crowd who had been watching Randy closely for some minutes now took Cox aside. "I don't think he should be driving any-place right now,'' Alicia Tracy told Cox. "I think this man must be in shock, he's just so devoid of . . . devoid of anything.'' Tracy thought the enormity of the event might hit the man while he was driving to the hospital. Roth might have a bad accident when the reaction set in.

Cox thought so, too. It just wasn't human to be so distant, especially in the midst of a personal tragedy. Who knew when Roth might go off? *This guy is sitting on the edge of an emotional explosion,* Cox thought. "Well, I think we'll give him a ride,'' he told Tracy.

"No, no, you don't understand,'' Randy said when the police offered him a ride to the hospital a second time. "I have my truck here. I have to drive my truck over.''

The police persisted. "Well, we'll bring you back to your truck,'' Cox said.

"No. I've got all my stuff here, and I've got two kids somewhere here on the beach.''

Then Randy rose, shouldered the deflated raft, picked up two of the bags, and walked toward the parking lot some two hundred yards away. Tracy and Cox stared after him.

*What do you mean, you have two children here on the beach?* Tracy thought. *You have been sitting over there this whole time, rolling up your raft, and you have two children over here watching their mother die?* Now Tracy wasn't sure Randy was in shock after all.

As Randy strode away, Patti Schultz grabbed the two remaining tote bags and went after him. She too was concerned that he might be in shock. She told him she would be happy to drive him to the hospital. Randy again refused.

"Well, at least let me ride with you." Randy ignored her and walked off toward his truck. Schultz followed him.

As they neared the parking lot, Kelli Crowell caught up with him. "I've got your kids," she said, but it seemed like Randy didn't hear her. Crowell followed, trying to get his attention. A fire department official also gave chase, wanting more information for his report. Randy ignored everyone as he made for his truck.

The fire official finally got Randy to slow down. He asked him what had happened on the lake. How did the accident happen? Randy explained again about the boat and the raft capsizing. "I turned over the raft," he said, "and she was dead."

"Dead?" The fire official was incredulous.

"Well, unconscious," Randy said.

Crowell trotted back to the lifeguard station and got the two boys. They ran after Randy, sobbing. Randy stopped. He took the wet tote bags from Schultz and gave them to Tyson and Rylie to carry. Schultz got the impression that Randy was disgusted with the boys for weeping.

"Come on, boys, we're going to the hospital," he

said. Tyson and Rylie took the sacks and choked back their sobs.

Randy's behavior seemed increasingly surreal to Tracy and several other onlookers in the crowd. Tracy couldn't believe that he had simply ignored the two boys throughout the entire lifesaving ordeal.

*He hasn't said a word to them*, she thought. *He hasn't gone over to them, he hasn't put his arms around them. He didn't drop all his things and run to them and cry. He has done absolutely nothing. Those little boys are terrified, and their daddy's not even giving them a hug.* It made Tracy sick to her stomach to watch.

Patti Schultz stopped Tyson and Rylie before they could follow their stepfather. "Hi, what're your names?" she asked, hugging both boys. The boys started to cry again.

"Well, my name's Patti," Schultz said, "and I'm gonna ride with you to the hospital." Randy marched on toward the parking lot, carrying his rubber raft.

# 3

# Too Calm

**M**ike Helbock had been a paramedic for more than a dozen years. In that time, he had seen plenty of people die. He also had seen their loved ones react as life slipped away, and never before had he seen someone as casual about death as Randy Roth.

As Helbock hovered over the comatose Cindy Roth while the aid car screamed toward the hospital some eight miles away, he kept thinking about the man with the sunglasses. *Most people are frantic*, Helbock thought, *or if they aren't, they're almost rigid. Not that guy. For Pete's sake, that guy was practically nonchalant.*

The doctors at the hospital were on the radio. Helbock could tell from Cindy Roth's blue coloring that she hadn't had any air for at least ten minutes before the resuscitation efforts began. The doctors kept asking Helbock what was wrong with the victim; they didn't understand how she could have drowned so close to a life raft. Was she diabetic, the doctors wanted to know? Did she have some sort of seizure?

"I don't know, I don't know," Helbock could only report. "There's got to be some reason," the doctors told Helbock over the radio. "I can't find anything," Helbock said.

Why hadn't Roth alerted a lifeguard earlier? Helbock couldn't believe he hadn't asked for help far sooner. Someone had told Helbock that Cindy was found facedown in the water in the raft, that Randy had been swimming, and that he had "pushed" the raft to shore with Cindy in it. Helbock thought that meant that Randy had pushed the raft ahead of him while swimming toward shore, which Helbock thought was crazy. What was wrong with that guy, anyway?

About ten minutes later, the aid car pulled up to the hospital's emergency entrance, and Cindy was hustled inside. Helbock got ready to write his report. *There's something wrong with this whole thing,* Helbock thought. *The flavor of this call stinks.*

Randy turned his Izusu Trooper onto the freeway to follow the paramedic van. Patti Schultz sat next to him in the front seat. Tyson and Rylie sat in the back. The boys were still crying, but making an obvious effort to keep quiet. Schultz again had the impression that the kids were frightened of Randy, that Randy was a stern father who frowned on the kids showing any emotion. The boys said nothing.

Schultz tried to talk to Randy, but Randy answered in monosyllables. Even when they turned onto the freeway, Schultz noticed that Randy was driving very slowly. She was watching him closely. "His affect was off," Schultz said later, referring to Randy's demeanor. "He didn't seem to be reacting at all. I didn't want him to have a reaction on the way in, and endanger himself or his children."

Randy asked Schultz how long a person could go without oxygen before irreversible brain damage and death. Schultz didn't want to tell Randy directly that Cindy was probably already dead, fearing that it might trigger the pent-up reaction she saw as inevitable. She tried to be gentle.

"Well, the paramedics are giving her medication which will hopefully start her heart again," Schultz told Randy. "They'll do more at the hospital. She's going to have very good care."

"Well, how long then?" Randy asked. Schultz thought she should give Randy some hope. "Oh, maybe thirty minutes," Schultz said, knowing she was telling a white lie. "After thirty minutes of CPR."

Randy was silent for a minute. "What about without CPR?" he asked.

Schultz admitted that it wouldn't be very long. Randy nodded. "I thought it was about four minutes before the brain stops," he said. "I remember that from the CPR class I took."

Schultz said nothing to this, but was thinking: *If this guy knows CPR, why didn't he help his wife?*

The scene at the beach upset another bystander far more than she had realized. After the aid car left, Maureen Devinck gathered up her children and her belongings and went straight home. She was still marveling over the man's lack of apparent reaction to his wife's probable death. She could still see Randy casually deflating and rolling up his raft while his wife was dying only a few feet away. *That was weird*, Devinck thought. *You'd think he'd have been more interested in the condition of his wife than his boat, wouldn't you?*

Maureen's husband was home from work when she arrived. She looked at her husband and immediately burst into tears. She imagined herself on the beach, with paramedics rolling her back and forth to empty her stomach of water, shoving tubes down her throat, and her own husband so seemingly indifferent to her plight.

"Think about it," Maureen told her husband. "If

they were doing CPR on me and I'm laying there and looking dead and there's no response and they're flipping me back and forth and emptying my stomach . . . I just can't imagine you would sit at the end of my feet and act so . . . unresponsive. He didn't ask, 'Is she gonna be okay?' He didn't even, you know, go, 'My God, where's the ambulance?' It was really, really weird.''

That was when it hit Maureen: she was sure in her heart that the man had murdered his wife. "I think he killed her," Maureen told her husband and a neighbor who had come over. "Do you think I should call the police and tell them how I feel?"

But Maureen's husband and the neighbor told her she was just suffering a reaction from the trauma of the events. "Oh, Rennie, there's such a large range of shock," the neighbor said.

"I know, but it just seemed weird," Maureen insisted.

Maureen's husband didn't think she should call the police. "Rennie, I'm sure if that's the way he was acting, the police are going to catch on," he said. "If there's anything to it at all, the police are going to investigate."

As it turned out, just as Devinck was having this conversation, the police were indeed preparing to investigate, and for exactly the reasons that Devinck had pinpointed.

# 4  Randy's Story

As Maureen Devinck sensed, Patti Schultz suspected and Mike Helbock knew, Cindy Roth was beyond saving. Shortly after 6:30 P.M., the pretty young mother was declared dead. Tyson and Rylie Baumgartner were orphans.

Like most major hospitals, Overlake Hospital in Bellevue, Washington employed a social worker to help family members cope with grief. D'Vorah Kost was with Randy and the boys when the doctors told them Cindy was gone. The boys were in heavy shock. Tears streamed down their faces. Neither said anything, and Randy said nothing to them. It seemed to Kost that the boys were in one world, Randy in another. It was hard to believe they were even related.

Randy looked angry, Kost thought. He seemed very tight, almost sullen. Kost thought he was feeling defensive. He was still wearing his sunglasses. "I couldn't save her," he said several times to no one in particular.

Officials from the county medical examiner's office arrived. Randy briefly described what happened at the lake. Then a detective from the Redmond Police Department came into the room, and Randy told the

18

story again. "I'm not wearing these dark glasses to hide anything from you," Randy told him. The detective didn't say anything to that. Instead, he asked Randy to write a statement. Randy finished the statement a few minutes after seven P.M.

"We arrived at the lake approx 2:30 P.M., then needed to inflate the raft and inner tubes for the kids so it was sometime after 3:00 when we reached the beach," Randy wrote. "The two boys were going to float in the swim area as they had done with their mom before. Cindy asked me to row to the east side of the lake where it would be more romantic. I said it looks like a long way, she replied you're strong, you can do it. We rowed to the other side and paddled around awhile and started back. She asked if I would like to cool off with a swim and I said okay. We swam for about ten minutes and she said the cool water was giving her a cramp in her leg.

"I said let's head back. We were at the side of the raft where she was holding onto the rope and I said hang on, I'll go around and hold the other side so you can get in. As I was working my way around a wake from a passing boat about 50–100 yds away went by and the raft turned over on top of her. She coughed once and I hurried to right the raft which took about 30 seconds. She was already floating face down and I couldn't get her into the raft from the water. I managed to climb in and pulled her aboard and proceeded to row to the beach side where help could be found. Upon beaching a lifeguard was summoned by my son Tyson who was on shore and she started CPR."

The man from the medical examiner's office told Randy an autopsy would have to be performed on Cindy. "I don't want one," Randy said. Sorry, said the official; there wasn't any choice in the matter. Under the law, any unexpected, unattended death required an autopsy.

Now Kost asked if she could call someone for them,

and the boys said they wanted to talk to their grandparents, Cindy's mother and father. But Randy reminded them that Cindy's parents were visiting relatives in North Dakota and couldn't be reached. Randy said he would call Cindy's brother, instead. Kost offered Randy some pamphlets on grief and counseling facilities. Randy took the handouts but didn't seem very interested in them. Just after 7:30 P.M., Randy and the boys left the hospital.

At that point, the detective told Randy he wanted to impound the raft. Randy became very upset on hearing this, the detective later recalled, wanting to know why the police wanted it and saying the police had no right to take it. Cindy had been dead for less than an hour.

Redmond Police Detective Larry Conrad thought Randy's behavior was highly unusual. As he looked over the written statement, Conrad couldn't help feeling that his description of the drowning just didn't sound right.

The medical people were convinced that Cindy had been without oxygen for a substantial period of time. Why hadn't Randy called for help? There were scores of boats on the lake. Why hadn't he waved to any of them? Anyway, could a wake from a powerboat *really* have flipped the raft over? But most of all, there was Randy's demeanor. Calmly deflating the raft while his wife lay dying seemed peculiar, to say the least. And there was Randy's opposition to an autopsy.

Further, when Conrad thought about Randy's story, he was struck by the fact that all of the fateful decisions seemed to have been made by the dead woman: it was *her* idea to go to the lake, it was *her* idea to row to the other shore, it was *her* idea to go swimming. Randy made himself sound powerless, helpless, a mere hapless bystander. He hadn't comforted the boys; he hadn't cried himself. Instead, he appeared focused on mundane, pragmatic, mechanical tasks. To

Conrad, the picture simply had too many broken pieces.

Conrad called his sergeant and filled him in. The sergeant agreed something might be fishy about Randy Roth and the death of his wife of less than one year. But if anything criminal had befallen Cindy Roth, it hadn't taken place inside the city of Redmond, the sergeant pointed out. The city's jurisdiction ended at the water's edge. Whatever happened to Cindy had clearly happened somewhere out in the middle of the lake, and the lake was the territory of the county police. The sergeant called them to tell them they might want to take a hard look at Randy Roth and the death of his recent wife.

Susan Peters was starting up her barbecue at her new home in the foothills southeast of Seattle when the telephone rang shortly after 7:30 P.M. Her father was visiting for a couple of days from eastern Washington State, and Peters was looking forward to a quiet evening at home with her father and a couple of friends.

Peters had been a detective with the King County Police for five years, the last year with the department's Major Crimes Section. That unit handled all homicides, kidnappings and death investigations. In earlier years, it had investigated the crimes of Ted Bundy, the serial killer, and later, the still unsolved Green River murders. Sudden suspicious deaths, murders and kidnappings, while increasing, were still rare enough to make it uneconomical to have detectives available in the office around the clock. Instead, detectives were assigned after-hours cases on a basis of existing workload, and most frequently, simple availability. Thus, the problems posed by Cindy's death and Randy Roth's unusual behavior were routed to the first detective who could be found, who turned out to be Sue Peters.

Peters turned custody of her barbecue over to one of her friends, apologized to her father, and drove to the nearest county police precinct, where she started making telephone calls. She first talked to one of the county's marine patrol officers, who briefed her on the facts of the drowning as told to her by the Redmond sergeant. Peters learned that a Redmond detective, Larry Conrad, was interviewing Randy at the hospital.

Peters called the hospital and was told that Randy and Conrad had already left. She called the Redmond Department and reached Conrad, who told her all the aspects of the drowning that seemed troubling. Next, Peters discussed the case with her own sergeant. He agreed the whole thing needed a close look, and assigned Peters to work full-time on the case until they could be sure that the death of Cynthia Roth really was an accident and not something more ominous—like murder.

After leaving the hospital, Randy and the boys drove through downtown Bellevue. Rylie was now sobbing as quietly as he could. Later, Rylie would remember Randy telling him to quit crying. "There's no need to cry," he said. "Just be quiet. It's over with, there's nothing to cry about."

Much later, Randy would deny having said these things. "I wouldn't have been that insensitive," Randy would say. But insensitive was just the impression Randy had already made on countless people that day. Rylie tried hard to hold his tears in. "I tried my hardest," he said later, "but—I tried not to be loud, but tears still fell down my face."

Randy pulled into a Burger King, and he and the three boys ordered hamburgers and french fries. Little was said. Afterward, Randy stopped at a nearby market and rented three movies, all of them comedies. Randy and the boys then drove home, a large, two-story, four-bedroom house located on an estate-sized lot in rural Woodinville, about twenty miles northeast of Seattle.

The house was filled with Cindy's things: an extensive doll collection in glass cases in several rooms, plenty of girlish knickknacks or cute art in various corners. Cindy had painted the house in her favorite colors, pink and mauve. Randy hated it. Now Cindy was gone.

Randy made root beer floats for the boys, made sure the telephone answering machine was on, and put the rental movies into the VCR. The boys watched the movies numbly. Randy had the idea that the movies would help the boys keep their minds off the tragedy. But even in this, Randy's insensitivity seemed apparent.

As it turned out, one of the movies was *Weekend at Bernie's*, a black comedy about two men at a beach resort who manipulate the body of a dead man to convince everyone else that the man is still alive.

For two young boys who had just watched their mother drown, the battering taken by Bernie's corpse in the movie could hardly have been funny. At one point in the movie, Bernie's waterlogged body washes ashore, and at another, it is dragged behind a boat at high speed. Tyson tried to laugh along with Randy, but Rylie went up to his room to cry.

# 5

# A Probable Accident

Being a detective in real life is nothing like it is on television or in the movies. There aren't any car chases, and if a detective ever gets into a shootout, it's almost always because of a bad miscalculation. Sherlock Holmes, Hercule Poirot and Miss Marple may have been brilliant logicians, but in real life being a successful detective demands one thing above all others: sheer unrelenting, often mind-numbing, persistence.

Nor, in real life, do detectives spend all their time driving around looking for leads and getting into trouble, no matter what Philip Marlowe thought. In real life, a detective's best friend is the telephone, and that's where Sue Peters began the day after Cindy Roth drowned.

Peters was thirty-three years old, and the first woman the King County Police Department had ever assigned full-time to major crimes. Previously, she had investigated sexual assaults. She was in some ways symbolic of the changes that had come to the department over the previous decade as it evolved from a largely rural sheriff's department into a modern metropolitan police agency.

There had been a time earlier in Peters' career when one of her male colleagues in uniform had subjected her to harassment because of her sex, but that sort of thing was widely looked down on by most police officers, and if discovered by the department higher-ups, was dealt with harshly. The six detectives Peters joined in the major crimes office were all skilled, professional cops—men who would no more sneer at her because of her sex than they would fire their weapons at the ceiling.

The only question was whether one could do the work, carefully and fully, and Peters knew she would never have been assigned to major crimes if she wasn't capable of doing that. Still, Peters valued the rapport she'd developed with her fellow detectives, and wanted to show them she could pull her own weight on the job and retain their respect. In that, she was no different than anyone else in the unit.

Short—five three—and with light brown hair cut stylishly close, Peters was a natural athlete, having once held a tennis scholarship at Washington State University. She'd begun college intending to go into teaching and coaching, but veered away from athletics after a couple of years to take up police science. Her grandmother had been a radio dispatcher for a rural sheriff in the eastern part of the state, and when she thought about it, Peters realized that her interest in police work went back to the days when she'd visited her grandma in the sheriff's office and read all the wanted posters and heard all the war stories about desperados of the past. Peters retained some of the frontier West in her own personality. She lived in a log cabin in the foothills southeast of Seattle, and one of her greatest pleasures was hiking in the wilderness with her one-hundred-pound Labrador, Shay. She had a wry grin and a down-home way of talking, Her strongest epithet was "Holy cow!"

Peters considered police work a bit like sports, in at least one respect: it was competitive, with the crooks on one side and the cops on the other. But in police work, unlike sports, there was nothing artificial about the contest; it was for keeps.

The central question about Cindy Roth's death was whether her husband's story was credible, Peters realized.

Was it possible for Cindy to have drowned so quickly by accident? Could the raft really have been flipped over by the wake from a passing boat? Were there any witnesses to the capsizing? Did Randy try to get help, and if he didn't, why not? Who saw what happened at the beach, and what did Randy tell them? Was it the same story, or were there inconsistencies that might indicate Randy was lying? Why had Randy been so indifferent to the tragedy?

Peters still hadn't seen Randy, but according to Larry Conrad, the Redmond detective, Cindy's husband was extremely muscular in his upper body; he worked as a heavy mechanic at a car dealership. He was taller, heavier and much stronger than the dead woman. Because of Randy's size advantage, Peters thought it perfectly plausible that Randy had murdered his wife simply by holding her under the water until she drowned.

Peters doubted Randy's version of the events instinctively. She had been a competitive swimmer in school and knew something about rafting and the outdoors; it didn't seem very likely to her that Cindy could have drowned as quickly as Randy claimed without his interference.

A vital question was whether anyone at the lake—there had been hundreds, if not thousands, of people surrounding the incident—had actually seen Randy holding Cindy under the water. Peters knew only one way to find that out, and that was to start collecting statements from the known witnesses and check them for leads and inconsistencies. She reached for the telephone.

The woman on the stainless steel autopsy table in front of Dr. Donald Reay, the King County Medical Examiner, had been very attractive. She was five feet two inches tall and weighed about one hundred thirty pounds. Her hair was colored light brown to blond, although it appeared that she was a natural brunette and was apparently allowing her hair to return to its natural color. Her eyes were brown and showed evidence of careful eye-shadow application. Her fingernails were neatly manicured and extended perhaps a quarter-inch beyond the tips of the fingers. They were painted with pink nail polish, and on both ring fingers, three small, clear stones were set in the polish. The toenails were covered with the same color of polish. It was clear that Cynthia Roth, when she had been alive, had taken extraordinary care with her appearance.

Reay's job was to find out how Cindy died, and whether there was evidence that someone killed her. The autopsy, when it was over, answered the first question: Cindy had died from asphyxiation from freshwater drowning. But except for two small scratches on the left side of the neck, there was no evidence to indicate *how* the drowning occurred. The long fingernails, for example, showed no bits of flesh underneath, as might have been expected if Cindy had scratched someone trying to drown her. Reay read the routine report his subordinates submitted after the events at the lake, thought it over, and reached a conclusion: in the absence of any contradictory information, he would have to classify Cindy's death as a probable accident.

# 6

## "Why Wouldn't I Be?"

By the following Monday morning, six days after Cindy Roth drowned, Peters had made only slight progress. Reay had give her his tentative conclusion from the autopsy, that the drowning was probably an accident; still, Peters couldn't shake her doubts.

Meanwhile, she'd been able to reach only two of the witnesses; the lifeguard Michael McFadden, and a fourteen-year-old girl on the beach who had told Redmond police she had seen the raft "tip up," which might at least partially confirm Randy's story. McFadden told Peters that he too was struck by Randy's odd behavior on the beach, but attributed it to shock. Peters made calls to other lifeguards present on the beach, but no one had called back.

Like all detectives, Peters kept a running log of all her actions on the case—every call made, every message left, even to other police officers. The log was the backbone of the detective system. Each entry was dated and timed, and confined to the dry facts. Later, when other officers or prosecutors needed to know exactly what a detective had done, said, heard or seen, and when, the record would be there.

One thing Peters had discovered was that Randy was a convicted felon. He had pleaded guilty to a burglary charge in a county north of Seattle back in 1975 and had received a short jail term and probation. Peters was still checking to see if Randy had had contacts with other police agencies, but it was slow going; each of the several dozen police departments in the Seattle area have different record systems.

In any event, that morning Peters decided to call Randy and take a statement from him. This would represent her first encounter with the one witness who knew the most about what happened to Cindy. Peters placed the call and got Randy's answering machine.

Five minutes later, Randy called Peters back. Could he talk to her about the events at the lake? Peters asked. And would he mind if she tape-recorded their conversation? Randy was agreeable, if brusque. He was on his way to a memorial service for Cindy, he told her; he couldn't talk long. Peters expressed her sympathy for Randy's loss. Randy said nothing.

The rafting trip had been Cindy's idea, Randy said; she'd wanted to row across the lake to the far shore. Randy described the trip across, then the trip back. He told Peters how he and Cindy had decided to leave the raft for a swim, Cindy's cramp, his attempts to hold the raft steady so she could climb in, and the wake from the powerboat that caused the raft to flip over. He heard a single cough, Randy told Peters.

When he turned the raft right side up, Cindy was floating facedown in the water. By the time he got into the raft himself and maneuvered it over to Cindy, she was already unconscious, he said. So far, Randy's story was consistent with what he had first told the Redmond police and the medical examiner's office.

Peters kept her tone neutral. At this stage, she only wanted to hear Randy's story in his own words. At one point, however, she asked Randy whether anyone had seen what was going on as Randy pulled Cindy into the raft. Peters wanted to find out from Randy whether there were any other witnesses to the drowning, but also was a subtle way of asking if Randy had tried to get help from any of the numerous boats nearby.

"Not that I know of," Randy said. "It was my primary concern to get her across the water." That probably meant Randy hadn't signaled for help at all, Peters thought, which was strange for an accidental drowning but perfectly logical if murder had been committed.

The whole interview lasted just six minutes, but Peters was struck by Randy's matter-of-fact tone. There was no emotion at all, no grief. It was almost as if he had been discussing a blown engine, not the death of a mate. And it was even stranger that Randy insisted Cindy had given out just a single cough and had swallowed only a mouthful of water. The rescue people were certain that Cindy had swallowed a lot more than just a mouthful; so was McFadden. That was evidence Cindy had been under water a lot longer than Randy was willing to admit.

About the time the memorial service for Cindy Roth was drawing to a close, Stacey Reese was calling the police.

Stacey explained to the police operator that she might know something about the woman who had drowned. The operator connected her with Sue Peters in major crimes.

Sue Peters always answered her telephone the same way. "Detective Peters," she said.

Stacey told Peters that she didn't know whether it was important or not, but that she knew the man whose wife had drowned. "Oh?" Peters asked.

Yes, said Stacey. His name is Randy Roth, and he works where I work. "How well do you know him?" Peters asked.

"I've gone to lunch with him a couple of times," Stacey said. Beginning when? Peters asked. Beginning earlier in the year, shortly after she had started work at the car dealership, Stacey said. In fact, Stacey said, she and Randy had lunch together in a park only the day before Randy's wife had drowned.

"Really?" said Peters, to encourage her to go on.

Yes, said Stacey. Randy wasn't very happy with Cindy, Stacey told Peters. In fact, Randy told her he and Cindy weren't *really* married, that they only had a one-year "marriage contract." Randy told her the contract "was just about up." Randy complained about Cindy a lot, Stacey said.

"He said she was obsessive and nasty," Stacey continued. "He said she was too bitchy." Randy made it clear to her that he wanted to get out of the relationship. In fact, Stacey said, she had the impression that either Cindy or Randy, one or the other, was packing to move out when the drowning happened.

Still, moving out was one thing, and dying was another.

Tell me about Randy, Peters encouraged.

Well, Stacey offered, Randy was a Vietnam veteran. He talked a lot about Vietnam, and he talked about death a lot, too. "He said that in the last six weeks, four of his family members had died," Stacey told Peters. He'd said this just the day before the drowning.

Stacey faltered a bit, and Peters realized that she was frightened. It wasn't so much that Stacey was frightened of Randy, Peters sensed, as much as of the act of actually calling the police to report these suspicions. Peters could imagine Stacey's predicament: one day Randy tells her he doesn't like his wife, that he wants to end the relationship, that he was in Vietnam, that four of his family members have died in six weeks, and the very next day the unwanted wife is dead. It would make anybody wonder.

But what if the drowning was just a horrible coincidence? By calling the police to report the information, Stacey could be getting Randy in a lot of trouble. After all, he seemed a nice enough guy. And what if it got out at work that Stacey had said anything to the police? That would make her look like a troublemaker, like she was some sort of stool pigeon.

Peters assured Stacey that no one would know Stacey had called unless Randy were charged with a crime, and that was a long way off, if ever. Stacey said she understood that, but it still made her nervous. Stacey told Peters about a call she'd had from Randy two days after Cindy drowned.

"I asked him, 'Are you all right?' and he said, 'Why wouldn't I be?' " Stacey told Peters.

Randy's attitude was the thing, Stacey said. He was acting like Cindy's death was no big deal. Later the same night, Stacey told Peters, Randy had called her a second time, and this time he talked about the drowning. "He said it was a horrible thing," Stacey recounted. But then Randy suggested that perhaps Cindy had subconsciously *wanted* to die because their relationship was over. It gave Stacey the creeps.

But that wasn't all. Randy complained about the way Cindy had decorated their new house. "He said, 'It's going to take me fucking forever to get this pink and mauve out of here.' "

Randy called her a third time to ask her out to breakfast a few days later, Stacey continued. She turned him down, Stacey told Peters. It just felt all wrong, Stacey said. She had the feeling—it was only a feeling—that maybe, just maybe, Randy had killed his wife so he'd be free to make a play for her.

Then Stacey, growing more nervous, told Peters something that focused the detective's mind wonderfully: "You know that Randy was married before?" Stacey asked. "He told me the day before the drowning, while we were having lunch in the park, that his second wife died in a hiking accident. She fell off a cliff about ten years ago. They'd only been married about eight months when it happened.'

Peters' mind churned as she took in this development. So Randy Roth had been married before, and *that* wife had died too—also outdoors, also accidentally, it seemed. Very convenient, Peters thought. But *who* was the first wife? Where had the accident happened?

Peters pressed Stacey for more details, but Stacey had reached her limit. "I can't talk any more. I'm at work," she said, and hung up.

There had to be some way to find out who the first wife was, Peters thought. Too bad she hadn't known about the earlier wife when talking to Randy that morning; she could have asked *him*. That reminded Peters of the tape-recorded statement she'd taken from Randy about the circumstances of Cindy's drowning. She decided to take a copy of the tape over to the medical examiner's office to let people there listen to it. Maybe the medical experts would hear Randy's taped version of the drowning—at least listen to his voice—and decide there was just no way it could have happened that way. Maybe, after listening to Randy's own words, they would reconsider their tentative decision to classify the death as an accident.

Peters drove over to the county medical examiner's offices and met with Dr. Reay. Reay listened to the tape, and afterward Peters had questions. Based on Randy's story, did Reay now think Randy could have drowned Cindy deliberately? Was it possible for a person to drown so quickly? Was there anything at all to indicate murder rather than accident? For example, were there any marks on Cindy that might have indicated she'd been held under until she drowned?

Reay said he couldn't be sure, but he didn't think so. Yes, there were the two small scratches on Cindy's neck, but they could have come from the resuscitation violence. The tape didn't clarify the matter very much,

Reay said. Based on the available medical evidence, he said, he'd have to stick with the idea that the death was a probable accident.

Peters was only slightly disappointed. She was still thinking about Stacey Reese's phone call. Peters was growing more and more convinced that Randy Roth had murdered Cindy Roth, no matter what the medical evidence suggested, or rather, failed to suggest. But why? Why would Randy have murdered Cindy?

Tomorrow, Peters decided, she would start trying to find out who Randy Roth's *first* dead wife was. Maybe that would shed more light on the death of the second.

# 7

## "Something's Wrong"

**S**ue Peters liked to get to work early. It gave her a chance to reach people before they left home for their own jobs; it also allowed her to talk to other police officers before they went out on their shifts. Shortly after seven A.M., Peters called an acquaintance in the police department's marine patrol unit and recounted Randy's version of Cindy's drowning.

"That doesn't sound right to me," the marine patrol officer told Peters. "For one thing, people who drown, well, their bodies usually don't float. At least, not right away. I'd say you got yourself a suspicious drowning."

Fortified by this opinion, Peters made numerous telephone calls over the next hour, leaving messages at every number for people to call her. She was still trying to reach several of the lifeguards at the beach, including Kelli Crowell, and the driver of a boat which had been vaguely identified as one that might have caused the supposed wake. She called the manager of the car dealership where Randy worked, trying to get the names of some of Randy's coworkers. She called Cindy's brother in the hope he might offer some

insights on Cindy and Randy's marriage. She called a
police sergeant in Everett who had called her, for what
she had no idea. No one was available.

Then, just before nine o'clock, Peters got a call from
a woman who didn't want to give her last name.
Roseanne told Peters that she had been a friend of
Cindy's. She'd read about Cindy's death in the newspaper, and later had seen Randy at the memorial
service for Cindy.

Randy, she said, had acted strangely at the service.
People expresssing their condolences at his loss were
met with indifference, even rudeness. Randy had arrived with an urn containing Cindy's ashes. Randy had
simply left the urn on a table in an anteroom of the
chapel for Cindy's father to deal with and had just
walked away. "Something's wrong," Roseanne told
Peters.

In fact, the drowning itself was very strange, Roseanne continued, because Cindy was a very cautious
person. Her children were everything to her, Roseanne
said, and she never would have left them alone on the
beach. Roseanne thought Randy knew more than he
was saying. For example, did Peters know that Randy
had been married before? That his first wife had died
in an accident?

Here was a second person in a matter of hours to
tell Peters about the death of a prior wife of Randy
Roth. Peters was pretty sure the Roseanne woman—
who said she had known Cindy for years before she
married Randy—had never heard of Stacey Reese, so
it was unlikely that the two of them had cooked up the
story just to get Randy in trouble.

What was the name of the first wife? Roseanne said
she didn't know. But Cindy's best friend, a woman
named Lori Baker, worked at Silver Lake Chapel,
where the memorial service had been held. Lori Baker
had lived with Cindy and the boys before Cindy mar-

ried Randy, Roseanne told Peters. Maybe Lori Baker knew the name of the first wife.

Just as Peters hung up, the telephone rang again. This time it was a detective sergeant who had taken a call for her while she was talking to Roseanne. Call this woman back, said the sergeant, providing the name and a number. She's got something.

Peters dialed the number the sergeant had given to her. The woman answered right away. "Is this Mary Jo Phillips?" Peters asked. "This is Detective Peters with the King County Police. I understand you know something about Randy Roth."

Indeed she did, said Mary Jo Phillips, who then proceeded to tell Peters that she had been Randy Roth's girlfriend some years before. Now she was afraid Randy was about to kill her, too, because of what she knew about him.

# 8

## Mary Jo

**M**ary Jo Phillips told Peters that she was in her mid-thirties and the mother of five children. She'd lived with Randy for a time in 1986, she said. "He's had four wives," Mary Jo told her. *Four wives!* Peters thought. "I was engaged to him for awhile myself," Mary Jo added.

Mary Jo said she had been divorced just after she met Randy and didn't want to marry him. What's more, Mary Jo told Peters, she and Randy argued about life insurance—insurance on *her* life. A switch closed in Peters' mind. *That's got to be it,* Peters thought—*life insurance*.

After five years as a detective, Peters knew as well as any cop that guessing about motive in the absence of facts was pure foolishness. People did all kinds of criminal things for all kinds of reasons, Peters knew; by far the most common reason for murder was simple rage. Most people who murdered their spouses did so on the spur of the moment, usually for reasons that seemed by any objective measure to be utterly trivial: a deprecation or complaint taken too far, an insult, a

38

taunt, sometimes just an irritating habit that suddenly assumed unbearable proportions.

The disclosure that Mary Jo and Randy had "argued" about life insurance on *her* strongly suggested a possible motive for murder by Randy: money. It was rare indeed for a spouse to murder for cold hard cash; few had the stomach for it. But if it happened mostly on television or in the movies, that didn't mean it couldn't happen in real life. Could Randy Roth be capable of killing a wife for cash? It might explain a lot about his behavior.

And, of course, there was the wife who, according to Stacey Reese, had fallen from the cliff—if insurance was involved there, too, that might indicate some sort of *modus operandi*, "M.O." in detective talk, the peculiar signature of action and motivation that signaled premeditation and planning. If Randy had done it once, Peters reasoned, and it had worked, maybe he'd tried it again.

But *was* there any life insurance on Cindy Roth? Short of asking Randy directly, there wasn't any immediate way of finding out. It was becoming crucial to delve into the recent history of Randy's life with Cindy Roth, Peters realized. She needed to find someone who was close enough to Cindy or Randy to know if Cindy had been insured, hopefully someone who could also provide an idea of the kind of marriage Randy had with Cindy.

Peters now asked Mary Jo to tell her more about Randy's earlier marriages. Mary Jo was quite willing.

Randy's first wife, said Mary Jo, was named Donna. She was the mother of a son by Randy, who was named Greg. Mary Jo said Randy told her Donna had disappeared when Greg was just a baby. Mary Jo had the idea from Randy that Donna might be living somewhere in California. Greg had stayed with Randy.

Randy's second wife was Jan, Mary Jo said. She was the first one who had died. Randy and Jan had been living in Mountlake Terrace, a suburb north of Seattle. Randy had told her that Jan slipped during a roped ascent of Mt. Rainier and had fallen to her death, Mary Jo said. After the fall, Randy was investigated by the police, but nothing happened.

Was there insurance? Yes, Mary Jo said; Randy told her he'd received several hundred thousand dollars from life insurance on Jan.

Donna was the third wife, Mary Jo told her. Peters was confused. Wasn't Donna the first wife? No, wait, you mean Randy was married to two *different* Donnas? Right, said Mary Jo. The second Donna was much younger than Randy, maybe ten years younger. That marriage only lasted three months, Mary Jo said. The second Donna had left Randy because she was afraid of him. Peters asked Mary Jo how she knew that Donna #2 (as Peters began to think of her, to keep her straight from the first Donna) had been afraid of Randy, and Mary Jo told her that she had once met and talked with Donna #2.

Cindy, Mary Jo continued, had been Randy's fourth wife, and the second to die. Now Mary Jo was worried that *she* might be in danger herself because of what she knew about Randy. She had been keeping a diary that discussed Randy, Mary Jo now told Peters; when Randy found out about it, he wanted her to destroy it. Randy told her it was "too incriminating," Mary Jo said. Peters wondered what was in the diary that Randy might think was incriminating.

Tell me more about Randy, Peters urged.

Well, Mary Jo said, when she met him in 1986, Randy lived in Snohomish County, just to the north of Seattle. He was a Vietnam veteran who collected martial arts trophies. He had lots of weapons around the house, including handguns and a sawed-off baseball bat with nails sticking out of the business end that he kept in a corner of the living room. He is paranoid, Mary Jo added.

Randy really doesn't like women, she said, and didn't like little girls, although he seemed to get along fine with boys. He didn't drink or take drugs. He had never been physically violent with her, but was very strict with his son Greg.

"He has a military mindset," Mary Jo said. "He was in Vietnam. He told me he had killed people and mutilated women and children, and that afterward, he had to go through three months of brainwashing just to be safe to be in society again."

*Holy cow!* Peters thought. If Mary Jo was right about Randy, he was beginning to sound like someone who was certainly capable of committing murder.

Mary Jo filled Peters in on some additional details of Randy's life, including the fact that he had recently been investigated in connection with another large insurance claim—this one from the theft of tools worth thousands of dollars from his house. *More insurance,* Peters thought. And there was one more thing, Mary Jo said.

"Do you know Randy has a brother who is in prison?" she asked.

"Oh?" said Peters.

"He killed somebody," Mary Jo told her. Randy had told her a little about it, she said. There was something about bullet holes in the brother's car that somehow had led to his arrest. Randy was contemptuous of his brother for having been caught, Mary Jo remembered. " 'You *don't* get caught,' was what he said," Mary Jo added.

"Well, what happened?" Peters asked. "I mean, why did the brother commit murder?" Mary Jo wasn't exactly sure, but Randy told her that a friend or a member of Randy's family had been killed, and that Randy's brother had evened the score by killing the person who had killed the friend or sister. Or something like that.

*Wow,* thought Peters, as she hung up the phone.

Only the day before she had almost nothing to work with except a gut feeling that something was wrong about the drowning of Cindy Roth. Now, in less than twenty-four hours, the good leads had exploded: a possible love interest by Randy in Stacey Reese, possible hefty insurance proceeds from the death of a prior wife, an earlier police investigation into that death, an investigation into possible insurance fraud in the theft of tools from Randy's house and even a brother who was in prison for murder! Who said detective work was boring?

# 9 | Free Fall

The first thing to do, Peters realized, was track down the earlier investigation into the death of the second wife, the one named Jan. There might be details there that could shed light on Randy's more recent activities, maybe even the name of an insurance broker. That might help her learn whether Cindy Roth had also been insured.

Mary Jo's story about the death of the first wife—actually, the *second* wife, Peters reminded herself—dovetailed somewhat with the information from Stacey Reese and Roseanne. Mary Jo, of course, had more details: Mt. Rainier, climbing, ropes. That would be a start. Once she got that pinned down, she could look for someone who might know about life insurance on Cindy; maybe Lori Baker would know about that.

Mt. Rainier, the 14,410-foot dormant volcano that dominates the skyline southeast of Seattle, is one of the premier climbing meccas in the country. It was perfectly plausible that Jan Roth—Peters assumed Jan used Randy's last name—had fallen while climbing there. Each year, it seemed, several people were killed on the mountain. The peak was in Pierce County, the county immediately to the south of Seattle. Peters called the Pierce County Medical Examiner's Office to see whether they had any record of a Jan Roth having been killed on Mt. Rainier. The Pierce County officials told her they had no Jan Roth in their records.

Rats! thought Peters. Five minutes later, she called the state's bureau of vital statistics. An official there found a record for the death of a Janis L. Roth, who had died November 27, 1981 at a place called Beacon Rock State Park in Skamania County. Peters knew Skamania County was in the mountainous south-central portion of Washington State, along the Columbia River, about an hour east of Portland, Oregon.

The death certificate for Janis Roth said she had been twenty-nine years old when she died in a three-hundred-foot fall from Beacon Rock, a near vertical, ancient volcanic plug that rose some eight hundred feet above the Columbia River valley. The rock was at the center of a state park. *Another park,* Peters noted. The records identified the dead woman's husband as Randolph G. Roth of Mountlake Terrace. The death was classified as an accident. Was it the same Randy Roth?

Peters dialed the number for the Skamania County Sheriff's Office and was connected with Undersheriff Mike Grossie. Peters explained that she was investigating the recent death of a woman named Cynthia Roth, who had been married to a man named Randy Roth. Peters said she'd heard of a Randy Roth who had been married to a woman who had died in a fall in Grossie's jurisdiction. Her question was: was this the same man as *her* Randy Roth?

Grossie remembered his Randy Roth very well. He found the file on the fatal fall. His Randy Roth had the same birthdate as Peters' Randy and the same driver's license number. It had to be the same person, Grossie agreed. Grossie, who supervised and often conducted most of the criminal investigations for the largely rural county, went on to tell Peters why he was quite familiar with his Randy Roth.

Ten years earlier, Grossie told Peters, he was convinced that his Randy had murdered Janis Roth by shoving her off Beacon Rock to collect $100,000 in insurance on her life. He just hadn't been able to prove it.

# 10

## "Get It All..."

Talking with Mike Grossie convinced Peters she was on the right track. Randy Roth, she concluded, had almost certainly murdered Cindy Roth, probably for insurance money, just as he had killed ten years earlier for the same reason. But believing something and proving it are two entirely different matters. Peters decided to tell her supervisor what she had learned.

"Guess what I found out," Peters told Sergeant Frank Kinney. "Not only has Randy been married *four* times, his second wife died and he had a lot of insurance on her. Skamania County has a file on it, and they're gonna send it up."

Coincidences do happen, Kinney knew, but the odds of one man having two wives die in recreational accidents one decade apart did seem a bit long. Kinney had already agreed with Peters that Randy's version of his wife's death didn't sound right. Now here was the possibility of a pattern: murder for life insurance proceeds.

But Kinney, a veteran of more than twenty years in police intelligence and investigations, also knew that proving a case involving complex circumstantial evi-

46

dence—"no smoking gun," as he later put it, meaning there was no apparent eyewitness to the drowning besides Randy—would probably consume hundreds of hours of investigative time and require a tremendous investment in patience and persistence. It might well be that the only way to solve the case was to confront Randy with information that might lead him to confess.

And if Kinney was any judge of character after two decades as a cop, it didn't seem very likely that a man who'd murdered once for money was likely to confess to anything. Probably the only way to prove Randy Roth had committed murder would be to enmesh him in the web of his own deceits, to bring out the circumstances that, taken together, could lead only to the unavoidable conclusion that murder *had* happened.

It might take months, and the major crimes unit was already short-handed. *But then*, thought Kinney, *isn't that what we're paid to do? I mean, you can't go around murdering people, it's our job to stop that sort of thing and catch you if you do it*.

This was a job that looked like it would take more than one person. Kinney turned to a second detective sitting nearby, who had been listening with interest to their conversation, and asked him to back Peters up. Randy Mullinax and Peters had worked together before, and in Kinney's mind, tended to complement one another. Where Peters tended to be effervescent, enthusiastic and energetic, Mullinax was an expert interrogator and an experienced digger. Peters might get you to talk, but Mullinax could tell if you were lying.

Mullinax was thirty-nine years old. He'd been a policeman since 1978 and a detective for nearly a decade. He was a short, trim man with a high forehead, dark brown hair styled back, and a ready grin. One of his most noticeable attributes was his eyes. They fixed a person in place, so that one could not escape the realization that whatever was being said, a substantial portion of Mullinax's brain was listening, turning things over, evaluating, searching for meaning and connections, remembering.

From 1984 to 1987, Mullinax had worked on the Green River murders—the worst serial homicide case in the country.

Along with a score of other detectives, Mullinax had patiently reassembled the pasts of dozens of possible suspects, looking for something, anything, that might tie a killer to nearly fifty young victims. Criminal histories, driving records, divorce cases, credit card invoices, interviews with friends and coworkers, bar owners, streetwalkers, all contributed to a mountain of information on possible suspects that was funneled into a gigantic computer database, which Mullinax and others constantly sifted, looking for the one fragment that would tie everything together and bring the case to a conclusion. Although the day never came, those digging skills were exactly what would be required for the Roth case.

A year earlier, Mullinax had solved a kidnapping case that had baffled the police for almost two years. Mullinax first noticed that an earlier kidnapping case in another jurisdiction bore marked similarities in the type of victim. Mullinax sat down with a newspaper reporter and related aspects about one of the kidnappers' backgrounds that had never been publicly disclosed, in hope that someone who read the paper might recognize the person.

A day later, Mullinax got just one phone call. But that one call delivered a name, and when Mullinax then matched the past of the named man with the kidnapper's description of himself to his victim, Mullinax was able to arrest the man and get a confession, and thereby arrest two other men and solve the case. It was a matter, Mullinax thought, of collecting background on the suspect and matching it with the background of the perpetrator. Now Mullinax would do the same with Sue Peters on Randy Roth.

"It sounds to me like this guy Roth is a stone cold killer," Kinney now told Peters and Mullinax. "Let's get him. Find out everything you can about the guy. Where he banks. His insurance company. Where he grew up. His criminal record. His military record. Who his friends are. What he does with his time. His girl friends. Get it all. Take as long as you need to do it, but do it."

# 11

## Lori

While Randy Mullinax—Peters already began to think of her new partner as Randy the Good to distinguish him from the other Randy, who naturally became Randy the Bad—read over her log to familiarize himself with the case, Peters considered her next move. Her suspicions about Randy Roth might be valid, she realized, but she also knew there was still too much missing from the picture.

For one thing, she was having a hard time bringing Cindy Roth into focus. How on earth did this attractive, seemingly naive, church-going, outwardly happy mother of two, by all accounts a complete innocent, get tied up with someone like Randy Roth? What had happened? She knew she needed to find someone who could tell her more about Cindy, and particularly about Cindy's relationship with her new husband. Peters began looking for the woman Roseanne who described as Cindy's best friend, Lori Baker. Peters started at Silver Lake Chapel.

In her own mind, Lori Baker had been growing more and more suspicious of Randy Roth. At first, the

51

suspicions were doubts hidden deep within her own mind, and Lori saw them as an aspect of her own denial that her close friend Cindy was dead—that is, the seemingly irrational idea that Randy may have been responsible somehow made it easier to accept.

The truth was, Lori realized, she and Randy had never gotten along. Randy had always seemed stand-offish to Lori, jealous of her long friendship with Cindy, and that had been true from the first, even before he and Cindy were married.

Lori was thirty-three and an administrative assistant at Silver Lake Chapel, which over the years had grown into a large evangelical church with its own Christian school serving much of south Snohomish County. Cindy, during her first marriage to Tom Baumgartner, had attended the church along with many other young couples with small children. Then, in 1984, Tom was diagnosed with Hodgkin's Disease; within a matter of months he was dead, leaving Cindy alone with her two boys.

Never married herself, Lori was a competent, orga-nized blond woman of pleasant features who favored a direct approach to most matters and plain talk wher-ever possible. Where her friend Cindy tended to em-phasize her femininity and occasionally got rattled over more typically male tasks, Lori was of a more practical, take-charge bent. She'd become friends with Cindy after Tom Baumgartner died. As a young mother, recently widowed, Cindy had at times been overwhelmed with all the responsibilities of single parenthood. To help Cindy out, Lori moved in with Cindy and the boys and became something of a surro-gate parent. The boys attended the school at Silver Lake Chapel.

Then Cindy married Randy. Lori moved back with her own parents while she looked for a new place to live. She'd still been looking when Cindy drowned.

That night, Lori heard the news on television. She

immediately called the Roth house. No one answered, so Lori left her name on the machine. No one called back, and finally around eleven, Lori was able to get through to Randy. Was it true that Cindy was dead? Lori demanded. Randy said it was true. Well, said Lori, why didn't you call me? Randy lamely told her he'd intended to call her the following day. For the rest of the night, Lori alternated between being completely numb at the news and being furious with Randy.

Over the next few days, several people who had also seen the news broadcasts about Cindy's death talked to Lori. The story coming out in the newspapers and on television just didn't sound right, they told her. How could Cindy have drowned so quickly with Randy right beside her? Why hadn't he done anything to save her? On Monday, Lori attended the memorial service for Cindy and had seen firsthand Randy's apparent disinterest in the ceremony, and in the people who had come to pay their respects to Cindy's memory.

Thus, Lori was only a little surprised on the next-to-last day of July, a week after Cindy's death, to get a call from a King County police detective who identified herself as Sue Peters. Lori agreed to meet with Peters and Mullinax, and tell them what she knew about Randy and Cindy Roth.

"Is it true," Peters asked Lori shortly after they met, "that Cindy and Randy had a one-year marriage contract?"

Lori wasn't sure at first whether Peters was kidding. "What?"

Peters explained that the detectives had received information that Randy and Cindy had agreed to some sort of one-year trial marriage. "That's ridiculous," Lori said. "I never heard anything like that."

As a Christian, Cindy wouldn't even go on a trip

overnight with Randy before they were married, Lori said; the very idea of a woman who wouldn't take an overnight trip with a man unless she was married to him entering a one-year "trial marriage" instead was absurd. Peters marked this down as a lie on Randy's part, one calculated to signal to Stacey Reese his imminent availability. But did the lie mean that Randy had been planning to get rid of Cindy *months* before she drowned?

Peters and Mullinax asked Lori whether she'd talked to Randy since Cindy's death. Yes, Lori said. She told the detectives about the call she'd made to Randy on the night Cindy died. Randy had described the accident to her. He'd told her he'd given Cindy twenty minutes of mouth-to-mouth resuscitation. That was far different than Randy's previous admissions that he had attempted no resuscitation efforts.

When Peters and Mullinax asked Lori how Randy and Cindy had gotten along with each other, Lori told the truth: the marriage was disintegrating, Cindy was very unhappy about it and had been thinking of leaving Randy despite her strong opposition to divorce.

Well, how did Randy meet Cindy? Why did they get married?

That was the thing, Lori told the detectives. It was very strange. Randy just seemed to become a completely different person not long after he and Cindy were married. Lori told the detectives that Randy had met Cindy at a Little League ballgame, where his son Greg was playing, and Randy was coaching. Cindy liked to support Tyson and Rylie in their activities, and they were playing in Little League, too.

One night in the spring of 1990, Lori said, Cindy volunteered to work in the concession stand at the Little League field. Randy met her there and began an acquaintance.

Soon Randy had asked Cindy on a date, and Cindy was very pleased when Randy had all the boys go with them. For Cindy, the family was everything, the church was very important, and here was a man who seemed to feel the same way. Randy was very polite, charming in the extreme, almost chivalrous, Lori said; he called Cindy frequently, sent her flowers, planned activities for all of them, and just generally seemed to be a wonderful, strong, kind, and occasionally funny man. Cindy had asked Lori what she thought of Randy, and Lori was hard-pressed to see any drawbacks.

Cindy, Lori continued, was very much against divorce. She'd often said she would never marry a man who had been divorced. When Cindy found out that Randy had been divorced from Greg's mother, however, she'd made an exception—because it was Greg's mother who had left the marriage, not Randy. Cindy knew all about the wife who had fallen from the cliff, Lori said, and felt sorry for Randy and Greg because of the tragedy.

When she thought about it from Cindy's point of view, Lori said, getting married to Randy might not have seemed like a bad idea. Cindy had been a widow for more than five years; her boys were growing up, and Cindy thought having a man around would be good for them. Certainly the boys seemed to get along well with Randy and his son Greg.

Then, in August of 1990, Randy invited Cindy to go with him to Reno to see a car show. Cindy had turned him down, saying she couldn't go on an overnight trip with a man unless he was her husband. That was when Randy proposed and Cindy accepted, Lori said. Cindy's mother and father tried to talk her out of it, saying it might be too soon, but Cindy told them she'd made up her mind. Randy was the right one, Cindy believed.

After Randy and Cindy returned from Reno, Lori said, she'd moved out. Randy and Cindy lived for a few weeks at Cindy's house, then both Randy and Cindy put their existing houses for sale and found a new place in Woodinville. The new house was very expensive, Lori said; Cindy had paid the whole down payment with the money from her house, because Randy's house didn't sell right away.

It was after they moved into the new house, Lori continued, that things started to go wrong.

At first Cindy wouldn't talk very much about it, Lori said, but Lori knew her friend was depressed. Being depressed wasn't in Cindy's nature, Lori said. By December or so of 1990, Cindy had begun to confide in her, however, that the marriage with Randy wasn't working out as well as she had hoped.

For one thing, Randy wouldn't go to church, which knocked out a big part of Cindy's life. Randy also tended to be moody, Cindy told her. He criticized Cindy frequently, complained about her appearance, and insisted on taking over her finances. Sometimes Randy was mean to the boys, sneering at them if they didn't seem to be tough enough.

Once Lori saw Rylie crying and asked him what was wrong. Randy had hit him with a rake, Rylie said, because he wasn't raking leaves properly. And there were other things. On a couple of occasions, Cindy was unable to start her car; she was convinced Randy had disabled it to keep her at home.

Then, by the following spring, Lori said, Cindy began to suspect Randy was cheating on her. Confrontations began over this and over money. Cindy threatened to leave Randy, but somehow the incidents blew over, and Cindy stayed. That was how matters stood when Cindy drowned.

What about Cindy's finances? What was her situation before the marriage?

Well, said Lori, Cindy was pretty comfortable before the marriage. When Tom Baumgartner died, he'd been insured for several hundred thousand dollars. The money was enough to pay off the house Cindy had with Tom and buy a new house free and clear of any mortgage. Then, Tyson and Rylie both received Social Security survivor's benefits and a small amount twice a year from Tom's pension fund.

Without any house payments, with her investments from the remaining life insurance money, the income from Social Security and the pension, there was enough money for Cindy and the boys to live comfortably without Cindy having to work. In some respects, said Lori, Cindy was seen by some men as a good catch because of her financial situation.

Did she have any life insurance on herself? Lori was pretty sure she did; she remembered Cindy had a policy in her own name before she'd married Randy. Probably the records could be found at the Woodinville house, Lori said.

How about a will?

Cindy *did* have a will, Lori said, and it might be in a safety deposit box at a bank in nearby Everett. Lori knew about the box because when she lived with Cindy, they were both signatories; later, she'd been taken off the signature card and Randy had been put on.

As for the will, at one time, Lori said, before Cindy had married Randy, Cindy had named Lori as the executor of Cindy's estate and guardian of the boys in case anything had happened to Cindy. Lori didn't know whether the will had been changed after the marriage, but it might still be in the box.

Was there anything else about Randy and Cindy that Lori could remember?

Well, said Lori, yes. Randy's mother lived across Puget Sound with his sisters. She'd come to Cindy's memorial service. She seemed strange, Lori said.

And, she remembered Cindy telling her, Randy was a Vietnam veteran. He still had nightmares from the war. He'd had to kill many people. Once he and his platoon had wiped out a whole village, including women and children, Cindy told her. Cindy thought the war had affected Randy very deeply, and was trying hard to be understanding of his behavior.

Randy was very proud of his combat record, Lori added; one wall of the house in Woodinville had been given over to plaques, a formal photo of Randy in his Marine dress uniform and displays of military insignia. One plaque had been awarded to Sergeant Randy Roth, Ironman, for Randy's performance in some sort of physical conditioning competition while he'd been in the Marines.

One final thing: had Cindy ever mentioned that Randy was married one other time, and later divorced?

You mean there was another marriage that he never told Cindy about? Lori asked.

That's what it looks like, Peters and Mullinax told her.

Peters and Mullinax next drove to the Snohomish County Courthouse in Everett. There they looked for records relating to Cindy and Randy, and almost immediately came upon the will Lori had described. The document was dated December 12, 1985; as Lori recalled, it gave custody of Tyson and Rylie to Lori and also made her executor of Cindy's estate.

Whether the will had been amended after Cindy's marriage to Randy was unclear, but if it hadn't, that meant Lori Baker was entitled to legal custody of Tyson and Rylie, as well as Cindy's estate. Peters wondered if Randy knew about the will.

The detectives also uncovered information about Randy's marriage to Janis Roth in 1981, and her death. Randy, it appeared, had sued the state over the fall from Beacon Rock. The lawsuit was later dropped by Randy. The court file included a lengthy deposition by Randy which provided a wealth of background information and a detailed description of the events surrounding the fatal plunge.

As Peters and Mullinax drove back to Seattle while

discussing their discoveries, they considered what to do next. Discussions like this were vital to a detective team, and having them would be a routine Peters and Mullinax would follow every working day for the next seven months, until ultimately they would be able to anticipate each other's moves and thoughts by the slightest lift of an eyebrow or the merest change of expression.

At this point, they had the bare outlines: a man who had been married four times, the last time to a comparatively wealthy young widow, a marriage which had the effect of improving Randy's own financial situation considerably; obvious strains in the marriage; a possible attraction to another woman; a previous wife dead under unclear circumstances that had been investigated by police; questions about life insurance proceeds both times; inconsistent statements about what had happened at the lake; a brother in prison for murder; and finally, numerous eyewitnesses who described behavior that seemed at the very least indifferent to the last wife's death. Peters and Mullinax decided they needed to confront Randy with some pointed questions about his past.

That afternoon, Peters called Randy and asked him if he wouldn't mind stopping in at the detectives' office in downtown Seattle the following day.

"We have a few more questions we need to clear up," Peters told him. Randy said he would be happy to come in. In that, at least, he was dead wrong.

# 12

## The Interview

Randy Roth arrived at the detectives' offices on the first floor of the King County Courthouse in downtown Seattle just before eight o'clock on August 1, 1991, almost one year to the day after he had married his fourth and last wife.

This was the first time either Peters or Mullinax had actually seen the man they had heard so much about, the man Mary Jo Phillips had described as a hard-bitten Marine killer, the mutilator of babies, strangler of women, the man who spent three months in a military hospital just to be fit to live in society again.

The real Randy Roth, however, seemed ordinary in every respect.

He was wearing jeans and a polo shirt, but was quite well-groomed, Peters thought. His dark mustache was neatly trimmed, and he was wearing contact lenses rather than the thick wire-framed glasses some said he occasionally wore. Randy was polite, calm, and gave every appearance of being cooperative.

The detectives invited Randy into a large conference room and closed the door. Randy sat on one side of the table at the very end. Mullinax took a seat opposite, and Peters sat between them at the end of the table.

As envisioned by the detectives, this would be a low-key meeting, as relaxed as possible. The detectives wanted to get Randy talking, to observe his behavior, and see whether he would be truthful with them. They chose not to tape the conversation in order to induce Randy to speak freely.

Randy, of course, had no idea how much the detectives already knew about him. As far as he knew, this interview would be merely another routine discussion of what had happened at the lake, a formality so the case could be officially closed as an accident.

For the next three hours, however, Mullinax gently probed at Randy while Peters took notes. The questions covered Randy's family, his background, his work, his hobbies, his marriage to Cindy and the events at the lake. As the interview wore on, Mullinax worked deeper and deeper into Randy's story, carefully attempting to draw him out on ever more specific details. Randy admitted that Cindy's life was insured, but wasn't too clear on the amount; he thought it might be around $200,000.

Throughout the questioning, Peters and Mullinax were both struck by the utter lack of animation in Randy's voice. There was nothing casual about any of his responses, no smiles, no frowns, just as there was nothing to indicate grief or shock over his wife's recent death.

*He's so matter-of-fact about it,* Peters thought, mentally validating what others like the lifeguards and Redmond police had already told her. Peters formed the impression that, inside, Randy Roth was an extremely rigid person, focused to an extraordinary degree on his outward image, bent on maintaining his self-control and having contempt for others without a similar orientation; thus, Randy seemed "tightly wound" to her.

No matter what the question, Randy's tone remained flat, unemotional. Both Mullinax and Peters noticed this behavior; it was like Randy was shielding himself by going on autopilot, making no attempt to differentiate between the relative significance of the events.

After about two hours, Mullinax escalated the interview by bringing up Randy's prior marriages.

The new subject seemed to distress Randy, although he tried to conceal it. Mullinax again pressed Randy for details. Randy seemed to be reluctant.

He'd been married for the first time in 1975, he said, to a woman named Donna. *Donna #1,* Peters thought.

Donna was the one who wanted to leave the marriage, Randy said; she didn't want to be committed. He wasn't sure where she was now. It had been several years since he had last talked to her. She was Greg's mother.

Does she have visitation rights? Sure, Randy said. Have any family in the area? Well, I think she has a sister east of the mountains, Randy told them.

Did you marry again, before you married Cindy?

Yes, Randy said. My second wife was named Jan. Janis. She died in a hiking accident.

When was that?

Oh, 1980 or so. He'd been divorced for about a year from Donna when he met Jan at a Parents-Without-Partners dance. They'd been married the following March.

What was her background?

Well, Jan was from Texas, Randy said. She had a daughter from a previous marriage. The daughter went back to Texas to live with Jan's ex-husband after Jan died. The natural father had parental rights, he added.

What happened in the hiking accident?

Well, Randy said, she fell off the side of the trail at a state park. She hit her head on a rock. We'd been there before with the kids and I thought the place was safe.

Did anyone see the fall?

There were several people on the trail that day, Randy said. She lost her footing and fell. I was about eight or ten feet behind her. We were living in Mountlake Terrace at the time. We'd gone down to visit my parents for Thanksgiving. When the accident happened, it was just the two of us hiking.

Mullinax repeated his question because Randy hadn't answered it: Did anyone see the accident?

As far as I know, Randy now said, they were right there.

Who were "they"?

Randy was quiet. The interview was suddenly taking an ominous turn. Why were the police asking him all these questions about something that happened ten years ago? Why did they want to know about his other marriages? What did any of this have to do with Cindy?

Did "they" see the actual accident? Randy wouldn't say. Was there insurance on Jan?

At that point, Randy could have stopped the interview, saying he resented the implications of the detectives' questions and that he wanted to consult a lawyer. But Randy kept on talking, although, to Peters and Mullinax, his answers seemed to grow more evasive.

There *was* insurance on Jan, Randy admitted. It was about $100,000.

What did he do with the money?

He paid off his house in Mountlake Terrace, Randy said. That's what the policy had been for. He pointed out that both he and Jan were insured, not just Jan.

Okay. What about your third wife?

Well, said Randy, her name was Dawn. *Dawn?* thought Peters. *Oh, he must be referring to Donna #2.*

*He seems to be trying to keep us away from that marriage.*

Do you know her maiden name?

I'm not sure, Randy said.

When was this?

This was five years after Jan, Randy said. She was ten years younger than me. I met her at the store and we started dating, I guess, around Christmas. We were married in May. She moved into my house with her daughter. She left in September.

Why did she leave?

Well, she was hanging around with a wild crowd, and also, she slapped her daughter around. I asked her to leave, and we got a divorce.

Where is she now?

I think she moved to Utah or Colorado and was going to move back in with her first husband.

And then you met Cindy?

Yes, he met Cindy in 1990, Randy said, and until then he had no thoughts of ever marrying again.

Did you have any insurance policies when you met Cindy?

No, Randy said.

Do you have a criminal record?

Yes, Randy said. He explained that when he returned from the Marines in 1974, he began going with Donna. An old girlfriend got jealous. She'd set him up on a burglary charge. She had invited him to stay at her house. But when the old girlfriend found out about Donna, she called the police and accused him of burglary. He pleaded guilty, Randy said, but didn't have to do any jail time.

Was there a police investigation into Jan's death? Well, said Randy, there was. Also an autopsy. I don't know for sure there was an autopsy, but I assume there was one. About a month after the accident, a guy from the police came to my house and interviewed me about the accident.

How did you feel about that?

For about three weeks after, I felt like I was being watched or something, Randy said.

The detectives asked who Cindy's closest friends were, and Randy named Lori and a woman who did Cindy's nails. She also has friends from aerobics, Randy said.

Okay, said Mullinax. One other thing: how would you feel about taking a polygraph examination? We can do one right now, here in the office, and get it over with.

"This is beginning to sound like I'm a suspect in something," Randy told them. "Am I?"

"It's hard to say at this point," Mullinax told him. "We can't really say—maybe yes, maybe no."

"I don't think I want to do anything further without talking to a lawyer," Randy said. He added that he didn't really object to taking a polygraph, but thought he needed to talk to a lawyer first, and get some advice.

Okay, said Mullinax, then just a few more questions. Have you ever been fingerprinted? I think so, Randy said. Have you ever been involved in any lawsuits? No, said Randy, I've never filed any suits.

That was untrue, of course, as Peters and Mullinax had determined only the day before. But it was not the only lie Randy had told. There was a little wobble about mouth-to-mouth resuscitation for Cindy; Randy said he'd given her two quick breaths before giving her up as a lost cause, but told Lori Baker he'd given Cindy twenty minutes of CPR.

A larger wobble came when Mullinax asked Randy who paid the down payment on the new Woodinville house; Lori Baker had been positive the money had come from Cindy only, but Randy said his money was used as well.

A real big whopper had probably come over Cindy's will; Randy denied there was any will, and Peters and

Mullinax were pretty sure that a man like Randy had to have known about it, even if he hadn't realized it was recorded in the Snohomish County records. Probably there were lies about life insurance too.

One thing Randy had *not* lied about was his military career.

Randy told them that he'd served in the Marines for just one year. He said nothing about being in the Vietnam War, or even being in combat. Instead, he'd served as a company clerk, mostly on Okinawa in 1974. He'd left the Marines after his mother had written the corps asking for a hardship discharge for her son.

That Randy was not the embittered, battle-hardened veteran everyone seemed to think he had been came as no surprise to Peters and Mullinax; by now they had already calculated that, for Randy to have seen any fighting in the war, he had to have joined the Marines when he was fourteen or fifteen years old. That didn't seem very likely.

Additionally, Peters and Mullinax knew that virtually all U.S. combat forces had been removed from the country while Randy was still in high school. So much for wiping out villages, killing women and mutilating babies. At least militarily speaking, Randy was a fraud.

Mullinax discussed the interview with Peters after Randy left. Later, Mullinax would say it was one of the most unusual interviews he ever conducted.

"He responded the same when we asked him what he did for a living as to tell us about what happened when Cynthia died," Mullinax recalled. "His accounting of the situation was exactly the same; there was never any fluctuation in his voice, there was never any emotion. It left both of us with a very uncomfortable feeling about this man, what he was all about."

Both Peters and Mullinax were now certain that they

were hardly wasting their time in trying to determine whether Cindy was murdered. Randy Roth was the only person with the means and the opportunity to murder on two different occasions, since he'd been alone with both victims when they had their fatal "accidents."

And now that they'd learned that Cindy's life had been insured for as much as $200,000, maybe more, it also appeared that Randy had ample motive. The task would be to prove just what had *really* happened on the lake, and why.

As soon as he left the detective offices, Randy went to a pay telephone in the King County Courthouse. He put in the coins, dialed a number in Lynnwood, Washington, and left a message for George Cody, attorney at law.

"Tell him to call me as soon as he can," Randy said, and hung up. Randy Roth might not always tell the whole truth, but he was not stupid. He knew he was in real trouble.

# 13 | Donna #2

The following day, Peters sorted through the county's old marriage license records and discovered the name of Randy Roth's third wife—Donna #2, as Peters thought of her.

Donna Clift had been only twenty-two when she'd married Randy in 1985. Randy had told them the previous day that "Dawn" had divorced him in September of the same year, and that she'd left the state. But Peters thought Randy's fudging of Donna's name indicated that Randy didn't want them to talk to the third wife. That made Donna Clift someone Peters *did* want to talk to.

Peters ran the Clift name through the police computer and came up with information relating to a Judith Clift.

Judy Clift was actually the stepmother of Donna Clift, Peters soon learned. Donna had been married—briefly—to Randy Roth in 1985, Judy confirmed. She too had noticed the news item about Cindy's drowning. She hadn't known Cindy, Judy Clift said, but she wasn't surprised the police wanted to talk to people about Randy. When she heard Randy had remarried in 1990, Judy Clift said, she'd told her husband that Randy's new wife wouldn't live a year.

The next day, Peters and Mullinax went to interview Donna Clift at a dry cleaning store where she worked. Randy had been wrong about her leaving the state. Donna was willing, even eager, to talk about her brief marriage to Randy. It had been a strange experience in her life, Donna told them; and in the end, she'd had to get out. Why? Well, said Donna, the whole marriage had been a mistake.

Had Randy ever discussed life insurance with her?

As a matter of fact, he had, Donna told them. But she wasn't interested in being insured, so they'd never bought any. Not long after that, Randy became completely indifferent to her; that was when she'd moved out. Randy had become impossible to understand.

Donna said Randy had told her his mother and sister were dead. His mother had been driving to the Washington State Penitentiary in Walla Walla when she was killed in a car wreck. His sister had then committed suicide in her mother's hospital room after she was pronounced dead. Randy told the bizarre story in a complete deadpan. But then, Randy hardly ever displayed emotion.

"I never saw him cry," Donna told them. "I swear, there was nothing there.

"He told me that he was in Vietnam. And I think it was really bad, because I know when he got out he had to be put in a hospital for three months to be rehabilitated. That's what he told me. He was in some kind of special forces, that's all I know."

Did he ever talk about killing people?

"Yeah," Donna nodded. "Women and children. He had a thing about coughs. He cannot stand to have or hear anybody cough. And I think when they went in and killed all those women and children, from what he told me, they *all* had that cough. I don't know. He was just really weird, you know? To tell me a thing like that.

"I left him," Donna said. "I'm scared of the guy."

On the following Monday, the police conducted a test. The question was: did Randy's raft really flip over in a wake from a powerboat?

To make the test as authentic as possible, Randy's raft was used. Two county lifeguards were asked to play the roles of Randy and Cindy. The police towed the raft to the middle of the lake and the lifeguards began treading water near the raft while Peters and Mullinax gave directions and watched. A third detective videotaped the test, while a fourth began making passes with his personal seventeen-foot ski boat.

From "fifty to a hundred yards away," as Randy had described the distance between the boat and the raft on the day Cindy died, the wake from the police boat barely caused the raft to rock, let alone flip over. The detectives ordered the powerboat closer and closer to the raft in an effort to generate a wake large enough to flip the raft over. Finally, the detective's boat was within ten feet of the raft, roaring by at high speed, churning a wake of nearly two feet.

Yet no matter how hard the two lifeguards tried, they were unable to flip the raft over. The reason, the detectives discovered, was that the flat, inflated bottom of the raft tended to adhere to the water's surface; indeed, it had been designed partly with that feature in mind. It was only after the lifeguard playing Cindy reached far over the inflated side by nearly climbing into the raft that the raft could be deliberately turned over.

The demonstration seemed to indicate that whatever had happened on the lake, the raft had *not* turned over. Therefore, it appeared that Randy was lying about that crucial part of his story.

Afterward, Peters drove over to the east side of the

lake. She parked her car and began knocking on the doors of the houses up the hill from the water. She wanted to see whether there were any witnesses who had seen Randy and Cindy the day of the drowning. After eight doors, Peters finally encountered one man who remembered seeing the raft the day Cindy died. He never saw the raft flip over, he told Peters.

The next day brought Peters and Mullinax more new leads. Donna Clift called and said that she now remembered the name of Randy's best friend. Would that be helpful? You bet, said the detectives. The man's name was Tim Brocato, Donna said, and she remembered also that he was a fireman in Lake Stevens, a town about an hour north of Seattle. Peters called the fire department and left a message for Brocato to call her.

Peters also talked to Patti Schultz, the off-duty paramedic who had worked on Cindy at the lake, who later rode with Randy and the boys to the hospital. Schultz told Peters that Randy told her that he had been trained in CPR. On the drive to the hospital, Randy asked her how long a person's heart could be stopped before resuscitation was impossible.

And Schultz remembered that Randy had two or three sacks of belongings that were all soaking wet. How could that be if the raft flipped over? If the sacks had been in the raft, wouldn't they have sunk? If they weren't in the raft, how did they get wet?

Meanwhile, Peters called Lori Baker. Lori had been doing some more thinking about Randy Roth after her conversation with the detectives two days earlier. She now told Peters that she remembered that Cindy had wanted Randy to sign a prenuptial marriage agreement before the wedding, but that Randy had refused. Lori said she remembered that Cindy told her Randy had complained about the proposal, saying that a marriage without trust was no marriage at all. Cindy had decided not to insist, Lori told Peters.

Now Peters told Lori about the will she and Mullinax had discovered in the Snohomish County records department, the will that awarded custody of Tyson and Rylie, as well as Cindy's estate, to Lori. Legally, Peters told Baker, it appeared that she was now the foster mother of two boys. What should I do now? Baker asked Peters. Get a lawyer, Peters advised.

Next, Peters called the state Probation Office for information about Randy's brother—the one who was supposedly in prison for murder. An earlier effort by Mullinax to find out whether the state prison system held an inmate named Roth had been unsuccessful. Peters had the idea that perhaps Brother Roth was out of prison and on probation instead.

The probation system did indeed have a Roth in their computer system. David M. Roth, born in North Dakota in 1957, was still incarcerated at the Washington State Penitentiary in Walla Walla. Peters called the penitentiary and asked to speak to the counselor assigned David Roth's case.

David Roth, it turned out, was serving a sentence for first-degree murder. David Roth had strangled a woman in 1977 and then used a rifle to shoot her seven times in the back of the head. After fourteen years, the woman was still unidentified. David Roth had never known the name of the woman he killed. Contrary to what Mary Jo Phillips said Randy told her about the killing, there was nothing in the file about any revenge motive; it appeared the woman had been an innocent hitchhiker. David was scheduled for release in 1997.

Just after lunch, Peters called Cindy's insurance agent, Bruce Timm, whose name she had obtained from Lori Baker.

After Peters explained why she was calling, Timm said he had already heard from Randy about a possible insurance claim from Cindy's death. Randy had called him on the Monday after the accident, Timm said. That, of course, was the same morning Peters first interviewed Randy, and the same day as Cindy's memorial service. To Peters, it was yet another indication that Randy was more interested in money than the fact that his wife had just died.

"How much insurance is there?" Peters asked Timm. The policy was for $250,000, Timm told Peters. But that wasn't all. Cindy already had an existing $115,000 policy that was completely paid for before she had even met Randy. Timm told Peters he had advised Cindy to keep Tyson and Rylie as the beneficiaries of the earlier policy, but Cindy was insistent on naming Randy as the new beneficiary. That meant Randy stood to collect on both policies, a total of $365,000. There could also be other life insurance he didn't know about, Timm acknowledged.

What had Randy said about insurance during the interview with them the previous Thursday? Peters looked it up in her notes. Randy had told the detectives he believed he and Cindy had insurance of about $200,000, and that was primarily to protect the mortgage. Now it turned out the life insurance was even more substantial than Randy had admitted. Randy had insurance on Cindy for more than three times the amount of the mortgage.

Now Peters was absolutely sure Randy had a motive for Cindy's death. No wonder Randy was so methodical when he rowed in toward shore that day at the lake. The longer Cindy went without oxygen, the more blue her face turned, and the greener Randy's own bank account became. Peters wondered what Randy had been thinking while he watched Cindy on the sand that day at the beach. *Die, baby, die,* probably.

With Cindy dead, Randy likely thought he was in

line to receive assets worth more than half-a-million dollars, not to mention the boys' Social Security and pension money. That could be why Randy was insisting there was no will. It was almost certainly why Randy was insisting there'd been a terrible accident.

# 14

## Going to
## the Prosecutors

**S**hortly after eight o'clock on Wednesday, August 7, 1991, Peters and Mullinax sat down with Lee Yates, a senior deputy prosecutor in the King County Prosecutor's Office, and asked him to file a murder charge against Randy Roth.

Yates, a diminutive, trim man with a precise way of speaking, was in charge of the prosecutor's filing unit, which screened most police cases before charges were filed. Yates had made a career of prosecuting criminals, and had long experience with the legal demands of developing and presenting complex cases. But on this particular morning, he had a lot of doubts about the adequacy of any case against Randy Roth.

Peters and Mullinax sketched the case they thought they had against Randy: a man who far too casually rowed into shore with a dying wife, and who never tried to summon help; a man who showed absolutely no emotion as violent efforts to resuscitate Cindy commenced; a man who stood to gain at least $365,000 in insurance with the death of his wife; a man who had lost a previous wife to a recreational accident, and who had collected a substantial insurance payout on that incident a decade earlier. Further, the detectives told Yates, Randy was a man who seemed to have an outside-the-marriage love interest in Stacey Reese.

Finally, the detectives said, there were all the lies Randy had told: the Vietnam war hero who never was, the noble brother serving time for a get-even murder that was really just a hideous crime, the bizarre tale about the mother and sister who died so tragically, but really hadn't, and all the evasions about insurance and wills and other financial affairs.

Even Randy's many versions of what happened at the lake and at Beacon Rock ten years earlier seemed in conflict. Randy Roth, said the detectives, was a man who somehow murdered his wife and now stood to gain substantially from his actions.

Well, said Yates, what does the Medical Examiner's Office say? Was Cindy Roth deliberately drowned? Can that be proven? Were there, for example, marks and bruises that seemed to show violence before death?

That was a problem, Peters and Mullinax admitted. The Medical Examiner's Office had conducted a quick autopsy and was so far classifying the case as a probable accident. Now the body had been cremated, so it wasn't possible to develop any new information on that front. The best the medical people could say was that there was no way to say for sure that it *hadn't* been murder.

Yates understood perfectly well what the detectives were saying; based on their description of the events, he too shared a suspicion about Cindy's death.

But he was responsible for deciding whether to commit substantial public resources to the prosecution of the case. The worst thing that could happen, he knew, would be to bring a criminal charge that could not be proved; in that case, if Randy were acquitted, he could not be charged again with the crime, because of constitutional guarantees against double jeopardy.

It would be far better to make sure the case was airtight before issuing a charge, Yates said.

Besides, Yates continued, there are some potential legal problems in your theory of the crime.

It's likely, for example, that you'll never be allowed to bring up the death of the earlier wife. Roth's lawyers would be sure to claim that the first death and the insurance payoff would have no relevance to Cynthia Roth's death. The law, Yates told Peters and Mullinax, provided only narrow grounds for allowing evidence on possible wrongdoing that wasn't part of the actual charge.

Any actual charge on the earlier death would have to be made by Skamania County, Yates said, which had the only legal jurisdiction. They'd already declined to prosecute, Yates pointed out.

In a trial on the death of Cindy, any evidence about Randy's involvement in the first death would be considered a "prior bad act," as the lawyers called them. The law prevented prosecutors from using earlier negative events as evidence if they were likely to prejudice a jury against a defendant, and thereby make a fair trial impossible.

The only way the death of Janis Roth could be used in a trial about Cindy Roth, Yates continued, was if there were some sort of obvious connection between the two deaths; just getting money from insurance probably wouldn't be enough, he said.

Much the same reasoning would apply to Randy's lies, like his non-existent Vietnam, experiences, or his burglary conviction, or his physical abuse of the children; none of this would be relevant to the charge of the murder of Cindy, and so would have to be excluded.

That also goes for most of what happened at the lake the day Cindy drowned, Yates continued.

Just because Randy acted like a cigar store statue while paramedics worked feverishly on his dying wife didn't mean anything, at least under the law, Yates advised. Previous cases had already held that such "demeanor testimony" couldn't be allowed, particularly since the testimony usually represented the *opinion* of witnesses, who had no expertise to discuss the "proper" range of emotion under traumatic circumstances.

Roth's lawyers would therefore try to knock testimony about Randy's behavior out, too, and in Yates' opinion—he had prosecuted just such a case that had been reversed on appeal—the defense lawyers would be successful.

That didn't leave much, Yates said. You can establish that Cynthia Roth drowned, and that Randy Roth stood to gain a substantial sum of money from her death. But because the medical examiner can't establish with certainty that Cindy drowned at the hands of another, you lose. Right now, you need a lot more information before we can file anything, let alone a murder charge. But as matters stand now, once you knock all this stuff out, most of your case is demolished. Sorry.

Peters and Mullinax were badly dejected as they left the prosecutor's office. It didn't seem right that, because of the technicalities of the law, Randy Roth might go free, and even possibly collect more than a half-million dollars while thumbing his nose at all of them.

But when Peters and Mullinax got back to their office, Peters learned that Randy's best friend, the firefighter Tim Brocato, had returned her call. Maybe, Peters thought, that will jar loose some new information. Peters called Brocato. Brocato sounded nervous and reluctant on the telephone, but agreed to meet with Peters and Mullinax the following day.

* * *

Meanwhile, Sergeant Frank Kinney, Peters' and Mullinax' supervisor, began to consider some other options to Deputy Prosecutor Yates' lack of enthusiasm. Kinney discussed the matter with his counterpart at the police department's criminal intelligence section, and a decision was made to ask another lawyer in a different part of the King County Prosecutor's Office to take her own look at the case.

# 15 Brenneman

At forty-two, Senior Deputy Prosecutor Marilyn Brenneman was one of those organized people who somehow manage to juggle a demanding professional career with being the mother of four children. Her demeanor drew from her childhood roots on the Georgia coast, and the exterior of her personality seemed at once both soft and light, sometimes even airy, punctuated by a pleasing laugh and a genuine wit.

But this approachable side of Marilyn Brenneman masked a mental side that was relentless. Her memory was phenomenal, her logic unassailable, her articulation nearly flawless. Someone could sit down with her to have a conversation about food or flowers or clothes or any number of other ordinary topics and never suspect, never guess, that behind her ready laugh and smiling eyes was the brain of a legal barracuda.

She had taken a circuitous route into the law, but once having arrived, realized—as others quickly did as well—that she had a marvelous talent for the thrust-and-parry of the courtroom. The secret of Brenneman's success as a senior deputy prosecutor in the

King County Prosecutor's Fraud Division was thorough preparation.

Once Brenneman had tried a rape-murder case in which, try as they might, the police could find no physical evidence to link the suspect to the crime. While interviewing the surviving victim, Brenneman discovered that the rapist-murderer had torn eyeglasses from the victim's face during the attack, flinging them across the room. The eyeglasses had never been tested for fingerprints by the police, although they had been carefully preserved as potential evidence.

Brenneman arranged for the glasses to be tested, and a fingerprint was almost immediately found on the inside of the lens. The print matched the suspect's small finger. Because the suspect initially had denied that he was anywhere near the victim, the fingerprint turned out to be crucial evidence.

"That was no more than a week or two before trial, and it taught me a valuable lesson," Brenneman was to say later. "No matter how thorough the investigation is, you cannot leave a stone unturned. You need to interview everyone, you need to follow up on every lead, and you need to ask the police. You must not *assume* that they've done these things, and that they had resulted in dead ends."

That was largely how Brenneman handled almost everything for the fraud division's special operations unit, which advised the police on such matters as undercover work, wiretaps, and often, sting operations. Later, as the cases progressed, the SOU conducted the prosecutions, particularly those that resulted in racketeering or conspiracy charges, or complex financial manipulations.

Sometimes it could be overwhelming, never more so than when it was time to research the legal issues likely to arise in a case. Frequently, special police operations raise important constitutional issues, and that means hours of reading old, obscure cases from other times, other circumstances, looking for a way to do legally what the police need to do practically to obtain a conviction.

Such a volume of work usually made the eyes grow weak before their time, but to win, it was necessary. And if anything, Marilyn Brenneman was in the law game to win.

It wasn't only that Brenneman saw trials as some sort of competition, although there was some element of that. There is something of the performer encased in every trial attorney, and prosecutors are hardly an exception.

"I do like that," Brenneman once said. "I like having a captive audience. I enjoy speaking in public, even to hostile groups. I enjoy persuading people of things I feel strongly about. And, I enjoy the sort of detail that's involved in putting on a complex case."

In Brenneman's mind, the courtroom was a sort of theater, where the art of law calls upon the prosecutor to bring to life a picture of the events in the minds of the jury, to tell a story that gives the jury the facts and the understanding it needs to reach the truth.

But Brenneman was mainly in the practice of law, and in the prosecutor's office for that matter, because of a deep-seated commitment to the public good.

Her job, as she saw it, was to act as the public's surrogate when it was necessary to deliver justice; without a system of effective justice—particularly when the strong victimize the weak, as is often the case when crimes occur—the very underpinnings of social agreement that allow people to live together in at least some degree of harmony would be wrecked, to everyone's loss. So Brenneman took her responsibility very seriously indeed.

Now, in early August of 1991, as officers from the county police department asked if she would be willing to look over a complex, circumstantial case involving a man who might have murdered two of his wives to collect on their life insurance policies, she was both intrigued by the challenge the case promised and fully aware that if murder had happened, it was the responsibility of those charged with the public trust to try to prove it.

It was only later, much later, that Brenneman realized just how much the Randy Roth case would represent so many subtle, continuing issues about the contemporary relationships between men and women. The distinction was, in the case of Randy Roth, that those differences had been taken to the extreme.

# 16

## "I Know Things about the Man"

On the following day, while Marilyn Brenneman was still familiarizing herself with the details of the Roth case, Peters and Mullinax set out to Snohomish County to conduct more extensive interviews with a number of witnesses, including Mary Jo Phillips; Cindy's mother and father, Hazel and Merle Loucks; and Tyson and Rylie Baumgartner, who were staying with them. From everyone they talked to, the two detectives added to their store of knowledge about Randy's life and behavior.

Randy, it seemed to Peters, was a something of a puzzle; while there were many distinct parts, it was difficult to fit them into a coherent whole. As Mary Jo, the Loucks, and the Baumgartner brothers talked about Randy and their experiences with him, Peters came to see him as a peculiar mosaic, in which some pieces seemed to stand out, jagged and jarring, while others, perhaps the most important, remained muted or hidden. Randy, she realized, was something of a cipher.

Based on others' descriptions, Randy was alternately a cold, calculating, methodical person, or he was a warm, passionate, caring person. Sometimes he was boastful, and at other times he was diffident, uncertain. Some saw Randy as a natural Lothario, while others saw him as so strait-laced that even kissing seemed risqué. Sometimes he was generous with his time, his help, his advice and his money; other times he was so stingy most people would consider him a surly tightwad. Who was the real Randy? It was hard to know with someone who seemed so proficient at posing as what others wanted to see in him.

Perhaps the most interesting information about Randy came from Tim Brocato, his longtime friend. Brocato, the detectives immediately perceived, was very afraid of Randy.

Brocato was about six feet tall, with short red hair and a freckled complexion. He lived in a new home not far from Marysville. He was waiting for them alone, and anxious.

To Mullinax, an expert in reading behavior and body language from his previous training as an interrogator, Brocato seemed hostile and defensive. He sat in a chair in the living room and refused to meet Mullinax's eyes. Every few minutes, he would rise from the chair and peer out the windows, as if he was expecting Randy to pull up outside any minute.

Peters and Mullinax both quickly sensed that Brocato knew important information about Randy. The difficulty would be in finding the key to open him up. Certainly Brocato seemed reluctant to talk to them, yet both detectives sensed that Brocato was struggling with himself; it was as if he wanted to talk, but something inside was getting in the way. What was holding him back? The detectives told Brocato it seemed to them he knew some important things, and that he needed to let them out. This agitated Brocato further, and finally Brocato told them, "I know things about the man that could come back, that could cause harm to me and my family."

Randy, Brocato told them, was a Vietnam War veteran. He'd been a killer in Vietnam. He'd strangled women and mutilated children. The detectives shook their heads. It wasn't true, they told Brocato; Randy had never served a single day in Vietnam, and he'd never killed anyone, unless it was his two wives.

Brocato was stunned. Were they sure?

There was no doubt, the detectives said. Randy himself admitted to them that he'd never been in combat.

Peters and Mullinax saw that Brocato was making a gigantic mental readjustment to this new information.

What sort of things did he know about Randy that might come back? the detectives asked. Brocato paused as if thinking things over. It wasn't anything specific, he said, it was more of a feeling, but just before Jan died Randy had asked him if he could ever kill his wife.

"I thought it was just crazy talk," Brocato said. But then Jan *died*. After the death, Randy had acted strange, almost ominous—as if he were telling Tim without actually putting it into words that he was responsible for Jan's death. Once, he said, a detective from Skamania County had interviewed Randy about Jan's fall. Afterward, Tim said, he'd asked Randy about the questioning, but that Randy had deflected him by saying he didn't want to tell Tim anything he'd "have to lie about later."

Peters and Mullinax listened quietly as Brocato went on to describe his long, often strange relationship with Randy. It was obvious that Brocato thought Randy had killed Janis; now Brocato believed that Randy had killed his last wife as well. But still Brocato seemed to be holding something back. When that blockage was removed, whatever it might prove to be, both Peters and Mullinax knew that Brocato might be the most important key to unraveling the secrets of Randy Roth.

On the same day, in her own mind, Brenneman worked out the broad outline of the case. What was it that tied all of Randy's behavior together?

*Motive,* Brenneman thought: Randy had to be an insurance crook. His history seemed to display a pattern in which insurance companies appeared to be the target; two wives were dead because they had been insured for substantial sums of money. Randy discussed insurance with a third wife, Donna Clift, and with a potential wife, Mary Jo Phillips. There was also the burglary claim filed by Randy for thousands of dollars.

The more Brenneman thought about Randy, the more she began to see the patterns in his behavior. Randy, she decided, was probably a person who had a basic need to control. Money, people, things, situations, whatever arose in Randy's life, Randy had some sort of compulsion to be the one *who had control*.

The techniques Randy used to control the women in his life also seemed part of a pattern: keep them home, keep them isolated from other men and their former best friends; retain control over all the money; intimidate them with war stories and their implied threat of potential violence; disrupt their transportation; belittle their self-image; work to demean their self-esteem.

All of these behaviors seemed present in Randy Roth's life, throughout his marriages and dating relationships, to the point that two of his wives were now dead—seemingly worth more to Randy in that condition than as mates. Murder, of course, is the ultimate form of control over another person.

But Randy wasn't born this way. And while Brenneman wasn't consciously thinking about these issues— she was mostly interested in getting Randy charged with a crime—she *was* interested in Randy's past.

Very interested, because Brenneman had an idea for getting around the legal problems previously cited to the detectives by Lee Yates.

It seemed to her that "prior bad acts"—such as the death of Janis Roth a decade earlier—*could* be included in a trial based on Cindy Roth's death if enough information was developed to show the striking behavioral parallels between all of the acts. There was a connective scheme here, Brenneman thought, a scheme in which Randy was a man who sought out women, wooed them, married them, controlled them, and then murdered them for insurance companies' money.

The only way to prove that, Brenneman knew, was to burrow deep, to go back down the previously hidden corridors of the life of Randy Roth.

As the summer wore on, those dark passages were to expose a personality as complex, as charming and as deadly as anyone could ever have imagined.

# THE LOVER

# 17

# The Badlands

About forty miles due west of Bismarck, along the hard steel rails of the Burlington Northern line, lies the small hamlet of Glen Ullin, North Dakota. It was to this place that the ancestors of Randy Roth came in 1895, German-speaking immigrants from southern Russia.

Today, Glen Ullin is a quiet little town of around twelve hundred residents, sandwiched between the tracks and State Highway 49. There is South Street, which runs along the tracks and, with its single signal, gives access to the feed silos and the loading docks and the farm machinery sales office, and there is a residential area perhaps ten blocks by four, where small, neat houses of varying ages and conditions nestle under poplars and cottonwoods.

The people of Glen Ullin are comfortable with who they are and a bit suspicious of travelers; in the two taverns along South Street, the pleasant talk is of gamebirds like wild turkey and pheasant, the roads and the seasons, and of course, of feed and livestock, because this southwestern corner of North Dakota is cattle country.

But there is little talk about the Roth family; in a small town, one learns to say little more to a stranger than one would be willing to have said about himself.

Certainly the family Roth—pronounced "Rothe" as in "both," in these parts—is well known in Glen Ullin. Randy Roth's parental uncle is one of the area's most successful cattle raisers, and also happens to be a commissioner in a neighboring county. In later years, as news of Randy's troubles in Seattle made its way to Glen Ullin, many may have shaken their heads or clucked their tongues, but they did so behind their own doors—certainly not among outsiders.

But if it is fair to say that a life is the result of a series of individual choices, it is also fair to observe that the world of one's origins may have a powerful effect on those choices. That is no less true of Randolph Gordon Roth, who was conceived in Glen Ullin in early 1954, and whose subsequent character was deeply affected by the conditions of his birth. One of those conditions is inescapably the land itself.

Tens of thousands of years' erosion by wind, rain, heat and cold have carved the landscape of southwestern North Dakota into increasingly fantastic shapes the further west one travels. For this reason, this country is called the Badlands.

The Badlands are a place of extremes. In the winter, howling blizzards rage down through Canada from the frozen Arctic, occasionally driving temperatures to as low as sixty below zero, freezing cattle in their tracks and bringing death to the unwary traveler; while in the summer the intense furnace of the sun burns down mercilessly, sometimes topping 110 degrees in the shade, what little of it there is. Rainfall usually averages less than fifteen inches a year.

In the summer, all around, as far as the eye can see, a reddish-brown ocean of parched soil forms timeless waves stopped in mid-surge. Conical buttes, rounded domes, flowing hills, rolling knolls, sulphurous vents, naturally burning coal seams, slashed here and there by hidden coulees or deep ravines, all make the Badlands a real-world embodiment of an earlier age's vision of Hell itself.

It is a harsh, unforgiving environment, one capable of killing without thought or mercy; it is a fact of nature, and one that was transmitted to Randy Roth from his father, and his father's father and his father's father's father for almost one hundred years.

The Roth family story is similar to that of many thousands of other immigrants who came to the Badlands around the turn of the last century. Like the Roths, many of the new arrivals were from south Russia, where they had lived for several hundred years as so-called German-Russians—German-speaking colonists who settled in the Volga River region at the invitation of Peter the Great.

Near the end of the last century, many of the German-Russians along the Volga began emigrating to the United States, where railroads like the Northern Pacific were selling land cheap around hamlets like Glen Ullin.

Almost all of the immigrants were incredibly poor, devoutly religious, and stoic, even fatalistic, in the face of privation, pain, disease and death—traits that Randy Roth retained deep within his own core years later. Few spoke English, and most tended to be clannish, clinging to friends and relatives from the old country, frequently intermarrying with cousins.

In the beginning, large extended families, parents with their married children and their children, lived together in houses made of sod or sandstone, isolated from other families for sometimes weeks at a time, particularly in winter when the ferocious blizzards made travel impossible.

Most believed the relationship between men and

women was ordained by God. God was first in the hierarchy, and the oldest man, the family patriarch, had the final responsibility of interpreting His Word. Often the only book in a household was a family Bible, and this was frequently printed in German.

A man who helped his wife with work around the house was ridiculed as soft or henpecked. Women were expected to follow their fathers or husbands' commands without question. Boys were favored over girls.

While the men worked from dawn to dark with their livestock, with plowing and with cutting and baling hay, the women were expected to do all the cooking, baking, washing, mending, food preservation, milking and vegetable gardening. They also raised the family's chickens and turkeys, and collected their eggs. They churned milk into butter on a daily basis, and in large families baked up to six loaves of bread a day.

Without running water, the women were expected to fetch the water necessary for cooking and washing from nearby streams or wells and to tend the fire that heated it.

Meals were served first to the man, who received the largest portions, and who usually ate alone; later the woman and the children ate what was left over. The need for farm labor called for large families, so most women were pregnant every year for a dozen to fifteen years. Women were responsible for all child care.

Except for Sunday trips to church, most women were tied to the farmstead in near complete isolation for years of unrelenting drudgery, often virtual chattels. Thus, the status of most of the immigrant farm wives was only slightly higher than that of a farm animal, often valued by many men more for her production capacity than for any romantic notions. Such a deeply rooted view of women's "natural" place persisted through several generations, even down to that of Randy Roth.

The Roth family's roots in the Glen Ullin area began when two brothers, Gottlieb and John Roth, started homesteads around 1896.

Gottlieb's younger son was Andrew Roth, who was about ten when the families reached North Dakota. Andrew married in 1907, and a son, William, was born nine months later, the first of seven children born between 1908 and 1930. Andrew started his own farm south of Glen Ullin not far from his father's place early in the century. He died in 1948, when his son William was forty.

William Roth married in 1926 at the age of eighteen. He and his wife Anna lived on father Andrew's farm until 1977. William and Anna Roth had five children, all born in the 1920s and 1930s. The fourth child born to William Roth was Gordon Roth, Randy Roth's father, in 1935.

Thus, the Roths were farming and ranching families, working to make their living along the edge of the Badlands. It was for many years a precarious life, punctuated by droughts, livestock diseases, crop failures, wildly fluctuating farm prices, economic depressions in the 1920s and 1930s, and compounded by the ravages of the Dust Bowl years. It was a life in which wastage was sinful, in which parsimony was a virtue, stoicism a requirement, and in which men, women and children often died young, whether from disease, from accident, from ill-chance, or even God's will.

Like many of their fellow German-Russians, the Roths were Protestants, who made up about three out of four of the German and German-Russian immigrants. Whether it was because of their sheer numerical dominance, or for some other reason, the Protestant immigrants to the Glen Ullin area tended to do better materially than their Roman Catholic fellow countrymen; indeed, as time passed in the area, an economic and political gulf between the two religious groups began to widen. Only rarely did Protestants and Catholics intermarry. Such alliances were frowned upon in the patriarchal setting that tended to dominate both religious groups.

Randy's mother, however, was a Catholic. Born in September, 1938, as the oldest of fourteen children born to Paul and Mary Messer, Isabelle Messer came into the world at a time when her father was out of work, as were nearly one out of two North Dakotans in the 1930s. While the Messers were from further west in North Dakota, near the small town of Richardton, Paul and Mary Messer lived in Glen Ullin for much of the 1940s and 1950s.

Just how the farm-dwelling Protestant Gordon Roth and the town-dwelling Roman Catholic Isabelle came to know each other is not entirely clear. In addition to being of different economic and religious backgrounds, both were quite young. Gordon had made it through the eighth grade, after which he went to work on his father William's ranch outside of Glen Ullin.

Sometime in the early spring of 1954, Isabelle— known by her family and friends as Lizabeth—became pregnant. Lizabeth was fifteen, Gordon barely eighteen. In September, Lizabeth turned sixteen. It was not until December 9, 1954, when Lizabeth was over eight months pregnant, that Gordon and Lizabeth married. Three weeks later, the day after Christmas in 1954, Randy Roth was born in a Bismarck hospital.

Illegitimacy was hardly unknown among the immigrant North Dakotans; it was looked upon with scorn, however, as might be expected in a society so permeated by traditional religious values. The divergence of religious faith between the Roths and the Messers was also a serious obstacle in the marriage.

Years later, a thousand miles west in Washington State, as the marriage of Gordon and Lizabeth finally unraveled, Randy Roth was to tell friends that he blamed himself for the fact that his parents had even married in the first place; his father, Randy said, bitterly blamed Lizabeth for entrapping him in the marriage by becoming pregnant. For her part, Lizabeth blamed Gordon for having seduced her.

Those conflicts between Randy's mother and father, coupled with the two families' traditional views about the primacy of men's control over women, were to play significant roles in the development of Randy's personality. Worse, the more bitter Gordon grew about the marriage, the more Lizabeth turned to her religion for refuge, with consequences that were later to be seen as rather bizarre.

In any event, Gordon and Lizabeth soon moved to Bismarck, where Gordon obtained work with his Uncle Elmer as a plumber. Within a year another child arrived, Darlene; then in 1957, a third, David. In the late 1950s, Uncle Elmer moved to the Seattle area, where he initially found work with the Boeing Company. Gordon, Lizabeth and the three small children soon followed. Later, Gordon and his uncle worked as plumbers in the Seattle area, frequently on new housing projects that were springing up north of Seattle in the boom years of the 1960s. By 1970, Gordon and Lizabeth had five children, including two younger daughters born in Washington State.

But by 1971, Gordon had decided he wanted out of the marriage. He told friends that Lizabeth was driving him crazy with her deepening religious convictions. Worse, the three older kids were running wild, Gordon told friends; Lizabeth seemed incapable of controlling them. Gordon disciplined the kids with his belt, just as William had done to him when he was a child, but Lizabeth raged at him when he did so. Lizabeth was particularly protective of David, who seemed extraordinarily dependent on Lizabeth.

In September of 1971, four days before Lizabeth's

thirty-third birthday, the thirty-seven-year-old Gordon
served Lizabeth with a divorce suit. Lizabeth did not
contest the divorce and, indeed, was not even represented in court. Gordon agreed to give Lizabeth the
family home in Lynnwood, and pay $70 a month per
child in child support, or a total of $350. The house
payment was $220, which left Lizabeth very little room
to maneuver. Gordon retained ownership of his vehicles, a separate piece of real estate and, interestingly,
two life insurance policies on himself. Lizabeth and
her children were left to fend for themselves, a situation which soon landed Lizabeth on public assistance,
much the same as her own father and mother had been
years before.

# 18

## Billy Jack

**Y**ears later, when Detective Sue Peters began searching for people who knew the Roth family as Randy was growing up, she would encounter numerous people who remarked on the desperate poverty of the Roth household. Moreover, many also remarked on Randy's fatalistic acceptance of *responsiblity* for that poverty. Somehow, in Randy's mind, it was he who was the cause of all his family's suffering.

That Randy felt particularly sensitive about the circumstances of his birth was made clear by a childhood friend to Peters years later.

"What was that like to Randy," Peters asked Belinda Howard in 1991, "when the parents were getting divorced? Was he upset?"

"Yeah," said Howard. "He didn't care for the adversity that was going on in the family. One thing, he was always very bothered by the fact that he was illegitimate. He would talk about that a lot. In fact, he talked about it so much that I went to my mother and I asked her, 'Was *I* illegitimate?' Because he was just really bugged by it.

"His parents had to get married," Belinda told

Peters, "because she's Catholic and he [Gordon] converted to Catholicism because of her, and she was, I think six or eight months pregnant, something like that with Randy—when they had to get married.

"And he used to talk about how, if it wasn't for him, his parents wouldn't have had to have gotten married, and his dad—his dad was pretty hard on his mom, and [while] I don't remember ever seeing anything [like] physical violence, he was just a tough guy. He was just kind of angry and—gosh, I don't know how else to put it."

Belinda told Peters that she began going steady with Randy in high school. Randy, she said, had given her a ring. Belinda was also from a broken family, and being around the larger Roth brood helped fill in some of the family life that Belinda missed. She loved Lizabeth Roth like a "second mom," Belinda said. But Lizabeth "was a little different."

"Can you describe her to us?" Peters asked.

"Well, very religious," Howard said. "Religion governed everything. Quoted the Bible a lot. Certain things on television couldn't be watched, because of religion. Went to tent revival all the time. Very concerned about her hair, it had to be perfect. I loved her, to put it bluntly."

While Belinda wasn't clear with Peters as to why she thought of Lizabeth as a "second mom," when one considers some of the social conditions of the late 1960s in King and Snohomish Counties, it's possible to see why. Most significantly, the late sixties represented an important cultural watershed between the traditional family values of the postdepression, postwar, fifties years and the experimental values of the mid to late 1960s.

The largest factor in this change was the increase in family transience, which was accompanied by disintegrations between parents, parents and children, and important social value groups, such as churches, schools, youth activities and the like. All of this social instability inevitably led to a reduction in the traditional beliefs about behavior that enforced personal conduct in smaller, more stable communities.

By the early 1960s, when the Gordon Roth family arrived in Snohomish County to the north of Seattle, the entire area was in the midst of one of its most sustained economic bursts.

Until the 1960s, Snohomish County was a primarily rural, agricultural county that began a dozen miles north of Seattle's city center. The arrival of a gigantic Boeing Company aircraft plant, coupled with the extension of major highways like U.S. Highway 99 and Interstate 5, transformed much of the area from smaller semi-rural villages into bedroom communities serving both Seattle and Everett.

Thus, throughout the sixties, seventies and eighties, towns like Edmonds, Lynnwood, Mountlake Terrace, Mill Creek and others grew rapidly as farmers converted pasturage to houses. Between 1940 and 1970, Snohomish County's population grew from just under 88,000 to 265,000, mostly concentrated along the highway corridors linking Seattle to Everett. The great bulk of the new residents were newly arrived families with small children, as was the family of Gordon and Lizabeth Roth.

The environment of southern Snohomish County was about as different from the high plains of North Dakota as could be imagined. In North Dakota, people *knew* one another; they knew each other's grandparents, uncles, brothers and sisters, warts and all. There was an existing social network in the churches, schools and the marketplace, regulated by the changing of the seasons and the distances that had to be traversed. Aberrant behavior was noticed and remarked upon, with the result that people tended to conform to social norms throughout their lives.

But in Snohomish County during the boom years and after, families tended to be far more psychologically isolated even if they did live in closer proximity. Often next-door neighbors knew each other in only the most superficial terms. Institutions which would normally have helped socialize young adults were shallowly rooted. Families moved around a lot, or broke up and reformed around new partners. The sense of time was foreshortened to the problems and opportunities presented by each week, rather than the longer view made possible by a more interdependent community.

In this setting, values tended to be more superficial, more material: clothes, cars, "toys" as Randy later described his desire for material goods, all of which became an element of *who* someone was, a definition of selfhood that revolved around the exterior image.

"In the last three years I've spent thousands of dollars on cars and bikes trying to find a way to fill that empty, worthless feeling," Randy once confided to a close friend. For Randy, as well as many of his contemporaries, the propensity to gather material things as the means of defining oneself was as much a part of creating the modern social mask as more primitive cultures once employed real masks or secret names.

But the bubble which helped create this new and mostly artificial environment popped in 1971, when the Boeing Company began to lay off workers. Coupled with the winding down of the Vietnam War and changes in worldwide demand for commercial airplanes, employment at Boeing plummeted from 95,000 jobs at the end of 1968 all the way to 37,200 by October of 1971.

In Washington State, the drastic reduction of jobs is still referred to today as "the Great Boeing Bust."

Tens of thousands of families streamed out of the state, belongings crammed into U-Haul trailers, in a desperate search for work elsewhere, until some wag finally saw gallows humor in the situation by printing bumper stickers that read, "Will the last person leaving Seattle please turn out the lights?"

Hundreds of thousands of other jobs were likewise lost: real estate agents, auto body repairmen, department store clerks, short order cooks, truck drivers, telephone operators, indeed, just about everyone whose economic livelihood depended on the huge payroll spillover from the Boeing Company.

Whether the great Boeing Bust had any immediate effect on the marriage of Gordon and Lizabeth Roth remains unclear, but that was the year that Gordon filed for his uncontested divorce from Lizabeth. And it also marked the beginning of Lizabeth's sharp decline into desperate economic circumstances—circumstances that were eventually to have a direct bearing on the personalities of Randy Roth and his brother David, and which go to explain something of the motives that drove both of them.

Belinda Howard was later to tell Peters that money "was very, very tight" in the Lizabeth Roth home, and that Randy had to work long after-school hours to bring enough money home to help his mother make ends meet. Others recalled that Randy, was the only licensed driver, was required to drive his mother, brother and sisters wherever they needed to go. Randy was also expected, at sixteen, to buy all the family groceries.

As a result, Randy found himself working a series of low-paying jobs while he was still in high school, either as a gas station pump jockey or a helper at a market, nursery, or similar work. Under the circumstances, it's not surprising that Randy began to resent his mother deeply, according to many of his closest friends.

In this value vacuum, Randy became increasingly incorrigible, resorting to vandalism of mailboxes and stop signs, hotwiring cars, committing petty thefts, unfunny pranks like squirting unsuspecting people with stolen fire extinguishers filled with paint, and similar anti-social acts that served as an outlet for his aggressions and frustrations from his family life, as well as a means of creating his own identity. In short, Randy became a juvenile delinquent.

Years later, Randy was to tell friends a story that probably carries some psychological significance. As Belinda Howard recounted the story to Peters, Randy told her that while he was in the Marines on Okinawa he had killed someone accidentally in a street brawl, and that he was financially responsible for the welfare of the family of the person he had killed.

To Peters, this story had all the earmarks of the way Randy twisted reality to suit his own manipulative purposes. The end that Randy desired was to gain the sympathy of Belinda; at the same time it showed Randy as a martyr, it also portrayed him as capable of murderous violence, however "accidental" or in self-defense. Yet Randy would be a good citizen and pay the damages, even if it took him the rest of his life.

After hearing this story from Howard, Peters and Mullinax were naturally curious to see whether it was true. A check with U.S. Navy investigators, however, showed the story was false; there was no record of Randy killing anyone while he was in the Marines, let alone that he was financially responsible for an entire family. And yet, there was a germ of truth in the story: Randy felt himself—by the fact of his conception and birth—to be "responsible" for his parents' marriage in 1954.

And with Gordon gone, Randy had to be "responsible" for financially supporting the family his birth helped to create. And ultimately, the logical extension: with responsibility came the right to *control*.

\* \* \*

Sociopaths, of course, are made, not born. In Randy's case, the conditions were probably present from his birth: the unhappy marriage of Gordon and Lizabeth, Randy's belief that he was the cause of their strife, coupled with the inherited taciturnity of Gordon toward the expression of feelings.

"Randy and his brother were brought up by their father, who didn't allow them to show emotion," Lizabeth Roth told a newspaper reporter years later. "He [Randy] was reprimanded for it. That's just the way he was brought up." In other words, Randy learned early to develop a very hard shell, and to believe that giving expression to emotional feelings was unmanly. In later years, Randy would tell friends that his mother used to discipline him by making him remain on his knees in the kitchen.

Moreover, as a child Randy was smaller than many kids. With his thick glasses, he was often teased as "Four Eyes." Randy hated the sneer; he hated being teased about anything. "You never teased Randy," a childhood friend remembered years later. "He couldn't laugh at himself."

People who teased Randy or insulted him were always the subject of Randy's retaliation. Randy constantly brooded on ways to get even. Randy thought of himself as different than other kids, sometimes as a pariah or an outcast, as he occasionally put it, other times as some sort of romantic outlaw.

The mask being cultivated by Randy in those early years drew upon icons of popular culture. One was the car. Randy loved working on cars.

"He always had to have the best car," one of his high school friends remembered. In high school, Randy acquired a used Pontiac GTO and spent hours working on its engine. At night Randy raced the car around Lynnwood and Snohomish County, running red lights and taking corners on two wheels. Driving recklessly and fast was as much a part of the image of

Randy the rebel as smashing mailboxes for fun. "With Randy, there was always the edge of risk," one friend recalled years later. "There was never a dull moment with Randy."

The other icon was a movie: *Billy Jack*, the story of a black-hatted loner who spoke sparingly and used his martial arts to clean up a corrupt town. The movie apparently appealed to Randy's search for the needed heroic image; years later, Randy's high school acquaintances recalled him wearing the character's black hat, jeans jacket and sheath knife with identical glowering machismo. Similarly, Randy worked out frequently and practiced martial arts. He never drank alcohol or smoked cigarettes and stayed completely away from the drugs that were then permeating the youth culture.

As he was growing up, Randy selected his friends based on the deference they showed him. "Randy couldn't stand to be made a fool of," recalled one friend. "He had to be the top dog. If he couldn't be at the top, he just wouldn't participate. He had to be the center of attention."

The departure of Gordon Roth in 1971 likely exacerbated these tendencies. Suddenly Randy was thrust at sixteen into the role of being the oldest male in the family, with the added pressure from Lizabeth of having to earn money to help support his brother and sisters. Randy became an exaggerated version of his view of his father, but a version imbued with all the self-doubts of a teenager trying to win his scornful father's approval.

"I've wondered so many times how it would be to have had a dad around when I needed someone to talk to or ask advice of," Randy later wrote a friend while he was in the Marines.

"I know if he wouldn't have always put me down I would be welding right now for $7.50 an hour and up. . . . I remember how he used to tell me, 'What do you want to weld for, that ain't no kind of special trade, you're already half-blind anyway.' That was only one of the confidence-building lectures I've received. When I mentioned construction work 'cause I like to drive he said it was 'seasonal.' Everything I've ever been good at and wanted to do has been criticized.''

After Gordon's departure, the family's rapid descent into poverty in a culture that tended to value personal worth by material possessions was scarring to Randy's still-developing personality, and later would be seen in Randy's desperate efforts to avoid financial difficulties by any means, including possible murder.

These forces came to bear on Randy at a time when developing a self-image was significantly affected by the attitudes valued by his peers, where one's importance in the scheme of things was determined by the things one had and the sort of person one *appeared* to be.

Seeming to be in control, being in command, of the forces affecting his life became an essential part of Randy's nature. The mask Randy displayed to the rest of the world was of someone who was quiet, confident, capable, tough, brimming with subterranean power and potential violence, mysterious, charged with the aura that there was always something more to be discovered.

On that foundation of sand, Randy over the years began to add to the legend in his own mind: war hero, martial arts expert, clever financier, mountain climber, scuba diver, lifesaver, motorcycle racer, strongman, whatever was necessary to project the armor necessary to protect the real Randy inside.

That Randy, as least initially, was just a sixteen-year-old boy saddled with overwhelming responsibilities, an irrational guilt over his own existence, and a clear incapacity to cope.

# 19

## "He Was Very Serious"

Years later, Belinda Howard described something of Randy's personality to Peters. "He was just the kind of person who, you know, was mysterious enough . . . where you wanted to break that and figure out who he was." That mask of quiet mysteriousness later became one of Randy's most potent tools in attracting and controlling women.

Controlling people was one of Randy's earliest defense mechanisms. Belinda recalled a trip she made with Randy and his family to visit Lizabeth's parents in Eastern Washington.

"Over there," she told Peters, "we had just a little argument. We were in his aunt's living room watching television and I was sitting on the floor with my back to him, purposely ignoring him, you know, giving the cold shoulder, and he was throwing little things at me, teasing me, and saying, 'Come on, turn around and talk to me,' and I was just ignoring him.

"It was nothing, no big deal. He wasn't trying to hurt me physically by throwing things at me. He was just trying to get my attention. After a while he got up and left the room, and a little bit after that I got up to go see where he went. And he did a complete turn-around.

"Now he was ignoring me and he would not speak to me, and I begged him for hours to speak to me and please tell me what was wrong, why wouldn't he talk to me? He completely turned the situation around, and when he finally did, after hours of—I mean, I was just emotionally broken down. I was crying and everything was horrible.

"He finally said, 'I'm too much like my father,' and 'We're breaking up.' That was all he said. Then he got in the car and he left, and I didn't see him for a couple of days."

Belinda's story was interesting in that it showed that even at sixteen or seventeen, Randy had already learned some of the techniques of control that were later to mark his relationships with other women.

Belinda's "cold shoulder" was likely seen by Randy as a challenge to his control over her; when attempts to cajole and tease Belinda into submitting to him failed, Randy withdrew and punished Belinda, to the point where Belinda was "just emotionally broken down." Years later, Randy was to employ the same techniques with Donna Sanchez Roth, Janis Roth, Donna Clift Roth, Mary Jo Phillips and Cindy Baumgartner Roth. Mary Jo referred to it as the "hot and cold" aspect of Randy's personality.

On another occasion, Belinda's mother—who didn't like Randy and tried to prevent Belinda from seeing him—went to Randy's house to pick Belinda up. Belinda's mother pulled her out of the Roth house and marched her to the car. Randy came out after Belinda and chased the car down the street, screaming at Belinda's mother and pounding on the windows.

"Why was he doing that?" Peters asked.

"I don't know," said Belinda. "I guess he was real possessive of me. I practically lived at his house. I was there all the time. And another time, my mother came over to get me and he bodily—she told me this the other day—he bodily threw her off the property." Belinda's mother had a friend with her, and Randy slammed the door on the friend's leg and held it shut while the friend was screaming for Randy to stop.

Randy's penchant for control extended to his lack of sympathy for injuries and illnesses suffered by others. Lizabeth for years had suffered from severe migraine headaches, often taking to her bed for long periods, throwing much of the burden of running the family onto Randy. Randy felt he had no choice but to accept this responsibility, yet at the same time resented his mother for this and had contempt for her suffering. Once Belinda experienced this side of Randy's behavior herself.

Belinda had just gotten her first car, she told Peters—an "old beater." Randy was driving the car, Belinda was sitting next to him, and one of Randy's high school buddies was sitting next to Belinda. Randy was driving the car fast through the residential neighborhoods of Lynnwood, Belinda said: "You know, rippin' and tearin' up and down the streets and practically two-wheeling around corners, just for the sheer pleasure of doing it, and as we went around, as we made a right-hand turn around a corner, the door behind the driver opened. . . .

"So I got up on the back of the bench seat where I was sitting, then leaned back and fell into the back seat and reached over and pulled the door shut." But as Belinda was trying to climb back into the front seat, the door opened again. Just then Randy put the car around another right-hand corner and Belinda flew out through the open door. "I just went flying right out the door and bounced across the street . . . ended clear across the street sitting on the sidewalk." Randy stopped the car, and Randy's friend ran back to where Belinda was sitting on the curb "totally dazed." Randy's friend checked her arms and legs to see if anything was broken and asked anxiously if she was all right.

But Randy's reaction to the accident was completely unexpected. "Randy parked the car and jumped out and ran over to me, and he crouched down and he grabbed my left upper arm and he squeezed it really hard and he said, 'If you make a sound, I'll hit you.' "

"Was he being serious?" Peters asked.

"He was very serious," Belinda said. "He was very serious. Yeah, I think that the incident scared him that if I had made—if I'd started crying or wailing like I'd been hurt or something like that and somebody had to call an ambulance or the police because of a so-called car accident, you know, it would have put him in a limelight which he probably wouldn't have cared to be in at that time."

"Did he show any concern for you being hurt?" Peters asked.

"Absolutely none," said Belinda.

Belinda Howard was not the only girl Randy dated while he was in high school. During the summer between his junior and senior years in high school, Randy met a sophomore-to-be named Theresa Mc-Guire.

Terri, as she was known to her family and friends, was an extraordinarily attractive, petite blonde. Almost from the beginning she adored Randy, no matter how Randy treated her. Even while Randy surreptitiously dated Belinda and another girl named Jan Johnson, Terri kept her faith in Randy. "I always knew he would come back to me," Terri later recalled. "I never pushed him or demanded; I never judged him or criticized him. I thought I could change him with love."

But Randy had learned to appear to be different people, as the occasion required. With Belinda, Randy tended to be the rowdy rebel; with Terri, he was the romantic protector. "I tried to please him as much as possible," Terri recalled. Meanwhile, Randy constantly told Terri that he wasn't good enough for her, a feeling that doubtless derived in part from Randy's own inner awareness that he wasn't the person he tried to appear to be, as much as the fact that the McGuires were much better off financially than the Roths.

But Terri also sensed in Randy a great yearning to be something more than what he was becoming. "I always told him, 'You can be anything you want to be.' " Terri said. By encouraging Randy and appealing to his better instincts, Terri thought she could help Randy rise above his grim surroundings, which by 1973 had become grim indeed.

"Randy never liked his home life, that was evident," Terri said. "He hated being there. Looked for any excuse not to be there. There was no laughter, no happiness. I could feel how he felt." There was constant bickering in the Roth household, punctuated by worry over money, Liz's headaches and frequent religious asides, which usually invoked the name of God to manipulate behavior. " 'Randy, God wants you to take care of your mother.' " Terri remembered Liz telling Randy. "He had total resentment against his mother." Inexorably, some of this sense of God the Punitive Demander began seeping into Randy's personality, along with the perception that his ultimate fate was really a matter only God could decide. That, of course, also relieved Randy himself of some of the responsibility.

Occasionally Terri caught Randy staring at Liz with what she privately thought was Randy's "evil eye." Randy began wearing dark glasses indoors so that no one could see what he was thinking. Liz kept telling him to take off his glasses, otherwise people might think he was a thief or something.

As his senior year unfolded, Randy spent increasing amounts of time over at the McGuire household, or the house of another close friend, Mike Conrad.

Sometimes Randy would stay at the McGuires until nearly two in the morning in an effort to avoid going home. Liz frequently called the McGuires demanding to know Randy's whereabouts.

When Terri and Randy were at the Roth house, Randy rarely interacted with the other family members, usually spending most of his time in his room with Terri or down in the garage working on his car. Even among his own family, Randy felt different. Other Roths smoked; Randy hated smoking. The Roths drank; Randy never drank. Randy preferred health food; the rest of the Roths ate whatever was handy.

By his senior year in high school, Randy had developed a reputation as one of the meanest kids in his school.

"Everybody knew you just stayed out of his way," Terri recalled. Other kids learned never to confront Randy or ridicule him. "Somehow accidentally your mirrors on your car would get broken, or a scratch would appear on your paint," Terri remembered. "You never teased Randy, never made him look like a fool."

Randy also got into a number of fights with other kids and was frequently suspended from school for brief periods. No other boy could approach Terri without getting the brunt of Randy's possessive anger.

"That's what they called it, the Wrath of Randy," Terri said. On several occasions Randy punched out other boys for touching her or even approaching her. Randy made it clear that Terri was his exclusive territory.

But while Randy played the role of the gallant knight with Terri, at other times he displayed less savory behavior.

To Sue Peters, Belinda Howard recalled an instance when she and her mother caught Randy breaking into their apartment by climbing through the kitchen window after jimmying it open. Belinda's mother later confronted Randy and asked him what he had been doing. Randy shrugged. "I just wanted to see if I could do it," Randy said.

The family of Randy's third girlfriend, Jan Johnson, also suspected Randy of having burgled their house. A neighbor saw a car that looked like Randy's parked in the Johnsons' driveway during the time of the burglary. Later, the family discovered a Purple Heart medal and a handgun had been taken from the house.

By the spring of 1973, U.S. involvement in the war in Vietnam was reaching its end. Randy, according to Terri McGuire, was completely indifferent to the issues of the war; if he said anything about the war at all, it was to vaguely conform to the sort of cynicism about its aims that was then widespread among young people. But the draft had been halted several years before, so Randy was in no risk of being conscripted. On March 29, 1973, the last U.S. combat troops were withdrawn from Vietnam. Five days later, on April 4, 1973, Randy joined the Marine Corps Reserve.

Terri later recalled why Randy joined. "He wanted to get away from home," Terri remembered. "Also, he couldn't get a job. He thought he could get some training that would help him." But why the Marines? "In Randy's mind, the Marines were the best, the elite," Terri recalled. "He thought if he was going to go into the service, it could only be the Marines, because they were the top."

But either the recruiter didn't spell things out for Randy, or, as Randy later claimed, the recruiter lied to him. Randy thought he could get the job training he needed to make his way in the world after leaving the Marines. Instead, when Randy signed up, he somehow failed to understand that his two-year active duty reserve commitment meant he wouldn't get any of the training he wanted. The Marine Corps generally despised two-year reserves as scrubs or fainthearts. Certainly, whatever job training the Marines had to offer wasn't going to be wasted on the likes of a two-year wimp like Randy. But Randy wasn't to find that out until it was too late.

In the meantime, Randy had about six months before having to report for basic training. In August of 1973, Randy confronted the same dilemma that his own father had encountered eighteen years earlier: Terri was pregnant.

The thought of becoming a father terrified Randy, Terri later said. "He said he knew he could never have been a good father," Terri recalled. Somehow it was all bound up in his relationship with Gordon, which had never been very good. What to do?

On the night of August 25, two days after Randy took his formal oath of induction into the Marines, a man wearing a ski mask held up a tire store in Lynnwood by knifepoint. One of Randy's high school classmates, Jesse Akers, was the only employee in the store at the time. The robber waved the knife in Akers' face and threw him to the floor, then tied him up and left him in a back room. The robber stole $240 and some eight-track tapes.

"I knew who it was right away," Akers said later. "I thought it was a joke and almost said, 'Hi, Randy. . . .' I knew it was Randy. He has the most recognizable, sort of bow-legged walk I've ever seen."

Akers called the police and told them he believed the robber was Randy.

Randy told Terri that he had committed the robbery, Terri later said. He gave her the money, which Terri used to terminate the pregnancy.

By the time the police got around to checking Randy out the following month, Randy was in basic training in San Diego. A Lynnwood police officer went to see Lizabeth, who said that Randy was in the military service and wasn't expected home until Christmas. The police went away that time. But they would be back.

# 20 | Semper Fi

In light of Randy's subsequent claims of military valor—indeed, his use of his Marine background to convince scores of his friends, girlfriends, acquaintances, enemies, and even his wives that he was one tough cookie—Randy's entire military experience is striking for how different it really was.

It wasn't just that Randy had never been in combat, let alone Vietnam, despite his war stories; instead, the reality of Randy's Marine Corps experience exposes him as a person who was simply incapable of adjusting to a situation over which he had no control.

For most of his life, Randy had hidden his vulnerabilities by asserting himself, by acting violent, and by committing outrageous acts that brought him admiration or at least fear; but in the Marines nobody feared the Wrath of Randy, and anti-social behavior was met with merciless discipline. In the Marines, Randy was "the lowest of the low," as he later put it, and *that* more than anything else Randy simply could not tolerate.

Meanwhile, Randy's attitude of defensive, posed superiority isolated him from his fellow Marines; in-

deed, it appears that he didn't have one single friend
by the end of his service career. Less than one year
after he reported for boot camp, Randy was begging
for help from his mother, his girlfriend, his congress-
man, anyone who could get him out of the corps.

The first ninety days of Randy's Marine career were
spent at the Marine Corps Recruiting Depot in San
Diego, California, a huge installation near the San
Diego airport where recruits were hazed by drill in-
structors, conditioned unmercifully, and where efforts
were made to sever the bonds between the recruits
and their girlfriends and families. For some reason,
Randy was never able to cast loose of those connections to his old way of living.

Within two days of joining the Marines, Randy was
pretty sure he wasn't going to like it. Everywhere he
went, somebody was yelling at him, calling him
"slime" or "worm" or even worse. For someone who
hated being ridiculed, the Marine Corps Recruit Depot
was not a benign environment.

Every morning, a drill instructor ran through the
barracks, getting everyone up at 5 A.M. The recruits
had just two minutes to get dressed and to make their
beds before inspection. Much of the rest of the day
was spent in physical conditioning, rifle drills and
studying military manuals. Just about the only conversation Randy had consisted of the words "sir yes sir,"
"sir no sir," and growling. All of his hair was gone,
and soon Randy's ears were sunburned and bleeding.
The slightest transgression of the rules was met with
harsh physical conditioning punishment. Once Randy
allowed himself a small smile of pride as he handled
his rifle in drills. The D.I. caught him, cursed him for
being happy and made him perform 500 squat-thrusts.
"The sarge said 'We don't need any bleep bleep bleep
bleep happy bleeping bleeps,'" Randy later recounted.

But Randy was better off than many of his fellow

recruits, in part because of the way he had honed his own physical condition before joining. By mid-October, Randy was outperforming many of the other recruits in rope-climbing, running the depot's obstacle course and similar exercises. After several weeks, Randy was made the guide of his platoon, which put him in the front rank. Ordinarily he would have been at the back of the platoon, where the Marines always put the smaller recruits, but being brought to the front was an honor.

However, by mid-November Randy was back in the rear again. "Well, I'm not the guide of the platoon anymore (not for awhile anyway)," he reported to Terri. "I had a little run-in with some guys from another platoon and they got hurt so the platoon commander is giving me time to settle down." Apparently, Randy's penchant for control through threatened violence was leading to excesses of his authority.

That so much is known about Randy's short-lived Marine career is primarily due to a fluke. As police were working to reassemble Randy's past in the summer of 1991, they were contacted by Terri, who gave the detectives an unexpected break.

Although sixteen years had gone by, Terri had kept a near-complete collection of sixty-six letters written to her by Randy during the entire eleven months of his Marine Corps service. And while the letters weren't ultimately needed in prosecuting the case against Randy for Cindy's death, they did provide a detailed look at what Randy's military career was *really* like, and how Randy worked when he was dealing with an audience of one.

The Randy-Terri letters are also remarkable for the insights they provide into Randy's personality while under the stress of Marine training and service. The letters show that as Randy's Marine career progressed, he grew progressively more isolated; as the isolation grew, Randy's need to control increased even as the scope of people and events he *could* control diminished. As Randy's compulsion to control grew more virulent, violent fantasies began appearing, as if Randy could somehow restore his own damaged self-esteem by claiming ever larger acts of aggression, eventually including descriptions of battles that never happened and heroic acts that never occurred.

At the same time, several major themes run through the letters that later appeared in Randy's adult behavior.

The first was Randy's unremitting struggle to define his self-image. That definition was in direct relationship with the fluctuations in Randy's control over the events of his life. At times, Randy displayed a remarkable degree of insight into his own personality, recognizing that his problems were rooted in his own confusion about who he was and how an adult should act.

For most of his life, Randy had centered his identity around his brusque, macho exterior, which in turn was tied to his risk-taking anti-social behavior, or his capacity for getting even, which ordinarily led others to validate the mask that Randy sought to wear.

But what was seen as outrageous or even funny in junior high school became obnoxious in high school, as the circle Randy could affect with such behavior grew larger. By the time Randy was in the Marines, the circle was vastly larger; no one was going to be either impressed or intimidated by Randy's antics or posturings, and that sort of behavior usually netted painful disapproval and discipline. In short, Randy was having a hard time growing up.

Randy realized this, the letters show, but was at a loss over what to do about it. Certainly he wasn't capable of taking advice from people he felt were constantly belittling him, although on several occasions Marine Corps noncoms tried to help Randy by showing him possibilities he couldn't see for himself.

"My sergeant made me go to a sociology class so I

would be easier to work with. He says I'm too isolated and mistrusting of my peers," Randy wrote on one occasion. On another, a sergeant tried to convince Randy to extend his enlistment for a year so he could qualify for the jet mechanic training Randy wanted, but Randy didn't want to do it.

The letters also show that Randy's feelings toward himself and his role in the Marines waxed and waned based on his relative success or failure in the corps. In the initial stages of boot camp, when Randy was doing well, he sounded aggressive, bragging, and the corps was great: he was by God a *U.S. Marine*; but later, when things went badly, it was because he was a mess, or more often, because the corps itself was a mess and a fraud.

One of Randy's biggest disappointments was in finding out that he would not receive any skills training. Randy was sure the recruiter had lied to him. "I've really been feeling down since Thursday," he wrote in late November of 1973. "It looks like I've wasted two years when I signed up in the Marine Corps."

Eventually the corps assigned Randy to clerk school, where he studied typing. For someone like Randy, who yearned to define himself by acts of derring-do, riding a typewriter was "sissy" work, a painful reminder of the "four eyes" taunts. Randy hated it.

As Randy became more miserable in the corps, his need to control Terri grew more acute. One of the most striking aspects of the letters is Randy's incessant protestations of love for Terri—repeated so often that it ultimately becomes a *burden* for Terri, an obligation, and thus a form of control. His entire future was in Terri's hands, Randy whined in virtually every letter; he did not know what he would do if she broke off with him. Terri had the power to ruin his life. Coupled with the violent imagery Randy also included

in his letters, Randy's bleatings had the quiet under-
current of a threat.

"You know honey, I've been thinking about it a lot
and it's really great that you're trusting, devoted and
loyal enough to stay with me and always love me while
I'm in here. I've talked to a lot of guys and found out
that their girlfriends left them after they joined the
service because they felt it was necessary to have
someone there at all times to love them," Randy
wrote.

While putting that burden on Terri, Randy also
generated a steady stream of commands, directions,
orders, advice and warnings, even down to instruc-
tions as to what clothes she must wear or not wear, or
how she must act with other people. In this way,
Randy tried to maintain control over Terri in much the
same way he would later attempt to control his wives.

Likewise, Randy's fearful jealousy is a constant
theme. In almost every letter, Randy threatens great
bodily harm to anyone who tries to move in on Terri;
if Terri doesn't do what Randy wants her to do, he
promises "to turn you over my knee," "give you a
spanking," or makes some similar dominating threat.
"I got a right to protect what's mine," Randy wrote,
as if Terri were a thing or a piece of property.

Another major theme is Randy's own disparagement
of himself, which became a constant tone as Randy's
year in the Marines progressed: he's a mess, no one
could possibly love him, he's confused, a misfit and
outcast. All of this worked, as Randy instinctively
knew it would, both as an excuse for his failures in the
corps as well as a snare to bind Terri closer to him.

By making Terri aware of these feelings, Randy was
trying to insure that Terri would never think of leaving
him. After all, it was Terri who believed that through
her love she could somehow transform Randy, make
him greater than he was, and if Terri did anything to

damage Randy's self-esteem, she would be acting contrary to her own view of herself.

But the letters also show that Randy felt far more comfortable expressing love for Terri on paper from twelve hundred miles away than he did in person. It was almost as if it was not Terri that he cared for as much as simply possessing her.

Throughout the fall, Randy wrote that he was looking forward to seeing Terri on his Christmas leave. All of his letters discussed possible plans for the two of them during the furlough. But judging from the letters Randy sent afterward, the leave was less than a success.

To Terri, Randy seemed distant and preoccupied. Despite the talk about rings and marriage, in the actual event Randy didn't seem very enthusiastic. Randy spent much of his time with his friend Mike, working on Mike's car. Worse, Terri discovered that Randy had seen Jan Johnson while he was home.

But as soon as he was back in San Diego, Randy tried to smooth things over. "The whole time I was home on leave I wanted to ask you to get engaged but I wasn't really sure whether I should or not," Randy wrote afterward. And, "That hurt bad when you told me I was neglecting you because I didn't think so, but I guess it looked that way. . . ."

After leaving boot camp, Randy was assigned to Camp Pendleton, where he would study typing. Randy was miserable. It was like the corps was saying that he was too little to be a real Marine, and that all he was good for was typing in some office. From his assignment to the clerk school on, Randy's unhappiness in the Marines steadily increased. As his unhappiness grew, so did his isolation, his concurrent violent fantasies and dependence on the emotional sustenance provided by his relationship with Terri.

At Camp Pendleton, Randy spent some of his off-hours in the nearby town of Oceanside, attending a martial arts facility, or *dojo*. Both Randy and Terri were interested in martial arts; Randy even told Terri that he had once studied with Bruce Lee, a martial arts expert who went on to become a famous movie star before dying of apparent head injuries in the late 1970s.

In late January, Randy wrote Terri about a big fight in the *dojo*, one in which Randy supposedly caused serious injuries to "five big hippies" who came in to watch the " 'ballerina girls practice.' " In the course of the fight, someone broke a chair across his back, Randy wrote, but he still got the upper hand.

Three of the hippies were sent to the hospital, Randy said, and the instructor at the *dojo* wanted Randy arrested. Eventually, however, the charges were dropped.

Just how much of this story was true was hard to say. Probably if Randy had really been hit over the back with a chair he would have been in the hospital himself. It *is* the sort of scene one sees in movies, but in the movies the chairs are *made* to come apart. In real life, a chair can break a person's back or at least severely damage their kidneys.

In any event, however, from late January forward to the end of Randy's military career, almost all of his letters recounted some sort of violent encounter, almost as a counterpoint to the unhappiness and belittlement Randy kept feeling. Years later, Terri came to believe that much of this reported violence might have existed only in Randy's imagination. Bored and frustrated as a clerk, Randy's legend-making machinery began working overtime.

By early February, Randy was more depressed than ever. While his typing skills had increased to twenty-two words per minute, he had just learned that he would be sent to a unit on Okinawa, farther than ever from Lynnwood, his car and the legend Randy had worked so hard in high school to create for himself.

By this time, Randy was sure the Marines were not for him. After discussing his situation with his chaplain, Randy decided to try to get a discharge. The way to do that, he reasoned, would be to have Lizabeth send a letter to the Marines contending that Randy was needed at home to help support Lizabeth and the other Roth children.

But before he could put his plan into effect, Randy was shipped to Okinawa, and there he began to sound increasingly desperate and worried that his unit would soon be sent into the field.

Randy was assigned to the headquarters platoon of M Company, Third Battalion, Fourth Marine Regiment of the Third Marine Division. While it was true that the company would have to go into the field, it was only Okinawa, not Hue in the Tet Offensive. Being part of the headquarters platoon also meant Randy's unit would have to do less maneuvering than the other units in the company and would have first crack at most of the amenities. Other Marines looked down on the members of the headquarters platoon as almost-Marines who couldn't quite hack it. None of this helped make Randy feel better about himself.

Randy was working mostly in the company clerk's office at a place called Camp Hanson on Okinawa. Because the headquarters platoon was considered the lower class of the unit, Randy and his fellows found themselves drawing much of the guard duty. That kept them awake much of the night and caused them to fall further behind during the day with their regular duties. The farther behind they got, the more they were ridiculed. The whole thing was a vicious circle, Randy concluded. He continued to resent the Marine system and remained isolated in his macho protective armor from even his fellow sufferers.

As soon as word got around that Randy wanted out, Randy's relationship with his fellow Marines went completely in the dumper.

"This place is just like hell," Randy reported. "Drug overdoses, murder, everything. . . . I only hope I can get out before I change too much because I can feel it already, filling me with resentment and hate." The noncoms were riding him unmercifully, Randy said, because of his discharge request. Randy often spent his off-hours sitting atop his locker, fantasizing. Most of the other Marines thought he was crazy, and soon Randy began signing his letters to Terri, "Randy, the Crazy One."

"Everyone notices me, but only because I'm inferior," Randy wrote, and then added, almost prophetically: "Someday when God decides to take a hold of me everybody is going to know it. I've got to have been put here for some purpose. . . . Most of my life has been one fall after another."

By early April, Randy noted that if his hardship discharge request was not approved he would have to ask for an unsuitability discharge. That, he told Terri, would require him to see a "crazy doctor."

But all Randy's talk about his unhappiness and his desire for a discharge troubled Terri. She talked to people she trusted, most of whom told her that Randy would be making a big mistake to get out of the Marines before his time was up. He would regret it all his life, Terri was told. Terri wrote back to Randy, reporting these reactions and suggesting that he consider sticking it out.

For awhile Randy stabilized, writing to Terri that while he still wanted a discharge, he now thought he could make it if he had to.

Still, the reports of violent episodes continued. Randy wrote Terri about several fights he had with other Marines. And in late April, Randy wrote that he had gone into town with two other Marines and had been attacked by eight Japanese civilians. One Marine he was with had his knee and his arm broken and suffered a fractured skull, Randy wrote. He himself was hit with a pipe that fractured his cheekbone. Randy claimed to have laid out four of the eight attackers. The Japanese police wanted to arrest him for his brutality, Randy said, but decided not to after learning that the eight Japanese were the aggressors. One of the attackers, Randy claimed, was in critical condition with a broken neck.

Whether any of this happened or was just a figment of Randy's imagination remains unclear, although, as Detectives Peters and Mullinax later discovered, there didn't seem to be any official Marine report of such an incident involving Randy.

What does seem clear about the reports of fights is that Randy was almost pathetically eager to have Terri see him as a powerful figure. That was made even more clear in another letter Randy wrote in late April, in which Randy described a fantasy that involved Terri.

In that fantasy, Randy became "Sir Randolph," a romantic knight errant mounted on a long, gleaming motorcycle chopper. Terri is working at the snack bar at a Lynnwood roller-skating rink, a local teen hangout, when suddenly Sir Randolph on his "Mighty blue Chopper" crashes through the doors of the rink, pulls a wheelstand across the floor, and skids to a halt in front of the snack bar.

"You can see fear in the eyes of all the boys at the counter as he dismounts his bike," Randy reported.

Sir Randolph pulls off his helmet and lets his dark hair fall to his shoulders (Randy hated his Marine haircut and wore a wig to hide it when he was home on leave). "The death-defying look on his face causes them all to scatter as he walks forward toward the beautiful woman at the snack bar," Randy wrote. In this manner, Sir Randolph rescues Terri from the roller rink, puts her "gently" on the chopper, "and gives a cold defiant look to the people around them" before burning rubber out of the establishment.

The significance of this fantasy is that it shows Randy's yearning to be back in an environment where he had status, or at least the belief that he had status, as Randy the Wrathful of Lynnwood.

But a second significance is also apparent: the point of the fantasy is *not* to be with Terri but rather to impress "all the boys at the counter." Terri is *an object* necessary to fulfill Randy's fantasy of gaining the fear and awe of "all the boys."

Despite Terri's advice, Randy continued to work on his hardship discharge. Meanwhile, whether it was because he wanted to convince Terri it was the right thing to do, or because of his deep psychological need to impress others, in early May Randy outdid himself. But first, in a letter postmarked May 9, 1974, however, Randy provided a subtle tipoff: he advised Terri to stand by for new adventures from Sir Randolph.

But it wasn't Sir Randolph talking in the next letter: Randy told Terri he was part of a force of twelve hundred Marines who had been flown into Vietnam, and then trucked to a village "somewhere between Laos and Cambodia, that covers a big area, but I forgot the exact name." A firefight ensued, Randy wrote, and two Marines were killed and four were wounded. Randy killed a North Vietnamese Army regular with his entrenching tool, he wrote. "Hell couldn't be any worse than this place," he said.

Three days later, in another letter, Randy said his unit was still fighting in Vietnam, but that now he was up for two medals for "something crazy I did the other night." He had managed to save a major and two captains from getting killed, he said.

"We all still can't believe we're here when the war is supposed to be over," Randy wrote. Years later, no one else believed it either.

Significantly, another letter postmarked May 21, 1974, makes no mention of Vietnam at all. Instead, the letter was filled with the self-disparagement that

Randy sometimes succumbed to when depressed. But
then the next letter, postmarked May 23, recounted a
huge fight in Vietnam.

In this battle, Randy claimed his unit was overrun
by the North Vietnamese Army, who outnumbered
them twelve to one.

"It was one of the worst fights I can imagine,"
Randy wrote (with unintentional accuracy), "and 85
of our men got blown to shreds and more than 40 were
injured." Eventually the Marines' perimeter col-
lapsed, and Randy and his comrades-in-mind were
forced to use their bayonets in close combat, he said.
"We fought like savage animals," Randy wrote. A few
days later, everyone went back to Okinawa, he wrote.

Altogether, Randy claimed to have spent two weeks
in Vietnam, even sending Terri a snapshot of the
terrain taken from the air that he identified as a place
called "Dak Pek." He told Terri that he and several
other Marines were able to get a day off from the
fighting to drive into Saigon to develop the picture,
which was certainly thoughtful of the NVA, particularly since the Laos-Cambodia border was nearly two
hundred and fifty miles from the South Vietnamese
capital.

A close reading of Randy's letters therefore clearly
shows that Randy's combat was all in his mind. But to
be sure, Detectives Peters and Mullinax checked with
the Marines and pulled Randy's service record. There
was no evidence that Randy ever left Okinawa. Still
later, the falsity of these stories was made apparent
when Randy's lawyers succeeded in getting all mention of Randy's *entire Marine career,* such as it was,
suppressed at his trial. Had Randy really been in
combat, it might have helped provide a delayed-stress
defense to the charge of murder.

# 21 | Busted

Meanwhile, life for Lizabeth Roth was seriously deteriorating. Early in March of 1974, while Randy was feeling sorry for himself on Okinawa, Lizabeth was evicted from a house she and her remaining four children rented in a poor section of Lynnwood. By now, Randy's oldest sister was pregnant and unmarried. She had also begun keeping company with a crowd of people involved with motorcycle gangs, some of whom were also involved with marijuana and amphetamines—"speed," in street talk. Soon Lizabeth was also involved with some of the same crowd, as was David.

Known as "Davy" in the family, Randy's younger brother was sixteen. He had dropped out of high school in the tenth grade to help support Lizabeth and the girls when Randy joined the Marines. If Randy was ill-equipped to deal with Lizabeth's adult-sized problems, David was in worse shape.

"David was really weird," Belinda Howard recalled to Peters. "David was *really* weird. I don't know for sure, but I really think David was into drugs. He was just a really sneaky kind of guy. He was somebody you just didn't want to be around or left in a dark room with. He was just weird.''

Belinda was right, Davy was into drugs, soon graduating from beer to marijuana, then Valium, Darvon and later "speed." But there were some extenuating circumstances. For one thing, Davy was different than the other Roth children. Where Randy was five feet eight inches tall, by the time Davy dropped out of high school he topped six feet five inches. He had a sharply receding hairline that made him look years older than he really was, and suffered from severe acne. By the time he was eighteen, he had only three teeth left in his head. Acutely self-conscious of his looks, Davy did not have one friend in the world, his lawyer later asserted. In fact, Davy's only real friend was his mother. Liz loved Davy, defending him all his life from Gordon, according to Davy himself. Davy feared his father, hated him and loved him all at the same time; after Gordon left home, Davy was to see his father only once more during his life.

But in early 1974, with Randy daydreaming about killing fields while clerking on Okinawa, Davy was the man of the Roth family, just as Randy had been before him. Now, with Darlene pregnant, Davy was asked to take on a burden he could not shoulder. Davy was unable to get steady work and soon spent most of his time looking for beer to escape his failure.

But Lizabeth's desperate circumstance worked to Randy's advantage. Soon Randy had Lizabeth use Davy's incapacity and Darlene's pregnancy as the basis for her request to let Randy out of the Marines. Terri helped Lizabeth write the hardship letter, she later told Peters. Lizabeth's letter was met with skepticism by Randy's Marine superiors, Randy later wrote Terri. One lieutenant on his review board asked him sarcastically why he thought he could take care of his family if he couldn't stop his sister from getting pregnant. The sneer made Randy smolder inside, touching as it did the scarred-over wound of his own birth.

But then in late July, 1974, Randy's discharge was approved. Randy wrote Terri the news. Then he asked that Terri keep quiet about the reasons for his discharge. "Just say my time was up, that would be sufficient, right?"

By mid-August, Randy was out and was back in Lynnwood. He immediately became engaged to Terri and found a job in a gas station. But despite Lizabeth's pleas, Randy had no intention of moving back in with his mother.

"There was no way he was going to move back in with her," Terri recalled. While Randy occasionally sent money to Lizabeth, he wanted to stay away from her as much as he could. Lizabeth was bitter and blamed Terri for Randy's estrangement.

Meanwhile, Terri's family allowed Randy to live by himself in the old family house, which Terri's mother and stepfather wanted to sell after Terri's mother remarried. Randy went off to work each day, and in the evening Terri would come over to be with him and cook for him.

But as September of 1974 unfolded, Randy went back to his old way of being hot-cold. Sometimes Terri came over, cooked dinner, and waited for hours for Randy to come home. Sometimes he never did. Terri was suspicious of Randy's behavior. But when Terri confronted Randy, he denied he was seeing anyone else and promised that she was the only one for him.

In mid-October, Terri went to see Randy at the gas station and saw him leaning into a car window, talking to a woman. "I could tell from his body language that something was going on," Terri later remembered.

Just the way Randy was posing for the woman in the car told Terri that Randy was cheating on her. The woman drove off and Terri confronted Randy with what she had seen. Randy denied he was being unfaithful. The woman was just a single mother, Randy said, who had hired him to fix her car.

But Terri knew Randy too well. "I could always tell when he was lying," she said; Randy tended to giggle softly when he lied, or he paused just before trying to make a feeble joke.

Not wanting to doubt Randy, Terri accepted his explanation. Later she found out from one of his acquaintances that Randy *had* been lying to her about the woman. Terri decided to see for herself. She walked over to the old house one evening when Randy wasn't there. The front door was chained from the inside, but Terri used a paperclip to get it open.

Inside, up in the bedroom, Terri found a woman's purse with its supply of birth control pills, and she knew at once that Randy had deceived her. The woman had a driver's license that identified her as a Donna Sanchez. Terri realized the woman was the same person she had seen Randy talking to through the car window two weeks earlier. Randy had been lying to her. Terri felt humiliated. She burst into tears. She thought about taking the Sanchez woman's purse, ripping everything to shreds, and mailing it back to her. Eventually she left the purse there and called her mother. "Come and get me," she said, "Randy's been seeing another woman."

Terri's mother drove over to the old house, gave Terri her keys, and told her to drive herself home. Then she sat down to wait for Randy to show up. June McGuire Kirkbride had thought something was off-center about Randy for some time, and ever since Randy had joined the Marines, June had wanted Terri to be free of him. There was something about Randy's eyes that bothered her, June told Terri. Randy had Charles Manson eyes, she said. Terri didn't believe her. But now Terri had caught Randy out, and June intended to use the opportunity to lose Randy for good.

A bit later, June heard a motorcycle come to a stop in the garage. Through the door to the garage June heard Randy and a woman laughing. The door opened and June saw Randy in the doorway with a woman. Randy was holding a little girl in his arms. Randy saw June and went completely pale, June remembered later. He put the child down and sent the woman and the girl back into the garage.

"We need to talk *now*," June told Randy. "How dare you do this to my daughter? You have one hour to get your things and get out of this house." Randy took less time than that.

"I didn't mean to do it," Randy told June. "I never meant to hurt Terri, it just happened." He gave June the keys to the house and rode away with Donna Sanchez, and moved in with her.

As 1974 ended, Lizabeth was again being evicted, Davy was becoming ever more involved with drugs, and Randy was again out of work. He was not able to keep away from Terri and kept cruising by Terri's house. June's new husband, Mel Kirkbride, started getting mad at Randy. Randy blamed Kirkbride for helping to break up his relationship with Terri. Meanwhile, Randy lost his job at the gas station.

At some point that fall, Randy returned to a pattern he had established while still in high school: he began committing petty crimes. No one now knows, except Randy, how many burglaries Randy committed in the fall of 1974. But in late January of 1975, Randy decided to get even with Mel and June Kirkbride by burgling *them*.

Waiting until the house was empty, Randy broke into the garage and took a set of tools, two television sets, a turntable and a stereo, along with Kirkbride's Purple Heart. Terri McGuire immediately concluded that Randy was the burglar because the house wasn't ransacked, because other items worth more money were left behind, and because none of Terri's things were disturbed; besides, Randy was quite familiar with the layout of the house from his previous relationship with Terri. There was bad blood with Randy over Terri, Mel Kirkbride told the police.

In early February of 1975, about ten days after the burglary, Randy and Donna Sanchez were arrested by Lynnwood Police and jailed on the burglary charge. Randy was also held for investigation of the earlier armed robbery at the tire store just before he went into the Marines. Shortly after his arrest, Randy was put in a police lineup, made to wear a ski mask, and was told to use words the robber had used during the tire store holdup. Randy's former classmate Jesse Akers immediately identified Randy as the robber. Donna was released and not charged with any crimes; it appeared she knew nothing about the Kirkbrides' burglary.

A week later, Randy was released from jail and ordered to stand trial on the burglary and robbery charges. In late March, Randy agreed to plead guilty to the burglary. The Snohomish County prosecutor agreed to drop the tire store robbery charge and to recommend that Randy be placed on probation, not sent to prison. The plea bargain also called for a pre-sentence investigation of Randy, including his current circumstances and his family background. The actual sentence—up to a maximum of fifteen years in state prison—would be set by a judge after the pre-sentence investigation.

A probation officer named James Stroklund conducted the evaluation of Randy.

"Randolph Gordon Roth is a 22-year-old unmarried Caucasian male who was born on 12-26-54 in Bismarck, North Dakota," Stroklund wrote. "He was born to the now-dissolved marriage of Gordon and Elizabeth [sic] Roth. At the present time his father lives in Washougal, Washington. Mr. Roth described his relationship with his father as being 'pretty good, better than my mom.' Mr. Roth noted there [are] a lot of emotional problems between his mother and his father. Mr. Roth went on to say that he has had very little contact with his father since his parents' divorce approximately sixteen years ago.''

That was wrong, of course, although it isn't clear whether the misinformation about the actual date of Gordon and Lizabeth's divorce came from Randy directly or was Stroklund's error.

''The defendant described his mother as being overprotective, easy to get along with, and she cared about him,'' Stroklund continued. After questioning Randy about his job history, Stroklund concluded that Randy was trying to con him because the dates didn't add up.

''I confronted Mr. Roth with the conflicting dates of employment that he provided me, and his only response was, 'I get my dates mixed up.'

''I discussed with Mr. Roth any possible drug use that he may have had and the only answer he provided was, 'I don't smoke or drink and I have never used any drugs.' His future plans are to get married when 'things are squared away' and to find a fulltime job.

''I have Mr. Roth's high school transcript from Meadowdale High School. this record reflects that Mr. Roth did graduate on 6-5-73 with an accumulated gradepoint average of 2.583. Mr. Roth informed me that when he graduated he had an accumulated gradepoint average of 3.5. There was no record of social interaction or discipline at that school.''

Randy told Stroklund that after getting out of jail he found a part-time job with Vitamilk, a dairy retailer in the Seattle area. After reporting that he verified Randy's employment by asking Randy to show him a paycheck stub, Stroklund moved to his conclusions about Randy:

''After interviewing Mr. Roth, and assessing the information that I have concerning him, I perceive him as being somewhat irresponsible, rebellious, obnoxious and immature. By this statement, I am saying that Mr. Roth has an attitude which indicates to me that he can 'damn well do as he pleases.' He provided conflicting information as to the dates of his employment and his only response was that he gets his dates mixed up. When he provided that answer to me, it was in a very obnoxious way. Mr. Roth falsified the information he provided to me about his gradepoint average." On the plus side, said Stroklund, Randy *had* graduated from high school and had served in the military.

"In my estimation," Stroklund concluded, "Mr. Roth is the type of person who would be benefitted by a short period of incarceration. I believe the exposure to incarceration would serve as 'shock treatment,' and as such would be therapeutic to Mr. Roth. By being exposed to incarceration, Mr. Roth would begin to feel what lays forth for him if he continues to be involved in crime."

Stroklund recommended that Randy serve sixty days in jail. However, the judge decided to accept the prosecutor's deal with Randy for no jail time, and Randy went free.

Randy soon was back with Donna Sanchez, and on the Fourth of July, 1975, he and Donna #1 were married in Washougal, Washington, where his father was one of the witnesses.

# 22

# Donna #1

Years later, when Sue Peters began searching for Donna Sanchez Roth, she wasn't exactly sure who or what she might find. This was Randy's first wife, married to Randy when he was just twenty years old, and presumably, someone who might know Randy best of all the wives Randy would later have or try to have. Donna #1, as Peters sometimes still thought of her, was also Greg Roth's mother. And if Donna #2 and Mary Jo Phillips were right, this Donna would have left Greg behind with Randy, only rarely having contact with her child. That seemed a bit odd to Peters as well.

Eventually, another detective tracked Donna #1 to California, where Donna had been working for some years. Donna's former employer said she might be living in the Bremerton area with her sister. The detective located the sister and conducted a telephone interview with Donna. A week later, Peters went to see Donna #1 face-to-face.

Donna was a bit different than the other Roth women. Of medium height, she was much taller than Janis or Cindy, for example. She was very pleasant

with Peters but completely convinced that Randy was
utterly incapable of committing murder. She also insisted tht Randy *had* been on secret killing missions in
Vietnam, and when Peters told her the records indicated otherwise, Donna told her the missions were so
secret no records were ever kept. *Well,* Peters thought,
*here's someone who's still convinced that Randy is a
hero.*

Donna was convinced that Randy had been through
violent combat in Vietnam. The missions were secret,
Randy told her. "There was a lot of killing," Randy
said. Once, he said, they had wiped out an entire
village. Randy had strangled a baby with a piano wire.
Randy was very proud of his service with the Marines,
and collected military emblems and patches. After
work, Randy often practiced karate moves in the backyard. At night, he often awoke from nightmares. He
told Donna that the bad dreams were from the war.

About the time Randy married Donna, he found
work in a fiberglass factory about two blocks from
Lizabeth's house. The factory manufactured commercial fixtures for grocery stores and similar places.
Randy worked in the lamination department, essen-
tially gluing strands of composite material together. It
was dirty, low-paying work, but at least it was full-
time. Donna found a job in a bank.

Donna and Randy attended a Catholic church in
Lynnwood, and also saw Lizabeth and the rest of the
Roth children quite frequently. Lizabeth was often
sick with her headaches and usually went to bed when
Randy and Donna visited. Unlike Belinda, Donna
didn't feel close to Lizabeth at all.

In early 1976, Randy got a better job with a steel
manufacturing plant near Portland, Oregon. He and
Donna and Donna's four-year-old daughter moved to
the Portland area. Lizabeth later was to say that Randy
had gone to be with his father; it does appear that

Randy was becoming increasingly estranged from Lizabeth and the rest of the family. He could still talk to Darlene, but she was the only one, Randy told friends later.

Randy worked in the Portland area throughout the rest of 1976 and into early 1977. It appears that he and Donna Sanchez separated for awhile during this period. By early 1977, Randy was back in the Lynnwood area and trying to see Terri once more. At least, when he sought Terri out at the roller rink, he told Terri that he and Donna had separated; Terri never knew that Randy and Donna had ever married.

Soon Terri was seeing Randy three times a week at an apartment Randy claimed was his. It seemed to Terri that Randy and Donna *were* separated, because neither Donna nor her daughter were around, although a second bedroom in the apartment was filled with a little girl's things. But Donna's whereabouts during this period remain obscure. Terri later said Randy told her that Donna had gone to live with her sister in eastern Washington; what Randy didn't tell Terri was that Donna was pregnant.

# 23  Davy

By August of 1977, Davy Roth was in terrible shape. Unable to work, a tenth-grade dropout, isolated by his horrible complexion and his mouthful of rotting teeth, he was more dependent on Lizabeth than ever before, often cadging small amounts of cash from her so he could cruise the convenience stores for beer.

At six five and nearly 190 pounds, with his frightening face and missing teeth, with his receding hairline and his frequent drunkenness, Davy was virtually friendless except for his family. To them, Davy was just Davy—a sensitive, shy person when sober, who vented enormous amounts of pent-up aggression when he drank. Although he was only twenty years old, he looked far older, and therefore had little trouble buying alcohol.

Sometime in late July or August of 1977, as Lizabeth later told the story, Davy had injured his shoulder falling out of a tree. Lizabeth took him to a doctor, she said later, who prescribed Darvon for Davy. Davy began taking the Darvon, along with Lizabeth's Valium, and combining both with beer.

Davy had two prized possessions. The first was his

car, a 1963 Chevrolet Nova that Lizabeth bought for him to enable Davy to get out of the house. Davy was almost pathetically grateful to Lizabeth for this gift, and immediately began customizing the car by attacking it with cans of spray paint. By August of 1977, the car was most generously described as "multi-colored." It was, of course, a beater, but Davy loved it because it was real evidence of his mother's love. Inside the car, Davy posted a sign: "Ass Gas or Grass. Hardly anyone rides for free," followed by a question mark.

Davy's second prized possession was his .22 semi-automatic Marlin rifle, which he kept in the trunk of his car, along with a jar of shells given to him by Bob Hendershott, a friend of the Roth family who had once dated Darlene Roth. Bob was probably Davy's closest acquaintance outside his family, and indeed, Lizabeth Roth was later to say that Davy considered Hendershott a virtual brother.

Randy and Donna, meanwhile, had moved back to Mountlake Terrace. Randy found work again at the fiberglass factory, this time working in the mold-making department, a step up. Randy and Donna had less frequent contact with Lizabeth, in part because of the increased presence of several motorcycle people around the family, and the obvious presence of drugs like marijuana and "speed." Randy hated drugs.

Sometime around August 11, 1977, Davy drove to Silver Lake, a county park where many young people in Snohomish County gathered in the summer months to go swimming. Davy thought he might go swimming. As he was parking near the lake, Davy saw a young woman hitchhiking by the side of the road. The woman was tall, had dark hair, was somewhere in her twenties or early thirties, and was wearing a striped one-piece top and shorts made from blue jeans. Davy decided to try to pick the woman up. "She was not a bad looking girl," Davy later told police.

The woman accepted the ride from Davy and told him she was on her way home to a trailer park south of the lake where she lived with two men. Davy asked her if she wanted to drink some beer with him. The woman agreed, so Davy drove to a market and bought a case of beer. Then he and the woman drove to a nearby high school—the school Davy had last attended before dropping out—and parked in a wooded area. Davy had already taken a considerable amount of Valium earlier. Now, the beer began eroding Davy's inhibitions completely.

Davy asked the woman if she would remove her top and, Davy said later, the woman did. After some necking, Davy asked the woman if she "ever fooled around." According to what Davy later told a psychiatrist, he had never had sex with a woman before.

"Yes, but not with somebody like you," Davy later said the woman replied. "This made me mad," Davy said. Davy drew back from her and the woman replaced her top. Davy asked the woman if she wanted a peacock feather. The woman said she did. Davy got out of the car and opened his trunk to get the feather. As he did so, his eyes fell on one of the rubber tie-down cords he kept in the trunk. At that point, Davy said later, he decided to kill the woman who had just rejected him.

Taking a handful of peacock feathers in one hand and hiding the rubber cord in the other, Davy approached the woman from the passenger side of the car and gave her the feathers. While the woman was looking at the feathers, Davy reached into the car with the rubber cord and pulled it tight around her neck. Davy pulled with all his considerable strength and the woman struggled to get free. Her face began to turn blue, then purple. Davy pulled as hard as he could for as long as he could. The woman urinated on the car seat. The rubber cord snapped. The woman seemed dead, but Davy wasn't sure. He went back to the trunk, got another rubber cord and resumed strangling the woman. After a few more minutes, Davy decided the woman was finally dead. He opened the car door and dragged the woman's body into the bushes. As he was getting ready to leave, Davy saw the woman move. He went back to the trunk and got his rifle. He returned to the woman and shot her seven times in the back of the head.

Afterward, Davy was beside himself with rage for his stupidity. Why had he killed the woman? He wasn't exactly sure. He knew it was something to do with the fact that he had no friends, people thought he was ugly, no one seemed to like him. In rejecting him with the words she used, the woman had unthinkingly hit Davy at his sorest point.

Now Davy did a psychologically interesting thing. Reloading his rifle again and again, Davy pumped round after round into the car his mother had given him, eventually shooting out the rear window and filling the doors and fenders with holes. Nor was Davy finished. Finding a can of spray paint, Davy painted the roof of the car with some chilling words: "*death* To the *one* who enter."

Next, Davy drove away, stopping to get still more beer, and later consuming all of his remaining Valium and Darvon in an attempt to kill himself. He failed. Hours later, Davy drove back to Lizabeth's house, parked his car, and passed out for two days.

Two nights later, on Saturday, Davy was riding around, drunk as usual, in the eastern Snohomish County town of Gold Bar. A police officer stopped him for erratic driving. Someone had previously reported that a man was waving a rifle around at a park outside of the town. Searching the car, the officer found some marijuana and Davy's rifle. He arrested Davy for possession of marijuana, and seized the rifle and ammunition for investigation of carrying a concealed weapon. The Gold Bar officer also impounded the car and took Davy off to jail.

The following day, Sunday, August 14, 1977, a husband-and-wife berry-picking team found the woman's body. The Snohomish County Sheriff's Department began an investigation, which was severely hampered by the fact that no one knew who the dead woman was. She had no identification with her.

On the following day, August 15, 1977, Lizabeth and Davy's sisters and their boyfriends, along with Bob Hendershott, went to the Snohomish County Courthouse to bail Davy out on the marijuana and weapons charges. Lizabeth dropped Davy and Bob off at the place where Davy's car was impounded. Lizabeth and the others went home. Davy and Bob got the car, stopped to buy some Thunderbird wine, and began drinking it as they were driving around. Hendershott couldn't help but notice all the bullet holes and the missing rear window. Davy and Bob finished the wine, so they stopped to get some more. Hendershott went into a supermarket to get it.

As Hendershott got back in the car, Davy turned to him. "What would you do," Davy asked, "if I told you I killed someone?" Hendershott later said he didn't know what to make of Davy's remark, so he tried to change the subject. But Davy persisted.

"Well," said Hendershott, "I wouldn't tell on you." That was good, Davy told Hendershott, because he would kill again if he thought it would be necessary. Hendershott kept quiet.

Davy tried out a story on Hendershott. He'd just killed someone who had beaten him up while he was in high school, Davy said. He'd always promised the guy he would get even with him, and now he had.

But as Davy continued to talk to Hendershott, some of the enormity of what actually happened began to overwhelm him. Soon Davy was telling the real story: about the woman, about being rejected, the rubber

cords, the rifle. Finally Davy told Hendershott he was
worried that the body was soon going to be discovered.
He hadn't hidden it well enough, Davy said. Obviously, Davy hadn't heard about the discovery on the
previous day. Hendershott got the impression that
Davy wanted him to help move the body. Hendershott
finally told Davy to drop him off at a friend's house.
Davy warned him again to keep his mouth shut.

About an hour later, Davy returned to the place
where he had dropped Hendershott off. "It's gone,"
he told Hendershott. Davy looked very shook up.
Hendershott knew Davy was talking about the body.
"It's gone," Davy said again.

The following day, Hendershott and Davy went over
to Lizabeth's house. Davy wanted Lizabeth to give
him money to buy more Darvon and Valium. Hendershott later said he waited in the living room while
Davy talked to Lizabeth in the kitchen.

"I could hear them talking about something," Hendershott said later. "I couldn't make out anything they
were saying and then I heard Liz ask Davy if he was
crazy. And Davy said no, pretty loud. And then they
were just quietly mumbling in the kitchen again."

"Could you tell what they were doing or what they
were talking about?" Hendershott was asked.

"I couldn't tell what they were talking about, I kind
of figured they were talking about what Davy had
done, and I heard them rustling a newspaper and I saw
her go back in the kitchen like she was going to show
Davy something. And she came out of the kitchen
with the newspaper into the dining room and I said,
'Let me see the paper.' So she handed me the paper
and it was opened up to . . . an article and it was about
a woman's body that had been found . . . and it said
the apparent cause of death was a gunshot wound to
the head."

Lizabeth, it seemed to Hendershott, was scared for

Davy. But at that point, Hendershott was scared for himself. He believed that Davy would kill him if he told the police what he knew.

Three days later, however, Bob Hendershott *did* talk, giving a lengthy statement to the Snohomish County Sheriff's Department that was based on what Davy had told him. The county's homicide detectives decided to arrest Davy for questioning in the murder. They also obtained search warrants for Lizabeth's house and Davy's car.

On August 30, 1977, the sheriff's deputies went to Lizabeth Roth's house and served the warrant. They also gave Lizabeth a subpoena to appear before the county's inquiry judge to see what she might know about Davy and the murder. While searching the house, the deputies found numerous peacock feathers, but there was no sign of Davy. Asked by the deputies where Davy was, Lizabeth said she did not know. Asked where Davy's car was, Lizabeth was also ignorant. A neighbor told the police that Davy and his brother had put a tow bar on the car and had taken the car away.

Who was Davy's brother? the police asked. Randy Roth. That afternoon, another team of deputies went over to Randy's house in Mountlake Terrace and found Davy's multi-colored, shot-to-pieces Nova under a tarp on the side of Randy's house. Randy made no objections as the police hauled the car away for a thorough search.

Where was Davy? No one knew, or if they did, no one was saying. But by this time, Davy was a thousand miles away in North Dakota, working on a relative's farm, hoping the whole nightmare would blow over.

# 24 | Debbie and Tim

The search of Lizabeth's house, the seizure of Davy's car, and the disappearance of Davy were not the only important events in the Roth family on August 30, 1977. On the same day the police were turning Lizabeth's house upside down for clues to Davy's culpability in a murder, Donna Sanchez Roth was giving birth to a son. At twenty-two, Randy Roth had just become a father.

Apparently, Randy had mixed feelings about Gregory Roth's arrival. Later, Terri McGuire was to say that on the night Donna gave birth to Greg, Randy had spent the night with her.

Randy, she recalled, was agitated about something. Whether it was the birth of Greg, or the police investigation of his brother, only he knows. Randy told Terri nothing about these two events, but Terri thought Randy was nervous, almost frantic. Later Terri was to speculate that Donna left Randy in early 1977 to prevent Randy from convincing her to terminate the pregnancy.

Terri was sure Randy hated the idea of being a father. She said Randy told her that night that he'd just had a vasectomy to make sure that he never would be a father. That August night, however, convinced Terri that she could never be happy with Randy; although she was to see him once more a few years later, Terri finally decided that love wasn't going to change Randy, no matter what. Terri began living her own life, and Randy drifted away.

Terri seems to have been right about Randy's attitude toward fatherhood, however. Randy, at least initially, saw the new baby as handcuffing him to Donna, according to what he later told friends. All the old feelings about his own mother and his father, particularly his father's sense of being trapped in marriage because of Randy's birth, came flooding back. Although he tried to drive the feelings away and assume the pose of the proud daddy, Randy soon began to identify with Gordon; his freedom, Randy told friends, was being restricted by Donna and his new role. In later years, Randy would tell friends and other women that he resented Donna because he felt she had become pregnant to keep him in the marriage.

But for the time being, Randy continued living with Donna in Mountlake Terrace. Soon he made friends with a young nineteen-year-old man at the fiberglass factory, and if Donna wouldn't do exactly what Randy wanted her to do, at least his new friend was a loyal follower.

Tim Brocato was a naive newlywed from Buffalo, New York when he first met Randy. His wife Debbie had given birth a few months before Donna. Soon the two couples were doing things together. Randy, of course, was the leader.

Tim admired Randy and looked up to him as someone worth emulating. Randy was older, a war veteran, wise in the ways of the world, quick to offer help or advice, Tim thought. At first, Tim believed most of what Randy told him.

Randy was very closed-mouthed about his age. Because of his demeanor, Tim thought Randy was probably in his late twenties. Tim was sure Randy had killed people during the war. Randy told him about secret missions, about the time Randy's platoon had wiped out an entire village. Randy kept telling Tim to read a book about Vietnam, saying his unit was mentioned in the book.

Randy told Tim women were dangerous. "You can't trust them," Randy said. "You can't tell them anything. It will be repeated. They'll stab you in the back." He could never work for a woman, Randy said; Randy couldn't stand to have a woman in authority over him. Tim was pretty sure Randy didn't like women and probably hated them.

But Tim's wife Debbie became good friends with Donna. Donna told Debbie about Randy's war experiences and his nightmares. Debbie believed the stories, too. From Debbie's point of view, however, it seemed like the marriage between Randy and Donna was failing. Randy was surly and uncommunicative with Donna much of the time. Debbie thought she'd never take what Randy dished out to Donna, but she put it down to Randy's war experiences.

Still, the Roth marriage staggered on, while both Tim and Randy continued to work at the fiberglass factory. The two couples visited each other frequently as the infants grew into toddlers. Debbie often thought Randy was far too harsh with the children. Greg was just about two, and Donna's daughter was only around five, yet Randy was very rough while spanking both kids.

Money was always tight for both couples, especially after Donna quit her job at the bank to have Greg. Another recession hit the area, this one the result of the tripled price of oil after the fall of the Shah of Iran.

Then, in the summer of 1979, there was a strike at the fiberglass factory. The strike lasted for several weeks. Both Tim and Randy went out. Randy was angry at the company and suggested to Tim that they torch one of the company's trucks. Tim refused. But on September 9, 1979, there *was* a truck fire at the plant. Tim knew he shouldn't ask whether Randy was behind it. Randy never went back to the fiberglass factory and instead got an on-call truck mechanic job at the dairy distributor, Vitamilk, in Seattle in October of 1979. As a diesel mechanic, Randy would be making more money than he ever had in his life.

A few months after starting at Vitamilk, in early 1980, Randy decided he'd had enough of Donna. One day she returned from church and was shocked when Randy gave her a divorce summons. A short, bitter dispute unfolded over the custody of Greg.

Later, Donna would remember standing over little Greg, who was lying on the bed. Randy stood at his son's feet, Donna at Greg's head, each of them tugging on their respective end of the child. It seemed crazy, but Randy simply wouldn't consider giving in on the custody issue, despite his anger at Donna.

"No one's going to take my boy away from me," he said. Donna thought it had something to do with Randy's own experiences after his father had left, or perhaps he was afraid that Donna would use Greg to control *him*. Randy seemed intense about the question, and Donna thought he might even turn violent.

In the end, Donna decided to let Randy keep Greg. Randy and Tim loaded up Donna's belongings, then drove her and her daughter to stay with Donna's sister in eastern Washington. Later, he told Tim and Debbie never to talk to Donna again, and they didn't.

# 25

## "Throw Your Mother in the Slammer"

**D**avy Roth stayed for about six months in North Dakota before returning to Washington State. By that time, in mid-1978, Lizabeth was living near Port Orchard, a small town across Puget Sound from Seattle, where she had a boyfriend who was thought by police to be a member of an Oregon-based motorcycle gang. The boyfriend in turn employed a man named Chuck. Chuck was asked to rent a small apartment in Port Orchard for Davy when Davy came home.

Davy moved into the apartment and tried to keep out of sight. Every night, however, Davy found himself drawn to the taverns in the area. Nor had Davy ceased his other drug use. Every night after the taverns closed, Davy smoked marijuana and hashish, took "speed," and continued drinking.

On January 14, 1979, a Kitsap County police officer working the traffic detail learned from an informant—never named—that a man named Chuck had rented the apartment for Davy. Police went to the apartment, but no one answered the door. Three days later, however, after checking with other residents of the apartment building, the police confirmed that Davy,

using the name David Flick, was indeed inside the apartment. They also learned that Davy was possibly armed with two pistols that supposedly had been taken from Lizabeth's boyfriend.

That night, just after two in the morning, the police went back to the apartment. One officer knocked on the door. "Who is it?" Davy asked.

"Terry," said the officer, and Davy, thinking the visitor was a friend, opened the door. Three officers crashed into the apartment and put their drawn weapons in Davy's face. Davy had been drinking heavily, smoking hashish and taking large amounts of speed. He later told police that he had not slept for three days before he was arrested.

The Kitsap County Sheriff's Department booked Davy into the county jail to hold him for the Snohomish County authorities. The following morning, two Snohomish detectives arrived to pick Davy up. He was still without shoes from the night of his arrest.

The two detectives handcuffed Davy and put him in their car for the drive back to Snohomish County. What happened next became the subject of a long legal dispute.

According to Davy, one of the detectives initially told him that he would just as soon shoot him as look at him. "I won't be any trouble," Davy promised.

On the way to the ferry that would take them back to the east side of Puget Sound, one of the Snohomish detectives told Davy they were interested in asking him about a murder and that the victim was still unidentified.

Did Davy know the woman's name? Davy said he didn't and that he didn't know anything about the murder. But the detectives persisted in asking Davy questions about the killing, until finally Davy asked them why they were bothering to ask him for details, since it was obvious they already knew everything

about the crime from their "snitch." Who was that? the detectives asked Davy.

"Hendershott," said Davy. This admission served to convince the detectives that they were on the right track in suspecting Davy. "There's no doubt in my mind that you killed that girl," one of the detectives told Davy.

A few minutes later, as the detectives drove onto the ferry boat, one of the detectives brought up Liza-beth. According to his later testimony, the detective told Davy that it appeared to him Lizabeth knew all about the murder.

"It's probably a burden for your mother to carry," the detective said he told Davy. The other detective reminded Davy that his mother had been before the county's inquiry judge, where she'd given sworn tes-timony. That was an oblique suggestion that perhaps Lizabeth could be charged with perjury, or possibly even aiding and abetting Davy in the murder.

"He was very concerned about his mother," the detective later testified. "Asked me if his mother would get into any trouble. And I told him the trouble was his problem, not his mother's problem." After that, said the detective, Davy gave a full confession to the murder.

That was not exactly the way it happened, Davy testified later. Instead, the detectives threatened to put Lizabeth in jail.

"Well," Davy testified later, "I wouldn't answer any of their questions, saying I didn't know [the an-swers]. They brought up what they wanted to know. [And they said] they will get it out of her, arrest her and send her to prison."

"What did you say to that?" Davy was asked.

"I told them that they didn't have anything on her because she didn't know."

"What was their response?"

"They said they were sure they could get her for something, [like] aiding and abetting."

"Did you reply to that?"

"I told them to let her out of it, that I would tell them what they wanted to know if they would."

Thus, the question later arose as to whether Davy had made a voluntary confession, or whether it was coerced by the detectives by threats to jail Lizabeth.

In the months after Davy's arrest, his lawyer concentrated most of his efforts in trying to get Davy's confession suppressed, that is, ruled inadmissible, which would make it just as if it had never happened. That would give Davy the best shot at beating the murder charge, Mark Mestel thought.

Ironically, Mestel's strategy—to use pretrial hearings to severely limit the facts the prosecution would be allowed to later present to the jury—foreshadowed the strategy that was adopted years later by Randy's lawyers in the death of Cindy. In further irony, Mestel was later to become the partner of one of the two lawyers Randy would have in his own trial twelve years hence.

Mestel sincerely believed that the police threatened to send Lizabeth to jail in order to get the confession from Davy. Indeed, it was possible, Mestel reasoned, that Davy was so concerned for his mother's well-being that he might have told the police *anything,* whether it was true or not, if it would keep Lizabeth out of jail.

Mestel therefore hired a psychiatrist to examine Davy. The psychiatrist eventually concluded that Davy was so attached to Lizabeth as to make the voluntary nature of the confession unlikely; that instead, "within a reasonable medical certainty," Davy was so upset about the prospect of Lizabeth going to jail that he was unable to make a clear judgement about his rights, and therefore to freely confess.

"This is not a normal parent-child relationship," the
psychiatrist noted in his report and later in his testimony. Davy had for so long relied upon Lizabeth for
every necessity, indeed, for all of his love, that threatening to jail his mother was virtually a sure-fire way of
getting Davy to admit to almost anything.

But after a hearing, in which the detectives denied
threatening Lizabeth, a judge ruled that the detectives
were simply more believable than Davy. The judge
allowed the confession to be used as evidence in
Davy's trial. Just as a jury was selected, Lizabeth fired
Mestel. Lizabeth's boyfriend then traded a motorcycle
to another attorney in return for the new lawyer's
agreement to defend Davy. Because the new lawyer
needed time to prepare for the case, a mistrial was
declared, and the case was postponed to the fall of
1979. Thus, David went on trial for murder at about
the same time that Randy's marriage to Donna Sanchez Roth was reaching its final months.

Meanwhile, Randy was expressing disgust about
Davy's situation to Tim Brocato. His brother had
raped and strangled a girl, Randy told Tim, adding an
offense that hadn't actually happened and omitting the
rifle shots to the head. Davy was weak, Randy told
Brocato. The cops had pressured him and he had given
in. He was also stupid, leaving the body where it could
be found, Randy told Tim. "You don't get caught,"
Randy said. Tim formed the impression that Randy
was mad at Davy for not telling him about the murder
so that the brothers could have moved the body before
it was found. After finding out about the murder,
Randy said, he'd tried to hide Davy's car at his house
under a tarp, but the police found it. The car was a
wreck. Tim got the impression that Randy was as
disgusted with the condition of the car as anything else
Davy had done.

* * *

Davy's trial opened in early November of 1979 with the judge and the prosecutor wearing bullet-proof vests. Police had been told that Lizabeth's boyfriend was an important motorcycle gang member, and somehow the rumor began circulating that Liz's boyfriend was likely to shoot the judge and prosecutor dead right there in the courtroom if the trial didn't go well. So the judge and the prosecutor were both a little nervous.

It didn't help matters at all when Lizabeth and one of her daughters began praying out loud in the courtroom during the trial, even going so far as to get down on their knees and chanting. Those present in the courtroom during these scenes were never very sure what exactly Lizabeth and her daughter were saying, however.

"It was gibberish," one of those present said years later. "It was unintelligible." Some people thought Lizabeth and her daughter were speaking in tongues. Davy's judge, Thomas McCrea, kept ordering Lizabeth to keep quiet. Lizabeth and her daughter would resume their courtroom seats and settle down for a bit, only to get back on the floor minutes later. Meanwhile, Lizabeth's boyfriend sat motionless, impassively staring at the judge through dark glasses. Police in the courtroom kept their eyes on the boyfriend's hands. The whole scene was bizarre in the extreme, several participants later recalled.

Davy's new lawyer, Paul Acheson, knew that because the jury would hear about Davy's confession he would have to find an alternative version of the events. The real killer, Acheson told the jury, was Hendershott himself. Davy was just a mark, a fall guy, someone Hendershott knew could be set up to take the rap for him. Hendershott owned a .22-caliber rifle too, Acheson would argue, and often borrowed Davy's multi-colored car. Immediately after telling the police about Davy, Acheson noted, Hendershott left to go to Alaska.

"The testimony that the state will present," Acheson told the jury, "will be mostly through a confession that they extracted from the defendant. The defense will show that Mr. Roth is twenty-two years old and he is a very shy person, very reserved. He talks very little. His mother will tell you that he had hardly ever had a friend. In fact, *really* hardly ever had a friend. He went to school. He was a poor student. He quit in the tenth grade after the family broke up. And he quit, thinking he would go to work to help support the family. But he was unable to ever get a job. It was in this kind of posture or context that he met a person by the name of Hendershott, Robert Hendershott.

"And the testimony will be that he became fast friends, according to what Davy thought. Davy thought they were the very best of friends. In fact, his *only* friend. And they knew each other about two years. And Davy helped him work on his car. In fact, Davy would do almost anything for him. And he would even call him his 'brother.' And he was the only friend that Davy ever had in his whole lifetime, and he admired him very much and would have done anything for him.

"Well," said Acheson, "there was a time when Mr. Hendershott told Davy about the killing. He said that he in fact had killed the hitchhiker and talked about it. Told him what the situation was and told Davy, 'Now, don't you tell anybody, Davy, because if you tell anybody we are not going to be friends anymore.' "

After telling the jury that Hendershott became nervous and decided to finger Davy for the crime that he had actually committed, Acheson discussed Davy's confession to the detectives. "And they got him on the ferry and they started putting the pressure on him to confess. 'Come on, come on. Tell us all about it. We know that you did it.'

"So they outlined the whole thing for him, telling him, 'Now you did this and you'd better tell us about it.' Well, Davy didn't know *what* to do. He said, 'Well, I don't want to tell you anything.' They said, 'Well, by God, you'd better be telling us something, because among other things, we're going to throw your mother in the slammer.' "

Under this pressure, said Acheson, Davy decided to agree that he had done the crime.

"In a fogged state of mind, which was colored by drinking and smoking marijuana and taking speed, the pressure that the policemen were putting on him and talking about—he was friends with [Hendershott] and talking in reference to his mother, talking about throwing his mother in the slammer and not wanting to lose his friend—he said *he* did it, so they just laid it out for him and they wrote it all down. 'This is what you did. Right, Davy?' And sure enough, Davy signed it."

Of course, there was much more to the evidence against Davy than just the confession. By this time, the authorities had subjected Davy's rifle to a ballistics analysis by the Federal Bureau of Investigation. An FBI agent testified that the bullets found in the dead woman's head had been fired from a .22-caliber Marlin rifle just like the one found in Davy's possession. The markings on test bullets fired from Davy's rifle were the same as those found on the death bullets.

That was a problem for Davy's lawyer. Acheson tried to mitigate this testimony by asking the agent whether he was *sure* no other brand of .22 rifle left the same sort of markings as those left by Davy's Marlin. The agent said he was sure. The bullet markings were drastically different than those left by other rifle makes, the agent said, citing, "for example, a bolt action Remington .22." Those bullets were completely different in their lands and grooves than the Marlin bullets, the agent said.

The state finished its case, and then Acheson tried

to present evidence on Davy's behalf, calculated to promote reasonable doubt in the jurors' minds.

First, Acheson presented testimony from a Roth family friend who knew Hendershott. The family friend testified that Hendershott once was drunk and had threatened to engage the police in a shootout; he was known as a violent person, the family friend said. And Hendershott *did* own a .22 rifle. "Yeah," said the friend, "he had a .22."

Next, Acheson called Lizabeth as a witness. After some discussion about the Roth family and Davy's problems, Acheson asked Lizabeth to describe Davy's personality.

"He took over after his father left and his older brother left to go to his father, which meant he didn't talk to us," Lizabeth said, apparently referring to the period when Randy and Donna were living near Portland and were estranged from Lizabeth. "And so he [Davy] took over. He tried to take care of us. He has always been kind of quiet, but everyone knows him to crack a joke now and then. Especially when there would be hard feelings. He would crack a joke and break it up."

"Did he have many friends?"

"No, he didn't have time for that," said Lizabeth.

"Now, during the time Davy was growing up, did he ever have the habit of taking blame for other people?" Acheson asked.

"Oh, yeah," said Lizabeth.

Lizabeth said *Hendershott* had actually asked her to read the newspaper to find out whether the police had discovered the body of a woman. She knew nothing about the murder until Hendershott brought it to her attention, Lizabeth said.

Next, Acheson put Davy himself on the stand. Davy said Hendershott had borrowed his car one night in August. When Hendershott returned it, Davy said, it was riddled with bullet holes.

"Did Bob [Hendershott] have a .22 rifle?" Acheson asked.

"Yes, he had a rifle," Davy said. Acheson rested his defense.

The prosecutor now asked Davy one important question. "What kind of rifle was it that Mr. Hendershott had, Mr. Roth?"

"A Remington, bolt-action," Davy said, and with that one sentence, after the FBI agent's earlier testimony that the death weapon could not possibly have been a Remington, Davy torpedoed his own defense. Then the prosecutor maneuvered Davy into claiming that the bullet holes weren't in the car when he was arrested on August 13, 1977. That, of course, was clearly untrue, as the reports the arresting officers made that night showed. To the jury, there was only one possible conclusion: Davy was lying.

An hour or so later, the lawyers began their closing arguments. The prosecutor exhibited the skull of the dead woman, pointed out the bullet holes in the skull, then left it out on the table for the jurors to stare at while he gave his summation.

"Ladies and gentlemen of the jury," the prosecutor said, "if anybody can conclude with a reasonable doubt that the defendant did not intend to kill this girl when he wrapped a cord . . . around her neck and held tight to [her] and dragged her from the vehicle and then went back to his vehicle, loaded his gun then went back to the girl and put seven bullets in her head, if anybody can conclude that he didn't intend to kill the girl, I would hesitate to know what we constitute intent to kill."

In his closing argument, Acheson tried hard to cast doubt on the facts assembled by the police against Davy. There were alternative explanations, he said.

"I think that if you take a look at all of the evidence, you can see there is evidence which would tend to establish that Mr. Hendershott was in fact the one who killed this person.

"Hendershott was a good friend of Davy's," Acheson continued, "and I think he would have known that Davy was the kind of person that he could put it on and Davy would have no idea how to get out of it. And he could tell Davy, look, if you say anything different you are just not going to be my friend.

"And I think that would have been very important to Davy. Davy never had a friend in his life. Have you ever known anybody who never had a friend, not even one, except maybe his family? I've never known anybody. Davy is the only guy I've ever known who has never had a friend, not even one. And I think that tells you something about Davy, what he is like, a little bit about how he might be thinking, how he thinks."

Acheson closed by asking the jury to see that there was reasonable doubt that Davy had committed the crime. But in his closing argument, Acheson had gone perhaps a bit too far. The jury indeed considered what Davy's lack of friends meant, what he was like, and how he thought. And after thinking this over, very quickly the jury decided Davy was guilty of murder.

Later, Lizabeth claimed that the FBI had framed Davy with the ballistic evidence.

Davy Roth was sentenced to a life term in the state penitentiary in early February of 1980, just fifteen days after Randy served Donna with the divorce summons. Davy might be going to prison, but now Randy would be free.

# 26

## Jan and Jalina

By the fall of 1980, Randy was enjoying his new life as a bachelor father. From things he said to Tim, Tim got the idea that Randy was spending a lot of his time in singles clubs and playing the field; Tim also guessed that Randy was having an adulterous affair with Greg's married babysitter.

Exactly why Randy therefore decided to marry again remains the subject of dispute. Years later, deputy prosecutor Marilyn Brenneman would conclude that it was sometime during this period that Randy first *consciously* formed the intent to murder a spouse for the life insurance proceeds. And there is inferential evidence to support that idea. Why else would Randy have remarried? Randy, of course, maintained that nothing could have been further from the truth.

While Brenneman's theory would seem powerfully validated by what was later to be learned of Randy's behavior with his many wives and girlfriends, his psyche remains a complex subject. Thus, while Randy's duplicities would be easily documented, his motivations may have been far more contradictory.

Terri McGuire, for one, came to believe that Randy

was caught on the horns of a deep-seated, almost unbearable contradiction: because of the unhappiness of his own upbringing, Randy desperately wanted to have a happy marriage and a fulfilling home life.

But Randy, because of his upbringing, was fundamentally incapable of loving another person; instead, what Randy *really* loved was the power to control his partner, all the better to avoid the emotional pain he had suffered ever since childhood.

As a result, in Terri McGuire's mind, and in the view of several others who knew him well, it was Randy's yearning for happiness, love and stability that drove him into his serial relations with women, relations in which every new woman would be the answer to the bliss that he sought but so far failed to achieve.

Compelled by this desire for a perfect family life, Randy tried hard to project himself in ways he believed women would value, but because the image he worked so hard to create was fundamentally false—as even Randy himself knew—the relationships quickly broke down under the weight of reality. Along with intimacy comes knowledge; knowledge without forgiveness and love soon turns to indifference, or even hate. Randy's marriages couldn't be perfect, because neither Randy nor his wives could *be* perfect.

An imperfect marriage, to Randy, was one to be disposed of. That was where the money or other things of value came into play. Unlike his own father years before, Randy showed a marked capacity to come out of his marriages with more than he brought in.

Randy, of course, has never discussed his marriages in any of these terms; throughout the investigation and subsequent trial, Randy insisted that he was the dutiful, loving husband and father in every case. That remains his position today, even as he appeals his conviction for murder.

In any event, whether for coldly calculated profit or from some more deeply personal desire, Randy at some point in the late fall or early winter of 1980 attended a dance sponsored by a group called Parents Without Partners. Some said the dance was at Halloween, while others insisted that it was on New Year's Eve. But it was at a Parents Without Partners function that Randy met a small, vivacious woman named Janis Miranda. Randy married her within three months.

Janis Miranda was twenty-eight and had been divorced from her husband Joe Miranda since September of 1975. She was four feet eleven inches tall and weighed just about one hundred pounds. She had a seven-year-old daughter named Jalina, who was almost as tall as she was, and a best friend named Louise Mitchell. Janis loved to dance.

Jan first met Louise Mitchell in Dallas in September of 1975, about the time her divorce from Joe Miranda became final. Jalina was then about two. As single parents, money was pretty tight for both women.

Life had dealt Jan a few rough shots; she knew what it was like to be poor and lonely, and there were times when only Jalina's presence helped Jan cope. Finding a friend like Louise to talk to and share things with was vitally important to Jan—in much the same way as Cindy Baumgartner and Lori Baker were to share their own lives a decade later.

The two women lived together and did almost everything together; like Lori and Cindy, they had joint bank accounts; they also had a small life insurance policies that named each other as beneficiaries in case something happened. Janis worked as an assistant in a medical office in Dallas, had ambitions of someday studying child psychology, and drove a green 1976 Pinto that still wasn't paid for.

In the summer of 1979, while Davy Roth was awaiting his trial and Randy's marriage to Donna Sanchez Roth was staggering toward its end, Louise Mitchell decided to return to the Seattle area, where she had grown up years before. Jan and Jalina visited Louise several times, and then in January of 1980, just as Randy was divorcing Donna and Davy was being sentenced to life in prison, Jan decided to move to Seattle permanently to be near Louise.

For the first six months, Jan and Jalina lived with Louise in north Seattle. Jan got two jobs, one at a pediatric clinic and the other as a cashier at a discount store, driving the loyal green car back and forth to both places. In August, Jan was able to rent an apartment across the street from Louise's place. With Jan working day and night shifts, as well as weekends, Louise took care of Jalina, as well as her own children.

Louise later said she remembered exactly when Randy first met Jan. It was at the New Year's Eve dance, she said. Randy seemed quite taken with the petite, energetic Jan, and they soon began dating. Randy later said he had actually first met Jan at Halloween, but that they didn't start dating until after New Year's. An acquaintance of Jan's also later said she remembered someone fixing Jan's car sometime before Christmas and thought that Randy was the mechanic. The friendly car mechanic approach, of course, was one Randy had already used with Donna Sanchez.

Years later as she looked back, Louise was fairly clear on what Jan saw in Randy—financial security. After all, Randy was at that time making around $14 an hour working on Vitamilk's diesel truck engines. He also told Jan that he owned his own home, and for someone like Jan who had missed the real estate boom of the 1970s and had lived in some pretty awful places, a man who owned his own home seemed like a good catch. As a bonus, Randy was attractive, seemed kind and even-tempered, and was unfailingly chivalrous in his demeanor. He didn't drink and he didn't smoke and he didn't use drugs.

The truth was, Jan was tired—tired of working two

jobs, tired of scrambling every month to pay the bills, tired of seeing too little of Jalina, and even that little was hardly quality time. While Jan wasn't entirely sure she loved Randy, she thought she might after being with him for awhile. So in late February of 1981, Jan and Jalina both moved into Randy's Mountlake Terrace house, the one he had previously shared with Donna Sanchez Roth, and a new family was instantly created. Two weeks later, Randy and Jan were married by a judge in King County. Louise Mitchell and Tim Brocato were witnesses.

Jan also quit her two jobs. The people at the pediatric clinic worried about her. Shirley Lenz, receptionist at the clinic, thought Jan was rushing into the marriage too fast—words eerily similar to those used a decade later by Cindy's parents, Hazel and Merle Loucks.

But Jan wasn't concerned, "Oh, Shirley," Jan told her, "he's going to take care of me." Others, including Dr. Bill Forney, one of the clinic physicians, also thought Jan was moving much too fast.

But Louise knew that Jan sometimes tended to act impulsively; it was more in Jan's nature to *do something* rather than stand around and dither. Randy seemed like her best chance at getting some stability into her life, and Jan had made up her mind to take it.

But reality surfaced not long after the marriage. Well, said Randy, I don't actually *own* the house, not yet, you see. I have a, well, it's called a *lease-option*. That's where you have an option to buy it, if you want—and if you can get together the down payment.

So far, no down payment, Randy told Jan. Oh, said Jan. How much money do *you* have, Randy asked. Not much, Jan admitted. Well, said Randy, there's always your car. But that would be no help; Jan told Randy about the car payments she still owed—and now Jan wasn't working any more. Who was going to make the payments?

That's when Randy, according to Tim Brocato,

came up with the idea of reporting the green Pinto stolen to the police and making an insurance claim to Jan's car insurance company—"to get out from under the payments," as Tim put it later.

On March 24, 1981, just two weeks after Randy and Jan were married, the green Pinto was abducted from the Roth lease-optioned driveway. Actually, as Jalina said years later, Jan and Jalina drove it to a junkyard. Randy, with Greg, followed behind in his own car, an old station wagon.

"Randy and my mother were talking while I was in the room," Jalina recalled years later, "and they were planning on that night crushing the car and collecting the insurance on it." Later that night, Jalina remembered, Randy and Jan woke Jalina and Greg, got them dressed, and put them into their respective cars. Jalina rode with Jan in the Pinto.

"We drove to the junkyard," Jalina said, "and I kept [asking] my mother—she used to tell me anything I asked her—and I asked her 'Well, what are we gonna do with the car?' " Jan told her the car would be destroyed so that she and Randy could claim it was stolen. After leaving the car at the junkyard, Jan and Jalina rode home with Randy and Greg.

Randy apparently felt confident enough in Tim Brocato's loyalty at this point to tell Tim substantially the same story. But in Tim's recollection, Randy had said the car was "torched." That was like Randy, to take the more mundane demise of crushing and escalate it into torching. Actually, chances are the car was simply stripped for spare parts at the junkyard.

A side effect of the disappearance of Jan's car was that Jan was effectively stranded at Randy's house. Without a car, she had no way to see her friends, chiefly Louise Mitchell and the people at the pediatric clinic. That isolation in turn increased Randy's control over Jan and helped make her more dependent than ever on him.

"I didn't get a chance to see Janis personally an awful lot," Louise later recalled, "because after they were married, she didn't have her car anymore. . . ."

Jan and Louise did talk on the telephone virtually every day, however, and Jan was quite willing to confide in her best friend. It became apparent to Louise, as the spring of 1981 turned into summer, that Jan was having second thoughts about having married Randy.

"When I saw Janis," Louise remembered, "she seemed to be unhappy—not unhappy. What I'm trying to say is, [she thought] maybe she made a mistake, she jumped too fast into getting married. She had some doubts, because she was independent, and she didn't . . . she felt she didn't have the independence that she should. . . ."

Randy did introduce Jan to Tim and Debbie Brocato, and the two couples did spend time together. However, the relationship between Jan and Debbie was not as close as that between Donna and Debbie. Randy also introduced Jan to his neighbors, including a couple named Ron and Nancy Aden. Ron was a teacher. Both Adens were actively involved in a Snohomish County church, where Ron was the music director. After Donna left, Nancy Aden helped Randy take care of Greg and occasionally fed Randy and his small son. During the year between Donna's departure and Jan's arrival, Nancy Aden learned a bit more about her normally quiet neighbor.

"He told us he was in Vietnam twice," Nancy Aden later told Sue Peters. "He actually volunteered for the second time. He was in a special forces group that was a very small group, I believe, of around twelve men, who would be parachuted into an area, and they would need to survive on their own. It sounded very dangerous. They were doing reconnaissance work, and it sounded like he had been responsible for quite a few deaths of Vietnamese communist soldiers. It sounded real daring and quite scary. We would always say, "Why in the world would you ever volunteer for a second time under such circumstances?" and he said he enjoyed that kind of work . . . which I couldn't understand."

Randy also let Jan know about his "war record." Jan, of course, told Louise. Jan told Louise Randy had been in Vietnam as a member of a team that wiped out entire villages. Randy, Jan told Louise, had bad dreams about Vietnam, waking up screaming, and often couldn't get to sleep at all.

Sometime in mid-June Randy and Jan decided to take the kids on a camping vacation down on the Oregon coast, and along the Columbia River Gorge where Randy's father Gordon was living with his second wife, Sandy. Jan wasn't much of a camper or outdoors person, but she thought she would go along with the plan to please Randy. All throughout the week before they left, Randy kept talking about Beacon Rock, Jalina later remembered. "What's Beacon Rock?" Jalina asked Randy.

"And he told me that it was the second largest rock in the world and he wanted to show it to us. So I guess he had been up there before because he knew so much about it," Jalina told Mullinax years later. Later, Randy would deny ever having been on Beacon Rock before June of 1981.

As Jalina later remembered the camping vacation, she and Greg slept in a blue tent while Randy and Jan slept in the old station wagon.

On the day they got to Beacon Rock, Jalina recalled, the weather was pleasant. A number of people were visiting the landmark at the same time, and soon Randy was leading the way up the winding, mostly paved path to the top. Although Jalina was eight and Greg almost four, neither of the kids had much trouble with the walk. On the top, Randy and Jan told Jalina and Greg to make sure to remain in the center of the flat area and not to go under the pipe railings. At no time, Jalina later said, did anyone go off the path. After about a half-hour, Randy and Jan and the kids walked back down the path to the station wagon in the parking lot below.

Randy's recollection of the June walk to the top of the rock was different in some significant respects. In Randy's version, he and Jan and the kids were following a group of hikers up the path. At a bend in the path, the other group went off the path and up a shortcut that linked two ends of a switchback. The shortcut, Randy said, was initially fairly steep, but then flattened out before making a right turn that rejoined the upper level of the switchback.

None of the group ahead of them had any trouble with the shortcut, Randy said, and neither did he, Jan, Jalina or even Greg. Randy thought he remembered holding Greg's hand part of the way up.

Although Jan had begun taking in small children for daycare, Randy still took Greg to his initial babysitter—the woman with whom Tim Brocato believed Randy was having an affair. The woman had become angry at Randy when he decided to marry Jan; by continuing to bring Greg over—and perhaps seeing her as well—Randy apparently was attempting to mollify her.

Jan didn't like this, of course. In addition to the money Randy paid—about $200 a month for Greg's care that could have gone into the household budget instead, since Jan was already home taking care of other people's children—Jan suspected that Randy had rather more intimate interests in the other woman. She said as much to Louise.

Moreover, Jan told Louise, she and Randy weren't making love much anymore. Randy told her he'd had an infection after his vasectomy and sex was painful.

Jan accepted this, but it wasn't making the two of them any closer.

Meanwhile, Randy was showing far less interest in going out with Jan for dancing or movies or any of the other things they used to like to do. And when they did go out, Randy seemed insanely jealous. Once, Jan told Louise, he'd gone over to a complete stranger to complain that the stranger was looking at Jan far too often.

But Jan still wanted her house, and Randy finally agreed to begin looking for a house to buy. He would use his veterans' mortgage benefit to get around the down payment problem, Randy said. The VA allowed one hundred percent mortgage financing.

Eventually, in September of 1981, Randy and Jan bought a house in Mountlake Terrace for just less than $60,000. The mortgage rate was around thirteen percent, and because the whole house was financed, the payments were nearly $900 a month, including the property taxes. That pushed the Roth budget to the limit. Late that month, Randy and Jan bought $100,000 in whole life insurance, in case something happened to either of them to prevent them making the heavy mortgage payments. The life insurance, the agent told them, would take effect on November 7.

Randy wasn't happy about buying the house. The payments were too much, he complained. At night, after Jalina went to bed, she could hear her mother and Randy arguing about money. One result was that Randy agreed to keep Greg at home rather than send him to the babysitter. Randy didn't like that, either.

In mid-October, Jan wrote a letter to her mother in Texas that showed something of her new life with Randy. The letter was remarkable for its poignant hints of what was to come.

# 27

## "Randy Has Many Very Good Qualities"

*Monday Night*
*Oct. 12, 1981*

Dear Momma,
   It was good to talk to you again. Very sorry that Cleda felt so badly. Wish she'd go to Parkland and do whatever is necessary to help her. They can't help her if she stays at home. What is it going to take to get her there?
   How are Marc and Michael doing? Do they like school? Marc sounds like he is getting big. Let me know how tall they are if you can.
   Jalina is 4' 5" and weighs 65 lbs. She eats good but weighs the right amount for her height. I'm glad she wants to stay "just right."
   Thursday is school picture day so within 3 wks I should be sending you some pictures. If she has her tongue hanging out like in last year's pictures I'll throw them away again! That was a waste of money. You HAVE to pay in advance. That's the only reason I got them in the first place.
   Presently I'm not working but yet I am. I'm babysit-

*ting. Right now business is slow. I have a one yr old (Brook is her name), and she is only part-time. Then I have a 4 yr old boy at night 10 p.m.–8 a.m. His mom is an R.N. He comes about 4 nights a week.*

*Of course, also during the day I have Greg. He turned 4 on Aug. 30th and already ties his shoes, makes his bed and helps do other chores. He is quite mature because Randy would not tolerate a "sissy" boy. He is little for his age. Most people guess him in size to be just 3 or 3½ yrs. old. He is a good boy most of the time. Kids are kids no matter what. The other day he tried to shave and cut himself right below his bottom lip. Then another day he came home (from across the street) with dog mess in his hair!*

*Nevertheless, he is cute. He always tells me I look pretty when I roll my hair and put on fresh make-up. I try to do that every day before Randy gets home and of course when we're going out.*

*Randy is 5' 7½" and weighs 155 lbs. He is a strong man. He used to be a karate champion. He has trophies and all that stuff but he doesn't do it much anymore. He tried to teach it again a year or so ago but he'd get so involved that he couldn't sleep, so he quit teaching it (That was just a part-time job.) Randy could have made good money in that field but it isn't worth it if it changes your personality plus keeps you awake at night!*

*Randy has many very good qualities. Sometimes his drawbacks are due to the time (2 years!?) he spent in Viet Nam. He used to have nightmares, some periods of depression, etc. for several years after his tour there. You probably wouldn't believe some of the things they had to do over there! He isn't proud of them but it's either you or the enemy. Also if you don't do what you're told, you go to the stockade! He was a Marine. If we ever have another war and Randy ever got drafted I wouldn't let him go. He's over draft age but in a National Emergency that can change. I'd* move to Canada first! So many guys got messed up in Nam. That was a dumb war. At least WWI and WWII were for our country!

The world itself can make you a hard, cold person, but so can war. He had to learn to be human again if you can understand that. One thing I can say is he NEVER, EVER messed with any type of drugs. We drink some when we go out but I haven't seen him tipsy yet! Also he never has smoked cigarettes even. I gave it up but sometimes I still miss it.

We go dancing about once every month to every six weeks. I wish we could go more but sometimes I get the urge and by 8 pm it's gone. I don't take to getting too old to Disco lightly! A couple of places we go to have couples our age but most are early 20s! This state still has the 21-yrs. age limit where alcohol is served. I find I tire more easily than I did at age 25! NO KIDDING!

We had a beautiful summer. What was the hottest temp. there this year? It must not have been hot enough to make the news up here. Seattle had three days of 100+ degrees and about 4–5 days in the 90's! I thought I was back in Dallas!

Well, gotta be going to bed. I'll try to finish this letter tomorrow before the mailman comes. That shouldn't be too hard "seeing on how" he doesn't come 'til after 2:30 p.m.! HA!

Tuesday afternoon:

I had to keep two extra kids this morning for a girlfriend of mine and they certainly kept me busy.

Once daddy asked to help me by keeping Jalina for a few more months but Momma I needed help and taking Jalina wasn't the answer. I was the problem not Jalina. Several times in my life Jalina was the reason for me to keep trying! Sometimes it was easier *when she'd visit people but after awhile I'd get lonely without her. She loves her Momma and I needed that.*

I'm the most secure and generally the happiest I've ever been BUT sometimes I don't know if that's what I want. That's strange but it's HARD on me trying to be a mother again for a 4 yr. old and playing house-wife isn't always fun. Sometimes I miss my indepen-dency! I love staying home very much of course and Jalina loves it to have me here when she comes home from school.

Randy is good to all of us and fair, but I sometimes remember liking to be my own boss. I've also never had it so easy if you know what I mean. We aren't anywhere near being financially stable but I alone am not struggling. We pay our bills, eat well and still go places. No matter what we make is never enough really. We want a basement, another bathroom, etc. but either we'll get it or we won't. Randy and I share things including money so it mainly goes for house payments ($871.000 a mo.!) and groceries and utilities AND insurance.

This house is half mine and if I chose to leave then I forfeit all rights (THAT'S HOW THE CONTRACT WAS DRAWN UP SINCE PRIMARILY THRU RAN-DY'S JOB STABILITY AND HIS INCOME & CREDIT WE GOT THIS HOUSE). If he passes away it becomes mine but his son has rights to half of it at age 18. There's no will drawn up yet.

I do love Randy very much HOWEVER SOME-TIMES I ask myself—IS LOVE REALLY WORTH IT? I don't know that answer yet.

Bye!

Love,
Janis

*Money Enclosed for you to use however you want! Your Happy Late Birthday Gift!*

# 28

## Trick or Treat

On Halloween night, 1981, Randy and Tim accompanied the kids as they made the rounds of the neighborhood with sacks collecting the evening's tribute. Randy seemed in a pensive mood, Tim thought.

"Could you kill your wife?" Tim later recalled Randy asking him. Tim looked at Randy as if he were crazy. "What do you mean?" Tim asked, "Well," said Randy, "I mean, like if there were an invasion or something, and she were going to be captured by the enemy."

Randy went on to say that Jan had asked him to kill her if she were terminally ill or were about to be captured in an invasion. Tim didn't give the conversation too much more thought. Later the same night, Randy told Tim that both he and Jan were insured for $100,000 in case anything happened to either one of them.

Tim put this conversation down to idle, crazy talk from Randy—just filling the airwaves, Randy trying to impress Tim with his stark, macho capacity to cope with any eventuality. Tim knew Randy liked to play the bad ass, to seem tough. The kids collected their candy, and later everyone went home.

Yet there was something about the Halloween talk that stuck with Tim in the following weeks. He could see that the marriage between Randy and Jan wasn't working. It reminded him of Randy and Donna. He knew Randy was cheating on Jan.

Tim liked Jan. To him, she seemed sweet, kind and caring, and more than a little vulnerable. Jan liked to dance, and she was normally a very upbeat personality. But as November of 1981 unfolded, Tim sensed that Jan was becoming increasingly despondent. Tim wasn't exactly sure what was wrong. Randy looked pretty glum himself. Randy complained Jan wanted to go dancing too often. He was getting sick of it. "Doesn't sound like you're happy," Tim told Randy. "Yeah," Randy said.

On the weekend before Thanksgiving, Randy asked Tim to use Randy's car to drop him off at Vitamilk. Randy told Tim he was going hunting, but Tim knew Randy *never* went hunting. Tim saw Randy get into a car driven by a woman who certainly wasn't Jan. Tim drove Randy's car back to Randy's house, where Jan was waiting. Tim didn't say anything about Randy's "hunting trip," however.

Still, Jan seemed miserably unhappy, very nervous and upset. She told Tim that she'd had a very bad dream the night before. In her dream, Jan said, she had learned that she was going to die.

Three days later, on the Tuesday before Thanksgiving, Jan asked Jalina to come into the bedroom she shared with Randy at the end of the house. They sat on the bed. Jan told Jalina that she might have to go live with her father—her real father, in Texas.

"I don't want to, Mommy," Jalina said.

"If something happens to me," Jan said, "you might have to."

"Well, I don't want to."

"You might not have any choice," Jan said.

"Nothing's going to happen to you, Mommy," Jalina said again. "Why are you saying that?"

"Well, if it does," Jan told Jalina, "I want you to know where this is." And with that, Jan removed the bureau drawer that was built into the wall of the bedroom. She showed Jalina a white envelope that was taped to the wall inside the drawer space.

"If anything ever happens to me, I want you to come and get this," Jan told her daughter.

"What is it?"

"It's some of the child support money sent by your real daddy, in Texas," Jan said, and replaced the drawer. Jan Miranda Roth had been a survivor for too long in her life to not put something aside for emergencies.

On the following day, as she was getting things ready to spend Thanksgiving with Randy's stepmother Sandy in Washougal—Gordon by this time had separated from Sandy and was living in a different house across the road in Washougal—Jan told Louise on the phone about her dream. Louise later recalled that Jan didn't really want to go to Washougal for Thanksgiving; she would rather be spending it with Louise and her children. Jan seemed to be thinking about divorcing Randy.

It was probably all her own fault, Jan told Louise; maybe she just wasn't meant to be married. Jan was reluctant to give up the house, as Randy told her she would have to do if she left him; but maybe she would, anyway. *There is something wrong over there*, Louise thought as she hung up.

# 29

## Beacon Rock

**E**xactly what happened that November day on Beacon Rock will probably never be known with certainty. Years later, Sue Peters developed a theory, one that at least fit with the physical facts of Janis' death. Peters guessed that Randy and Jan walked to the top of the rock, keeping to the trail all the way, never once venturing outside the railings, despite Randy's later insistent claims to the contrary.

Once at the top, in Peters' scenario, Randy suggested to Jan that they duck under one of the railings so that Randy could find a scenic spot to take a picture of her. Then, when they were both far enough way from any passersby and likely concealed from view by the trees, Randy simply shoved Jan over the side—three hundred feed down to the rocks below.

What is known is that shortly after 11 A.M. on November 27, 1981, a wild-eyed, apparently crazed Randy Roth came sprinting down the trail, passing a small group of hikers. Then, while the hikers were peering at each other in mystification, Randy came running back toward them.

"My God, have you seen my wife?" he asked. "I

think she might have fallen from the rock." Randy told them that his wife had climbed under a railing "to take a picture" and that she had disappeared. He'd warned her not to, Randy said. The hikers, Steven and Shelly Anderson of Washougal, Washington, told Randy that they hadn't seen anyone. The Andersons' dog, normally a well-behaved, gentle pet, raised her hackles at Randy, growled at him and lunged in his direction. The Andersons were amazed at their normally friendly dog's reaction to the stranger.

Randy wanted the Andersons and two others who were hiking with them to help him look for Jan. But Shelly Anderson didn't trust him. "He was freaked out," she said much later. "He was just—his eyes were crazy and he was freaked out."

This encounter with the Andersons, which probably took place within minutes of Jan's plunge over the side of the rock, was among the most significant pieces of evidence that Randy might have had something to do with Jan's death. For one thing, Randy said nothing to the Andersons about actually having *seen* Jan fall— only that she had "disappeared" while going to "take a picture," and that he thought she "might" have fallen. All of this was radically different than Randy's later story to almost everyone else, in which he said he had watched helplessly as Jan "cartwheeled" over the side.

In Peters' scenario, however, Randy's speech and behavior take on a certain logic. In this concept, after shoving Jan over the side, Randy began to descend on the pathway and soon encountered the Andersons and their dog coming up from below. In Peters' theory, Randy would have no way of knowing whether the Andersons, the closest witnesses, had seen anything incriminating. Randy could have been worried that, at the worst, the Andersons might have seen him actually shove Jan off the cliff, or at least be able to say exactly

A close-up of Randy Roth, taken during his press conference on August 9, 1991, in which he denied killing two of his four wives. (Peter Liddell/*Seattle Times*)

Randy Roth at about the age of six or seven. (King County Police)

Randy Roth and his high school sweetheart, Terri McGuire. Terri thought her love could change Randy, but she ended up testifying against him years later. (Terri McGuire)

Randy Roth astride his Honda in 1974. He is wearing a leather jacket given to him for Christmas by Terri McGuire. Shortly after this picture was taken, Roth was arrested for burglarizing the McGuire family's house. (King County Police)

Randy Roth at about age 16 wearing his "Billy Jack" hat. Roth admired the fictional movie hero played by actor Tom Laughlin. (King County Police)

Roth as a Marine Private First Class, early 1974. He hated the Marines. (King County Police)

Randy Roth being promoted to Lance Corporal by his commanding officer in the spring of 1974. Despite his later claims of having served in Vietnam, Roth never made it farther than Guam—and that was more than a year after the U.S. involvement in the war was over. (King County Police)

Cindy Baumgartner Roth with roses in about 1990. She was 34 when she drowned in Lake Sammamish in 1991. (King County Police)

The house that Randy and Cindy Roth bought in Woodinville, Washington. Randy sarcastically referred to it as "The Swamp." It was sold for a $50,000 loss after Cindy drowned. (King County Police)

The rear of the Woodinville house, with Roth's prized four-wheelers on a trailer and his dog Jackson, who failed to bark the night Roth burglarized his own house. Randy and Cindy had disputes about landscaping the rear of the house. (King County Police)

Many stolen goods found by police in the crawl space of Randy Roth's house on the day of the search. (King County Police)

Roth being escorted by jail guards during his trial. (Pedro Perez/ *Seattle Times*)

Roth, center, in his jail coveralls, during pretrial hearings, with his lawyers, George Cody, left, and John Muenster, right. (Jim Bates/*Seattle Times*)

Detectives Randy Mullinax and Sue Peters taking congratulatory telephone calls in their office after Randy Roth's conviction. (Alan Berner/*Seattle Times*)

Senior Deputy Prosecutors Susan Storey, center-left, and Marilyn Brenneman, center-right, being mobbed by news media after Randy Roth's conviction. (Alan Berner/*Seattle Times*)

Beacon Rock, an 800-foot-tall ancient volcanic plug where Janis Roth fell to her death the day after Thanksgiving, 1981. (King County Police)

Police attempt to reenact Randy Roth's story that his raft capsized on the day Cindy drowned. (King County Police)

where she fell, which could have posed other problems for Randy's later story.

So, Randy, after first passing the Andersons on his way down to the parking lot to report Jan's fall, suddenly realized he needed to determine what, if anything, the Andersons had seen. If the Andersons gave Randy any indication that they had seen too much, Randy could begin his immediate escape; if they knew nothing, Randy could continue with his "accident" story.

That was why Randy, after first passing the Andersons, then raced back to ask them if they had "seen" his wife, in the process already proffering two potential alibis: she was going to take a picture and voluntarily ducked under the rail against his advice and "disappeared," and he thought she "might" have fallen off.

Nothing in his initial statement to the Andersons indicates that Randy had any actual knowledge of what happened to Jan. But Randy was extremely agitated, probably at that point with fear of detection, which was likely why the Andersons' dog was alerted. "His eyes were crazy," Shelly Anderson remembered years later. "I mean, you could look through them. He scared me."

The Andersons, however, told Randy they had seen nothing. At that point, Randy wanted to enlist the Andersons as possible witnesses on his behalf by his request that they help him look for her.

But the Andersons didn't want to be anywhere near Randy, at least on the rock. Instead, they volunteered to walk back down to the bottom to summon help. Randy went back to the top. He said he would resume the search by himself.

Later, he was to claim he ran up and down Beacon rock four times in an effort to find a way to reach the place where he thought Jan had fallen—which location

he shouldn't have known if indeed Jan had simply
"disappeared."

Instead, it seems more probable, at least in Peters'
theory, that Randy went back to the top, looked for a
spot on the trail that seemed dangerous, and then sat
down nearby to wait for the authorities to tell them a
more likely story.

Within a few minutes after the Andersons returned
to the parking lot, Skamania County Deputy Sheriff
Ed Powell arrived at the rock. A few minutes later, so
did two volunteer members of an ambulance crew
trained in search and rescue techniques. Powell sent
the two ambulance people up the path to look for
Randy. The ambulance people met Randy about half-
way up.

Randy acted as if he was looking for someone who
might have fallen over the cliff. He explained to the
ambulance crew that he had seen Jan slip on some wet
grass or leaves and then "cartwheel" over the side.
That was the first time Randy was to say he had
actually seen Jan go over, although the ambulance
people didn't know that. The ambulance crew sent
Randy down to the parking lot to talk to Powell. The
ambulance crew went up to the place where Randy
said he had seen Jan fall. The crew couldn't find the
place immediately, based on Randy's description.

After getting down, Randy told someone that he
remembered there was a beer can near the spot where
Jan fell, so that information was radioed to the ambulance crew higher up. They found the can and realized
that a mountain rescuer would be needed. The spot
was too steep for anybody else.

Soon an expert rescuer, a man named Bill Wylie,
arrived. By that time the county's undersheriff, a man
named Ray Blaisdale, had arrived on the scene to
coordinate the rescue effort. Blaisdale introduced Wylie to Randy, and asked Randy to take Wylie to the

spot where Jan had gone over the edge. Wylie was a bit surprised to realize that the man Blaisdale had just introduced him to was the husband of the missing woman.

"He didn't seem to be involved in the incident at the time," Wylie remembered, foreshadowing words that were later used about Randy in connection with Cindy's death. "He was calm and standing off to the side and, wasn't presenting himself to be emotionally upset or pressing for information or anxious to get us to the top of the hill."

This demeanor was in marked contrast to the "crazed" look first exhibited by Randy to the Andersons, although no one was then aware of that.

Near the top, Randy pointed out the place where he said he and Jan had gone off on the shortcut. Wylie and Randy, accompanied by several others, climbed the shortcut and went to the place where Randy said Jan had fallen.

"He showed me the section of the trail cut that he described as where she had gone over the edge," Wylie said later. "He said that he was in the lead and that he was starting to go into the treed section, back into the treed section, and when he turned around, he saw her tumble over the edge, go over the edge."

This statement—that Randy was in the lead, and that he turned around to see Jan fall—was also in contrast to Randy's later descriptions of the incident. In those recountings, it would be *Jan* who was in the lead, with Randy following to provide her with "security" in case she slipped.

The place pointed out by Randy was relatively flat but bordered a fairly steep slope about ten by fifteen feet. The slope was covered with sparse grass and a few shrubs. Wylie guessed the slope area was about twenty-five to thirty degrees in inclination. Beyond that a sheer cliff dropped away for about three hundred feet.

Wylie wanted to know exactly where Jan had gone off the sloped area. Randy was vague, suggesting that it was somewhere in the middle of the lower edge of the sloping ten-foot area. He was very calm. As Wylie started to set up his equipment, Randy walked over to a tree near the edge and sat down. Wylie told someone to take Randy back down to the parking lot to keep him from getting involved in the rescue. "That's often a problem," Wylie said later. Relatives of accident victims, Wylie knew, tend to get emotionally involved in rescue efforts, sometimes dangerously so. Randy went back down the rock.

Neither Wylie or any of the others present could see any skid marks or other evidence that Jan had actually slipped down the slope Randy was indicating. There were no tufts of grass pulled out or broken branches that might have been expected as someone sliding headfirst might have grabbed on the way down.

Wylie looped his climbing rope around a tree, got into his harness, walked down the slope and then rappeled over the side. He got to the end of his rope, one hundred sixty-five feet, dropped to a small ledge, but saw no trace of Jan. Wylie thought he might try to climb a bit further down the rock to another ledge some distance below; maybe he would find Jan there.

But then, two Army air rescue helicopters from Portland, Oregon, arrived at the scene. Wylie was concerned that the backwash from the rotor blades might blow him off the ledge, so he hooked himself back onto his climbing rope and watched. The chopper was about one hundred fifty feet away from Wylie. In a few minutes, he saw a rescuer descend from the helicopter on a cable into a clump of trees about another one hundred fifty feet below him, and about the same distance to the right. Then Wylie saw a body basket being lowered to the rescuer in the trees, and Wylie knew that the air rescuer had found Jan Roth.

Wylie was puzzled; the place where Jan was found

was much farther away from the place where Randy had indicated Jan had initially fallen. To wind up one hundred fifty feet to the side from the straight line down the cliff that Wylie had followed meant that Jan's descent would have been perhaps as much as twenty or twenty-five degrees off line, a nearly impossible angle. Wylie knew that bodies bounced, but certainly not one hundred fifty feet. It was peculiar, he thought.

Down at the parking lot, Blaisdale was standing with Randy when the word came that Jan had been found. The rescuer asked that intravenous material be sent down on the cable. Blaisdale turned to Randy. "Evidently she is still alive," Blaisdale told him.

Blaisdale thought Randy was happy to hear this. "I would say that he was pleased and somewhat relieved," Blaisdale said later. Randy didn't act at all like he was worried that the rescuers had found a living Jan who would be able to accuse Randy of shoving her off the cliff, Blaisdale thought later. But then a few minutes later, the rescuers reported that Jan was definitely dead. Blaisdale asked if he could speak to Randy privately and told him the news.

"Well, why did they ask for the IVs?" Randy asked. Blaisdale said he had no idea. Randy didn't say anything but seemed upset. Later, Blaisdale was to wonder whether Randy thought the authorities were trying to trick him by saying Jan was dead when she really wasn't. Randy walked away from Blaisdale to stand beside his own car, the station wagon, holding his head in his hands. Blaisdale thought Randy was crying, but he couldn't see his face.

Finally Randy came back to Blaisdale's car and told the undersheriff that he'd seen a lot of dead people in his life but never a loved one. And then Randy said something Blaisdale thought was a bit strange: "She didn't smoke, she didn't drink, and I loved her very much." It was a weird sort of epitaph, Blaisdale thought.

The helicopter crew pulled Jan's body back up the chopper in the basket attached to the cable, then flew off to a nearby farm to transfer the body to the ambulance. Randy told Blaisdale that he wanted to see the body. They drove over to the farm in Blaisdale's car. On the way over, Randy again told Blaisdale: "She didn't smoke, she didn't drink, and I loved her very much." Strange, Blaisdale thought. Couldn't Randy think of anything more to say about his dead wife than *that*?

At the farm, one of the emergency medical technicians present at the ambulance suggested to Randy that he *not* view Jan's body.

"In this particular situation," the EMT said later, "sometimes it's best to retain the memories, the good memories, rather than the trauma of viewing [her] as she was at that time."

The EMT was trying to spare Randy's feelings. "She [Jan] had some gross injuries to the head and face and there was quite a bit of hemorrhage [bleeding] that had occurred." Jan was not a pretty sight.

But Randy was insistent on seeing her. "He was adamant," the EMT recalled. A decade later, Peters and Mullinax wondered whether the reason Randy was so insistent on seeing Jan's body was that he wanted to make sure Jan was *really* dead and that Blaisdale wasn't playing some trick on him.

The EMT unzipped the body bag so that Randy could look. Blaisdale went first. "I stepped out back away from the ambulance and then he [Randy] stepped up and looked. . . ." Blaisdale remembered. Blaisdale asked Randy if it was his wife in the body bag. Randy said it was.

Blaisdale took Randy back to his own car. Then, for the third time Randy told Blaisdale that he'd seen a lot of dead people—while he was in military service,

Randy added—but never a loved one. "She didn't smoke, she didn't drink," Randy said once more. "That's why I married her. I loved her very much." Blaisdale didn't know what to make of Randy's thrice-stated remark, but it definitely seemed like an odd thing to say.

*Imagine loving someone simply because they didn't smoke and didn't drink,* Blaisdale thought. *Imagine that.*

# 30

## Aftermath

In later years, Jalina was to grow confused about the events that happened that day at Beacon Rock. She came to believe that she and Greg had accompanied Randy and Jan up the rock on the same day that Jan died, rather than five months before. In Jalina's mind, as the years passed, the two events merged, so as Jalina remembered it, Randy and Jan had gone *back* to the rock after having climbed it with her and Greg once already earlier on the same day, the day after Thanksgiving.

The recollections of others present, however, show that Jalina confused the June trip with what she later heard about the November event. Jalina never was on the rock in November; instead, she stayed at Randy's stepmother's house to ride horses with Marcie Thompson, Randy's fourteen-year-old stepsister, and the two youngest sons of Gordon and Sandy Roth, Randy's half brothers.

A decade later, when Peters and Mullinax attempted to unravel the sequence of all these conflicting accounts—to determine the reliability of Jalina's admittedly hazy memory, and thus, Randy's credibility—

Sandy Roth was dead. As a result, it came down to Randy's word against his stepsister Marcie and his former stepdaughter, Jalina.

Just about everyone later agreed that Randy and Jan left by themselves to go to the rock about nine A.M. But while Randy was to say that going to Beacon Rock had been Jan's spur-of-the-moment idea as they were driving, Marcie remembered Randy telling the kids—but apparently not Jalina—that he and Jan were going to Beacon Rock to spend some time alone with each other.

That suggested Randy had previously *planned* to push Jan off the rock, and of course, also sounded remarkably similar to what Randy was to say about the "romantic" excursion of his and Cindy's in the raft almost ten years later, a parallel immediately noted in 1991 by Peters and Mullinax.

After Jan's death and the recovery of her body, Randy's whereabouts for much of the afternoon remain unclear. It appears that Randy left Beacon Rock by himself around two or three in the afternoon. Jan's body was taken to a funeral home in nearby Camas, Washington, where a pathologist performed an autopsy, concluding that Jan had died from severe brain injuries from a skull fracture that occurred in the fall. The authorities listed the death as an accident.

Apparently Randy was at the funeral home, because he was given a receipt for expenses to be incurred in cremating Jan's remains the following day, along with a death certificate.

Where Randy went next remains a mystery. Years later, Randy said he went to Sandy Roth's house and immediately told her what had happened. Others said, however, that Sandy Roth was at work that day and couldn't be located to be informed of the news. The discrepancy was important evidence on whether Randy was lying about the events surrounding Jan's fall. If it could be proved that Randy was lying about this fact, what else might he be lying about?

"We went into the back room and had a discussion," Randy remembered, "and I don't remember specific details after that. She [Sandy] decided that we wouldn't take the trouble to make a dinner there that night, that she would take us out for pizza." But Marcie said Sandy Roth was never present for the pizza dinner and thus couldn't have heard what happened next.

While waiting for the pizza, Marcie later remembered, Randy slid the receipt for Jan's cremation expense across the table to show her. He didn't say anything. Marcie looked at the receipt and didn't understand what it was, or who it was referring to.

"I don't know any Janis Roth," she told Randy. Marcie was thinking of Jan as "Jan," not "Janis."

"Yes, you do," Randy told her. "Think about it."

It suddenly dawned on Marcie that Randy was using the paper as a sly way to tell her that Jan was dead. Marcie became very upset and left the table to go into the bathroom. Jalina got up and followed her, according to Marcie. Marcie said she didn't say anything to Jalina about her mother. They then returned to the table and ate the pizza—"as if nothing had happened," Marcie recalled.

After returning to Sandy Roth's house in Washougal, Randy told Marcie that Jan had fallen while they were taking a shortcut, and that he had tried to grab Jan as she went over but missed. Then, Randy told Marcie, he'd run up and down the hill looking for Jan but wasn't able to find her.

At this point, perhaps ten hours after Jan's death, Randy's version of the events had evolved significantly from his initial statement to the Andersons just after Jan had "disappeared." It was a version Randy would stick with in the coming years, except for variations he would invent to later impress people such as Mary Jo Phillips.

In Randy's version of the events that night, he and Sandy Roth together told Jalina that her mother was dead.

"She was obviously curious as to where her mother was," Randy said later, "and I told her I'd talk to her later on, and Sandy and I both approached her in the living room. The other kids were sent down the hall, and we did talk to her and explained to her that she was involved in an accident and that she had been taken into [Camas]; that they had told me that she was dead."

Jalina remembered it quite differently.

"When did you see Randy next?" Mullinax asked her years later.

"The next time I saw Randy," she said, "it was late at night because I was waiting up for them [Randy and Jan] to come home. And I remember it being eleven o'clock because I was supposed to be in bed at ten. And he came home and I just remember he had on some jeans or something with a dark brown leather jacket."

"What did he tell you?"

"When he came home he was crying and I said, 'Why are you crying?' And he said that he wanted to talk to me, and I said, 'What about?' He told me to come and sit in his lap, so I was sitting in his lap and he told me there had been an accident.

"I kept asking, 'Where's my mommy?' And he said there had been an accident. And I said, 'What kind of accident?' and he told me she had fallen from the rock. . . ." Randy told her, Jalina said, that Jan was in a hospital in Washougal. Jalina was crying and Randy was hugging her.

Thus, in Jalina's memory, there was no Sandy Roth present and there was certainly no mention of her mother being dead, contrary to Randy's later story. In

Jalina's memory, she believed that her mother was still alive throughout the weekend and early into the following week.

The following day, as Jan's body was being cremated, Randy got up early to make some telephone calls. The first call he made was to the insurance agent who had sold him the $100,000 life insurance policy on Jan. Randy had written the policy number on the back of the death certificate he'd been given the previous day, which later seemed to show he'd been well-prepared for Jan's "accident."

Agent Darrell Lundquist vividly remembered the event years later. Lundquist was still in bed when Randy called. Randy said he wanted to make a claim of the life insurance on his wife. Lundquist thought Randy wanted to cancel the policy and claim the money that had been spent on premiums—maybe thirty dollars. You can't make a claim, Lundquist told Randy, unless somebody has died.

That's just exactly what had happened, Randy told the agent: Jan was dead. Lundquist was amazed. No one had ever called him less than three weeks after an insurance policy had gone into effect to make a claim. How did it happen, Lundquist asked. Randy told him Jan had fallen off a cliff. When, Lundquist asked. Yesterday, Randy told him. Now Lundquist was bowled over. *That* certainly had never happened before, someone calling the day after his wife's death—on a weekend yet, while he was still in bed—to make a claim. Well, said Lundquist, there was nothing to be done on a Saturday; Randy should come into the office on Monday, and Lundquist would begin processing the claim then. Randy agreed and hung up.

Next Randy called the pediatric clinic where Jan had worked before the marriage. Jan's friend Shirley Lenz—the receptionist who had worried that Jan was rushing too fast into the marriage—answered the phone. Randy explained that he needed Jan's Social Security number. Shirley Lenz said she didn't know what the number might be. Well, said Randy, couldn't Shirley look it up on Jan's job records? The records were in the doctor's private office, Shirley explained, and he wasn't in yet. She told Randy to call back.

Randy called back a half-hour later. Shirley had Jan's Social Security number but was puzzled. Why didn't Randy just ask Jan for her number? Well, he couldn't, Randy told her; Jan was sick, he said. Shirley thought that it was strange Jan was so sick she couldn't even give Randy her own Social Security number. Randy told Shirley nothing about the fall.

An hour or so later, Randy, Jalina and Greg started back to Seattle. On the way out of Washougal, Jalina later remembered, she asked Randy if they could stop to see her mother in the hospital. No, Randy said; the doctors weren't allowing Jan to have any visitors.

Back in Seattle, Randy stopped at Louise Mitchell's house to see if Jan had any mail there waiting for her. Louise wasn't there, and Randy said nothing to Louise's children about Jan's death and left no message for Louise to call him.

After getting home, however, Randy called Tim Brocato. "Jan is no longer with us," Randy told him. Tim immediately concluded that Jan and Jalina had left Randy and Greg; after all, the marriage had badly deteriorated, as Randy's apparent affair and Jan's despondency just the weekend before indicated. "What do you mean?" Tim asked Randy.

"Just like I said," Randy told him. "She's no longer with us."

"Did she go someplace?" Tim asked, still not getting it. Then Randy spelled it out for Tim: Jan was dead, d-e-a-d.

Tim was shocked. "Is there something I can do? Geez, I'm sorry," he stammered.

No, said Randy. "That's all I wanted to say," Randy told Tim, and hung up.

Tim told Debbie what Randy had said. Then he decided to drive over to see Randy, to make sure he was okay. When he arrived, Randy was baking cookies for the kids. "Are you all right?" Tim asked.

"I told you not to come over here," Randy told him, "and I meant it, I don't want you here." Tim left.

But by the following day, Randy was apparently feeling more sociable. He took Greg to the church attended by his neighbors, Ron and Nancy Aden, where Ron was the music director. After the service, Ron spotted Randy in the congregation and went up to shake his hand. Ron and Nancy had been trying for some time to get Randy and Jan involved with their church.

Ron shook Randy's hand. "Where's your better half?" he asked jovially. Randy looked straight back at Ron without blinking. "She's dead," he said.

Ron Aden couldn't believe it. Here was Randy, completely serious but without a tear in his eye. He pulled Randy over to the side of the sanctuary and asked him what happened. Randy explained that he and Jan had been hiking and that Jan had fallen off a cliff. Ron called Nancy over, and arrangements were made to have someone stay with Randy and Greg while the Adens took relatives to the airport.

Then the Adens rushed back to the church to be with Randy and Greg once more. "We felt like he was really kind of reaching out for some help and we wanted to be helpful to him," Nancy Aden said later. "We really felt sorry for what had happened."

Meanwhile, Louise Mitchell had been anxious to talk to Jan to find out how the trip to Washougal had turned out. She called Randy and Jan's house on Sunday, but no one answered. The fact that no one answered the telephone bothered Louise.

\* \* \*

Skamania County Undersheriff Ray Blaisdale was by this time developing doubts about Randy Roth and what happened to his wife.

For openers, there was the strange angle of Jan's fall. Blaisdale talked to the rescue workers, who told him they couldn't understand how Jan had come to be so far away from the place where Randy said she had gone over the side.

Blaisdale talked to the rescue worker Bill Wylie, who told him that Randy had said *he* was in the lead, not Jan. Randy had told Blaisdale it was the other way around. Wylie was sure about what Randy had said, because he'd asked him several times. But Blaisdale was equally sure Randy had told *him* Jan was ahead.

To Blaisdale, that meant Randy might possibly be lying about the events on the rock. Blaisdale also kept remembering what Randy said about his dead wife: "She didn't smoke, she didn't drink, and I loved her very much."

On Monday, November 30, 1981, as Randy met with insurance agent Darrell Lundquist to begin the process of filing his claim, Louise Mitchell called Randy and Jan's house again. Still there was no answer.

Meanwhile, Blaisdale called the pediatric clinic, looking for information about Jan. Why did he want to know? Blaisdale was asked. Blaisdale told Shirley Lenz that Jan was dead, that she'd died in a fall on the previous Saturday. Shirley couldn't believe it. Why hadn't Randy told her about Jan's death when he called asking for Jan's Social Security number? Lenz told the others in the clinic about Blaisdale's call. Everyone in the clinic got upset, Lenz later remembered, and there was quite a bit of discussion about Randy, and the suddenness of the marriage, and the death itself. People thought the circumstances were suspicious.

Next, Shirley called Louise Mitchell to see if Louise

knew anything more about Jan's death. Until that point, Louise had known nothing of the events of the weekend. She couldn't believe it, either. She immediately called Randy at work at Vitamilk and had a conversation that was eerily similar to the one Lori Baker would have with Randy ten years later.

"What happened to Janis?" Louise demanded. "Is it true that she's dead?"

"Yes," Randy told her.

"Well, why didn't you contact me?" Louise asked.

Randy didn't answer.

Louise didn't know what to say. Finally, she asked if Randy had contacted anyone in Jan's family in Texas. No, Randy said. Why not? He didn't have any of the telephone numbers of Jan's family, Randy said. Louise thought it was more a matter of Randy just not wanting to do it. Louise said she would make the calls and hung up, fuming at Randy's behavior.

Louise called Jan's sister in Dallas and told her the bad news. Jan's sister in turn called their mother, Billie Ray, and told her. Then Jan's sister called Joe Miranda, Jan's first husband, and left a message for him to call her.

That night, Billie Ray called Randy and asked what had happened to Jan. Randy explained. What about funeral arrangements? Billie asked. Randy told her there would be a memorial service for Jan on the following Saturday, December 5. Billie said she and Jan's sister would fly up for the services. Meanwhile, Sandy and Marcie drove up from Washougal to be with Randy. Randy was getting a lot of attention at this point.

The following evening, Tuesday, December 1, Joe Miranda called Randy. Joe told Randy he intended to take custody of Jalina. Randy explained that he was perfectly happy to have Jalina continue to stay with him, but Joe wasn't having any of it.

Well, Randy said, it doesn't sound like I have any

real choice in the matter, since you've got the legal right. Joe said he would be up to collect Jalina the following day, and hung up.

At this point, according to Jalina, Randy hung up the phone and told her that the call had been from the hospital and that the doctors had been unable to save Jan. "Your mother is dead," Jalina remembered Randy telling her.

The next day, according to Jalina, Randy told her the rest of the news: she would be going back to Texas to live with her real father. Jalina didn't want to go; she wanted to stay with Randy and Greg. But Randy explained that while he wanted to have Jalina with them, he didn't have any choice in the matter, since Jalina's real father had legal rights to her. But Randy promised he would try to get Jalina back. Jalina believed him.

Now, said Randy, they had to go see Jalina's real father at a motel. He told Jalina to pack her clothes. Jalina packed, but Randy wouldn't let her take any toys, or any of Jan's things, for that matter. But Jalina managed to surreptitiously take a pair of shoes that belonged to Jan and slip them into her bundle.

Then Jalina, remembering what Jan had said to her before going to Washougal, went into the bedroom, pulled out the drawer, and removed the white envelope. She was looking in it as she left the bedroom and saw that it contained cash, some checks and some papers. But before she could look closer, Randy saw her.

What's that, Jalina? he demanded. It's something my mommy told me to get if something ever happened to her and I had to go live with my real daddy, Jalina said. Randy took the envelope from her and looked inside. "She was holding out on me," Randy said, as if to himself. Then he told Jalina that he would take the money and use it to send her presents while she was in Texas with her real father. Jalina, who hadn't seen her father since she was about two and barely remembered him, agreed.

Next, Randy told Jalina not to tell her real daddy where Randy and Greg lived. Jalina agreed to that, too.

About half an hour later, Randy and Jalina arrived at Joe Miranda's motel. Joe was there with his new wife and his sister. Randy turned Jalina over to Joe and again said that he was willing to take Jalina if Joe didn't want her. No chance, said Joe, and Randy left. Jalina would not see Randy again for another ten years; he never sent any presents. Besides a fading memory, the only thing of her mother Jalina would have would be a single pair of dancing shoes.

# 31

## "I Don't Want to Tell You Anything . . . "

As December unfolded, Randy went back to the routines he had established before marrying Jan. Greg went back to the babysitter Randy had been using before Jan put her foot down. He continued to work on the trucks at Vitamilk. And he continued to see Tim Brocato.

Tim was very troubled. He asked Randy what had happened to Jan, and Randy gave him a terse description. When Tim pressed for more details, Randy clammed up. Tim realized Randy didn't want to talk about it. But Tim noticed changes in Randy's behavior. Randy seemed very nervous, keyed up. He would sit for hours in the darkness, not sleeping. He frequently threw up and was convinced someone was watching his house.

Tim finally had to admit it: he was pretty sure Randy had killed Jan. The Halloween talk about killing wives, followed by Jan's fearful dream, and then Jan's death, convinced Tim that Randy had murdered her. So Tim was afraid of Randy; his friend seemed capable of anything, especially now that he was so edgy. Randy, Tim remember, was the guy who could sneak up on

someone and garrote them without a second thought.
Hadn't Randy done those things in Vietnam? To babies, even?

By the first week in December, Undersheriff Blaisdale had talked to Steve and Shelly Anderson, the
hikers on Beacon Rock. The Andersons told Blaisdale
about their encounter with Randy on the trail.

Randy had acted "confused," the Andersons said,
and had asked them if they had seen his wife, saying
she had "disappeared" while trying to take a picture,
and that he was afraid she might have fallen. Blaisdale
noticed the discrepancies in the story, but did not
immediately recognize their significance. Everyone
agreed that Randy initially seemed to be in some sort
of panic, and it was always possible that because of
the trauma of the events, the Andersons themselves
may have gotten confused about what Randy said. But
Blaisdale still smelled something rotten about the incident and was determined to keep on digging.

Throughout December, Blaisdale interviewed people in Seattle who had known Randy and Jan. It didn't
take him very long to reach Louise Mitchell.

Mitchell was hardly Randy's biggest fan, but she
wasn't able to tell Blaisdale anything that shed much
light on the possibility of murder. And the more Blaisdale dug into Jan's past life, the more he realized that
it was possible that Jan might have killed herself. At
one time, Blaisdale discovered, Jan had felt suicidal in
Dallas.

Louise Mitchell told Blaisdale Randy and Jan's marriage seemed to be good, that she knew of no violence
between them. But, Louise said, she felt that Jan
wasn't entirely happy in the marriage. She'd lost her
independence, Louise told Blaisdale, and was beginning to feel that she'd gone into the marriage too
quickly. Louise told Blaisdale about Randy's "war
record," and told him that Randy did have a violent
temper and could be capable of violence. Louise

thought that Randy had once been arrested for assault. Louise told Blaisdale about the life insurance; Jan had told her about the policy, but Louise wasn't sure exactly how much it was for, although it was in the thousands, she believed. The insurance, she said, might have been Randy's prior to the marriage.

Louise also complained that Randy hadn't bothered to tell her about Jan's death, that she'd had to call him. Louise told Blaisdale that Jan was worried that Randy had been seeing another woman, Greg's former babysitter, and gave the undersheriff the woman's name. She didn't know what to think, Louise concluded. If Randy did have something to do with Jan's death, she hoped Blaisdale would be able to prove it.

Just before Christmas, an investigator for the life insurance company came to see Randy. Randy answered all of the man's questions but didn't volunteer much information. He told the investigator that Jan had slipped on some pine needles as she went over the cliff. That was pretty specific, and completely different than what Randy had told Steve and Shelly Anderson. The investigator thought that Randy's statements to the Andersons might have been made under emotional distress and therefore not very accurate. However, *this* Randy, the investigator thought, was calm and collected. "His answers were very brief, very concise," the investigator later recalled. "He didn't elaborate on any, *any* statements whatsoever."

Randy seemed very cold, very matter of fact, the investigator thought. The investigator filled out a report, wrote a statement of Randy's version of the events, and had Randy sign both. He left.

Meanwhile, Randy continued to see Greg's babysitter when her husband was not around. The husband, however, had grown suspicious of his wife's behavior around Randy over the previous year; she became teasing and more flirtatious when Randy was around.

The husband confronted his wife and accused her of having an affair with Randy, but she denied it, telling him he was imagining things.

One night in late December or early January, however, the husband came home early from a night school class and discovered Randy and his wife lying in front of the fireplace together. The husband later confronted his wife, who again denied there was anything going on between her and Randy. But the husband didn't believe her.

The following day, the husband went to Randy's house and confronted him there.

"I told him that I believed he was seeing my wife and I wanted him to stop," the husband said later. "And he said to me, 'No, I wasn't.' And I said, 'I have proof.' And he said, 'No, you don't.' And I said, 'Yes, I do.' And then he said, 'She wanted my attention.' "

"What did you respond?" the husband was asked.

"I told him if he did not stop bringing his son over to babysit and if he did not stay away from our house, I was going to go to the prosecuting attorney who was involved in the death of Jan, and tell them that he was involved with my wife at the time of Jan's death and was involved with her while they were married."

Randy again denied having an affair with the man's wife. But he stopped bringing Greg over for babysitting and he stopped seeing the man's wife.

"Did you go to the Skamania County sheriff?" the husband was asked years later.

"No, I didn't."

"Why?"

"I was afraid of him," the husband said.

The Skamania County Sheriff's Office would likely have been very interested in the husband's story, however. By early January of 1982, opinion was hardening that Jan's death was suspicious. By that time,

Blaisdale had discovered that Jan had been insured for $100,000, with Randy as the beneficiary. That at least provided a motive for Randy to kill his wife, Blaisdale thought.

In late January, Blaisdale dispatched a Skamania County deputy sheriff, Mike Grossie, to interview Randy at Randy's Mountlake Terrace house. After Grossie made the appointment, Randy called Tim Brocato and asked him to come over to "watch Greg" while he answered the deputy's questions. Years later, Marilyn Brenneman would suggest that Randy wanted Tim present so he could make sure Tim didn't say anything bad about Randy to the Skamania authorities without his knowledge.

Tim tried to eavesdrop on the conversation, but only picked up bits and pieces. One thing Tim apparently did *not* overhear: Randy told Grossie that he had been in the Marines for only ten months, and that he had seen no combat. Thus, Randy made Louise's earlier suggestion that Randy might have been a stressed-out war killer seem like some sort of sour-grapes fantasy on Louise's part. But Tim, not hearing this, continued to believe Randy was a combat veteran for years afterward.

Randy explained about the insurance and said he and Jan both considered it mortgage insurance, to help pay off the house. He confirmed calling the clinic to ask for Jan's Social Security number. He hadn't told anyone at the clinic, or Louise Mitchell, about Jan's death, Randy said, because he "didn't like to be the bearer of bad news."

What about the babysitter? Grossie hadn't talked to the woman's husband, but knew that Louise had said Jan was suspicious that Randy was having an affair with the babysitter. Randy told Grossie that the babysitter had watched Greg before his marriage to Jan, and that after the marriage the two women had become close friends.

Grossie asked Randy to again describe what happened on Beacon Rock. Grossie wanted to clear up the discrepancy over whether it was Randy or Jan who had been in the lead.

"He also stated that Janis was definitely in front of him on the whole climb and does not know where anyone got the idea that she was behind him in the climb," Grossie later reported. "He stated that with her in front he felt there was a little more security in case something happened, he would have been able to help her. He stated that when they got up to the top of the shortcut and she made a turn to the right, when she put her left foot down and put her weight on it, her left foot slipped off a rock, causing her to fall and go down off the side of Beacon Rock." Grossie did not ask Randy any questions about the Andersons' report that Randy had told them that Jan had simply "disappeared" while she was trying to take a picture.

Grossie did ask Randy to take a polygraph test, however. Randy didn't want to. "In regards to a polygraph test, Randy stated that he does not feel a polygraph test would be accurate. He stated that he does not want his emotional feelings to be interpreted as incrimination. Randy also stated he felt the polygraph would do more to prove a person guilty than to prove them innocent.

"In conversation with Randy, I could not tell if Randy was genuinely remorseful or if Randy was putting on an act," Grossie reported.

After Grossie left, Tim tried to talk to Randy about the interview. "Why was he here?" Tim asked. "Why are you being investigated?"

"I don't want to tell you anything you'd have to lie about later," Randy told Tim. After that, Tim decided to shut up about Jan. No way was he going incur the Wrath of Randy, Tim decided. No way.

# 32

## The Big Spender

It took awhile, but by early in 1982, the Skamania County authorities decided not to file any charges against Randy in connection with Jan's death. The way Blaisdale explained it later, he totaled up all the reasons to be suspicious about Randy, and all the reasons to believe him. When he added up the pluses and minuses, it just didn't seem to be a clear-cut case. Blaisdale discussed the matter with the Skamania County prosecutor, who looked over the case, too. The prosecutor concluded that it would be a difficult case to win, and suggested that Blaisdale drop the matter and go on to more pressing business.

That cleared the way for the insurance company to release the $100,000 in life insurance proceeds to Randy. The check came in April of 1982, and suddenly, after a decade of money problems, Randy was rich. The first thing he did was buy a new house. Randy put down $40,000 on a brand new, three-bedroom house in a new subdivision northeast of Seattle. He bought a new truck—Tim Brocato saw him pull $10,000 in cash out of his pocket—and he bought motorcycles for himself and for Tim. In June, he invited the Adens and their children to go with him and Greg to Disneyland for a week, with Randy picking up the entire tab. Later Randy bought two chainsaws, one for him and one for Tim, so they could cut wood in their off-hours and sell it for money. Randy landscaped his new house and bought toys for Greg. Later, when Tim and Debbie ran into money problems, Randy loaned them $4,000.

Tim was still uneasy about Randy. He was convinced in his own mind that Randy had killed Jan. But he was afraid to tell anyone—except Debbie—in case word got back to Randy. Tim thought Randy might kill him too if he became a threat.

Once, Randy pestered Tim for weeks to go snowmobiling with him. Tim kept making excuses. He didn't want to go anywhere isolated with Randy, in case he met with some sort of "accident," like Jan. But finally Tim agreed to go on the snowmobiling trip. He didn't want Randy to think he was afraid of him, even if he was. But before leaving, Tim told Debbie: "If I don't come back, it was no accident."

But as Tim kept trying to distance himself from Randy, Randy redoubled his efforts to maintain some form of control over him. Soon Tim saw Randy's generosity with the motorcycle, the chain saw and the $4,000 loan as Randy's way of trying to buy Tim's loyalty. At one point, in fact, Randy sent a letter to Tim, telling Tim that he didn't want "anything" to come between them. Tim was pretty sure he knew what "anything" was. But still Tim said nothing about his suspicions to anyone else, other than Debbie.

Randy, meanwhile, was working fewer hours at Vitamilk. His tax records later showed his wage income dropped by almost half in 1983, down to $16,951 from a high of $33,100 in 1981. Randy later said that his hours were reduced at Vitamilk because of layoffs at the firm. Randy, of course, also had the remains of his $100,000 payoff to fall back on. The following year, 1984, Randy's wage income was back up to $29,000.

In the middle of 1984, Randy decided to sell his house and buy another one in a better neighborhood. The new house cost around $90,000. Randy took the $40,000 equity out of the house he'd bought in 1982 and put it down on the new home.

But in deciding to buy the new house, Randy left Tim and Debbie in a bad financial fix. For some months, Tim and Debbie had been having a hard time paying all their bills. They wanted to buy a new mobile home to live in, and Randy had agreed to buy their existing mobile home and told them not to worry about making the payments on the old one, that he would take care of them when he bought the place.

But when Randy bought the $90,000 house instead, suddenly Tim and Debbie were left with a lot of overdue payments. In late 1984, Tim and Debbie filed for bankruptcy and listed the $4,000 loan from Randy as a debt. That meant Randy wouldn't get his money back. Randy was furious.

"If you think you're going to get away with this, you're crazy," Randy told Tim. For once, Tim got his back up with Randy.

"You caused it," he retorted. But Randy was insistent that Tim pay him back. He began leaving threatening notes at Tim's trailer demanding payment.

As January 1985 arrived, Tim broke down and decided to discuss the situation with Randy. Tim told Randy he just didn't have the money to pay him right then, and that if Randy would be patient he would try to pay him back later. But in the meantime, Tim told Randy, he was really hurting financially.

This seemed to make Randy feel better. Tim later recalled how Randy liked to feel superior to him, and Tim's move to file bankruptcy let Randy assert this superiority. Randy told Tim he'd try to think of something Tim could do for Randy to make money. Then,

Tim said later, Randy came up with a new idea: Tim should burgle his own house and turn the claim into his homeowners insurance company. " 'It's easy to get money that way,' " Tim later said Randy told him.

Tim thought it over and decided to do it.

"We went out in the backyard," Tim later recalled. "He said he would break in the back door. He said I should hit the window."

Tim smacked the window, but it wouldn't break. Also, it made a lot of noise. Tim started getting worried all over again. Randy was disgusted.

"So he just pushed the door in and, it was really a cheap door, and the frame was really bad," Tim remembered. Thus, Randy broke into Tim's mobile home while Tim watched. Tim never did break his own window.

Randy and Tim went through the house, picking up a radio, a music box, a VCR, and a few other things that Randy and Tim knew a burglar would probably go for. Tim chose the items. Then Randy and Tim drove over to Randy's new house and deposited the loot. Tim drove home and told Debbie what the plan was.

That night, Tim went to a social function at the fire department where he worked as a volunteer and got drunk. Debbie was at work and the kids were at a babysitter's. Tim came home early in the morning and called the police to report that his house had been burgled. A few days later, Tim went over to Randy's house, and together they filled out the claim forms. Tim didn't know what to write, so Randy made some suggestions.

" 'Tools' is always a good thing to put down," Randy told Tim. So Tim declared that some expensive tools that he had never really owned had been stolen. He signed the form. A month or so later, got a check for about $2,800 in the mail from the insurance company.

Later, this fraud became Tim's darkest secret.

When Peters and Mullinax finally caught up with him in 1981, it had been this crime that made Tim so reluctant initially to cooperate. But finally, after some serious soul-searching, Tim realized that his problem with having committed a felony fraud was minor in comparison to the likelihood that Randy had committed murder. Tim knew that if he told the police what he believed about Randy and Jan, the story of the fake burglary would inevitably come out. That, Tim thought, would probably cost him his by now fulltime, paid job with the fire department.

But what was more important, his job or the chance that Randy might have murdered twice, and if he got away with it, that he might do it again? And Tim believed that one reason why Randy had encouraged him to rob himself was because Randy was desperate to get something on Tim to hold over him to keep him quiet. As a result, when Tim finally told the story of the fake burglary to Peters and Mullinax, he felt a huge burden lift off his shoulders.

# 33 | Misty Meadows

**R**andy's new house was on a cul-de-sac in a small subdivision called "Misty Meadows," located a bit east of the Interstate 5 freeway. A power line ran behind the house, along with a graveled right-of-way that permitted vehicle access to the rear of the property. That more obscure access route would later figure in a charge that Randy himself took the advice he once gave to Tim Brocato and staged his own burglary when he would need money in 1988.

Shortly after he moved in, Randy made the acquaintance of his neighbors, Ben and Marta Goodwin, and their three children, two of them Mrs. Goodwin's from a prior marriage.

As in many aspects of Randy's past, there was no clarity on just how Randy and the Goodwins met. Randy later said he met the Goodwins when one of the Goodwins' children got into a schoolyard fight with Greg, and that he had gone over to the neighbors to straighten the matter out; Ben Goodwin remembered meeting Randy because Goodwin's son told him that Greg had to be home alone while Randy was at work. Ben later said he didn't think that was right, so he'd gone over to meet Randy and tell him that Greg was welcome to stay over at the Goodwins' house after school if he didn't have anyone to take care of Greg.

Later Marta Goodwin, like Nancy Aden before her, often invited Randy and Greg over for dinner; ultimately, the Goodwins were to buy a house right next to Randy's and were to become two of his closest friends—at least, until Randy did something a few years later that made Ben feel like tearing Randy apart with his bare hands.

In the beginning, Ben had at least one thing powerfully in common with Randy: both men loved rebuilding old cars. Randy frequently acquired junked or distressed vehicles, fixed them on his own time in his garage, and later sold them. Randy also had an interest in classic cars of 1950s vintage and worked to rebuild one of those. So did Ben, who had a 1950 Chevrolet that he was rebuilding as a hobby when he and Randy first met.

Ben *was* a Vietnam veteran, having been a twenty-year-old in an engineering battalion in 1968. Randy told Ben that he, too, was a Vietnam veteran. Ben wasn't sure he believed him; he wondered how Randy could have been in the war because of his age. Randy liked to tell war stories to the kids, then ask Goodwin to verify what he had said. Once Ben, trying to get into the spirit of the thing, told how his battalion had bulldozed a village during the war, and Randy came back with his stories about killing villagers, secret reconnaissance missions, "all kinds of strange stuff," as Goodwin later recalled.

But at home with his wife, Marta, Goodwin had his doubts. "Boy," he told Marta, "either he's older than he's saying he is, or he never was in Vietnam."

Randy talked so much about his wartime exploits, in fact, that Ben got irritated with him.

"Anybody like myself who had been in Vietnam . . .

people who went don't normally come back to the
States and talk about it," Goodwin said later. "And I
always questioned him about why he would . . . be so
talkative about it. But he seemed to brag."

Once Goodwin lost his temper over the subject.
"And I kind of got infuriated with him one time and
told him that the only difference between him and me
was, when I came home I gave away all my uniforms
and *his* are still hanging in his closet."

But apart from this difference of opinion, Ben and
Randy seemed to get along well. Soon Ben was spending time in Randy's garage working on his old car with
Randy's help. Randy was, after all, by now an accom-
plished professional mechanic, and had a large number
of automotive tools as well as expertise that Ben
admired. Being admired by Ben, of course, made
Randy feel superior to him.

Not too long after moving into the new house, in
early January of 1985, Randy and Greg went into a
nearby convenience store to buy some bread and milk.
Randy noticed the young woman behind the counter
and initiated a conversation. Within a few minutes,
Randy had asked her if she'd be interested in going
out with him. "Sure," the young woman said.

Donna Clift was twenty-two. She had a four-year-
old daughter from a marriage that had just ended in
Arizona. She had moved to the Pacific Northwest to
live with her father, Harvey Clift, and stepmother,
Judy. She had been living in the area for less than a
month and was interested in meeting new people.

The next night, Randy returned to the store and set
up a date with Donna. A few nights later, Randy took
her to a Chinese restaurant. Donna decided that Randy
was nice—well-groomed, polite, definitely interested
in her. The following day, Randy sent her flowers. And
then, over the next few weeks, more flowers. And
~ards. "He just really wanted to take me out," she

recalled years later. "Every other day I was getting flowers."

"Roses?" she was asked.

"Yes." The flowers came by florist.

Soon Donna was seeing Randy every day. Then other gifts began coming in. "I got a gold chain," she recalled. "He bought me contact lenses." Two leather coats. Donna asked Randy why he was doing all this for her. "I just want to make an investment in you," Randy told her.

Soon Randy was talking about marrying Donna. Donna's divorce still wasn't final in Arizona, so she put him off. But Randy was persistent. To Donna, Randy "seemed like the type of person that you would want to . . . he was really good to me at first. He just overwhelmed me."

One night, not long after Donna's divorce became final, Randy took Donna to a restaurant in downtown Seattle and proposed to her. It was Valentine's Day, as Randy later remembered it. This time Donna accepted. A few months later, Donna and her daughter moved into the Misty Meadows house with Randy and Greg. About a month after that, on May 17, 1985, Randy and Donna were married.

Donna was naturally curious to know more about this man she had married. Being forthcoming with details about himself was not Randy's way, however. He enjoyed cultivating his aura of mysteriousness. But Donna was no Jan, willing to accept Randy on Randy's terms; when Randy was away, Donna #2 began "snooping," as she called it, into his past.

Soon Donna was rummaging through closets and finding old bank records and cancelled checks of Randy's, including one bank statement that showed a deposit for nearly $90,000. Donna thought it had something to do with Jan but didn't want to discuss it with Randy. Randy told her that Jan had died in a hiking accident, and that he was suing the state for its negligence in failing to mark the trail as dangerous.

One day Donna was sorting through a closet and found what looked like a plastic box stashed back in the corner on the floor. At first she thought it was a box of cassette tapes. Then she noticed the box had the name Janis Roth on it, and she realized that the box contained Jan's ashes. Donna's blood ran cold. *It's weird,* she thought, keeping those ashes in a closet. She called Judy Clift, put the box on a table, and immediately drove over to see her stepmother.

A bit later, Randy came over to the Clift house. Randy seemed very agitated. "He just came over in a panic and he was sweating," Donna said later, "and I don't know why, but he was just really nervous."

Randy could see that Donna was very upset. He asked her what was wrong. Donna told him about finding the ashes. She couldn't understand why he would be keeping the ashes "just sitting there in the closet in a box."

Later, after Donna calmed down a bit, Randy told her more about Jan's death. They had been hiking in Skamania County, Randy told her, and they had been walking on a trail that had been mismarked as not being dangerous, when Jan slipped on pine needles and loose rocks. When Jan started falling, Randy told her, he grabbed for her but couldn't hold on. Randy made the story seem painfully tragic, and Donna cried. "I felt bad for him," she said later. "And I felt bad for her daughter."

But Donna was still upset about the presence of the ashes in the Misty Meadows house. To her, it just didn't seem respectful to Janis to keep her remains in a plastic box in a corner of a closet. Randy said he understood. One night he took the box and left. Later, he came back and told Donna that he had scattered Jan's remains across the surface of Silver Lake.

\* \* \*

Years later, Donna was to say that some time just before their marriage, Randy began talking to Donna about life insurance.

"We were sitting on the bed and he was showing me papers about different kinds of insurance," Donna recalled. "Different amounts of money were talked about. And you know, I really didn't think much of it at the time. I had my own life insurance policy, and he had talked to me about having him as beneficiary on it." Donna's life insurance was for a nominal amount of money: $3,000. The original beneficiary was her daughter, but Randy convinced Donna to make him the beneficiary.

But Randy apparently wanted more insurance. "So he could take care of my daughter," Donna said, in case anything happened to Donna. "Every time the subject was brought up, he would say, you know, this is what [her daughter] would get or, vice versa, if anything was ever to happen to him, then this is what I would get."

The life insurance discussions continued for some time, Donna later recalled. But Donna just wasn't interested in life insurance. She was only twenty-two years old, after all, and all the talk about death and dismemberment was, to her, *weird*, just like finding Jan's ashes in the plastic box in the closet. Dying wasn't anything Donna particularly wanted to think about. "It wasn't important to me," she said later. Randy seemed quite interested in the subject, however.

But it wasn't too long after the marriage that things began to go sour for Donna and Randy. "I mean just a couple of weeks afterward, he started being really cold toward me. He would leave for work in the morning and wouldn't come in and say goodbye to me. He wouldn't . . . there was nothing. He'd just leave. And he was really cold. He would never talk to me about it. I couldn't understand why he was treating me this way.''

And Donna soon discovered that in Randy's household she was almost like a piece of equipment, rather than a mate. Randy wouldn't include her in any of the family finances, or put her on any of the family legal papers.

''I was never on the checking account. I was never put on the house. All the vehicles were in his name. I had no access to anything,'' she remembered. ''If I ever needed anything, I had to go to him to get the money.'' Randy, in this regard, seems to have replicated at least some of his own father's behavior in maintaining strict control over the family budget.

A month or two after the marriage, Randy suggested that he, Donna, the kids, and Donna's father and stepmother go on a river rafting trip. Randy said he knew a place up in Snohomish County, on the Skykomish River near Gold Bar, where they could inflate rubber rafts and float down the river. Judy and Harvey Clift were game, so the trip was organized.

Donna, however, was in a funk on the day of the trip. ''I was really upset that day because he and I hadn't been getting along, and because he was being so cold to me,'' she said. Judy Clift took a short walk with her stepdaughter to see what was the matter. Donna told her that Randy had been acting like he could care less if she was around. Donna cheered up a bit after the talk, however, and soon Harvey and Randy were busy inflating the rafts.

Randy had a two-person raft. He suggested that he and Donna ride his raft, while Donna's daughter and Greg should ride with Harvey and Judy. Everyone piled into the rafts and set out. The trip was not a success.

Judy, for one, was worried about Randy's raft. She thought it looked pretty flimsy. She told Harvey not to get too far ahead of Randy and Donna in case Randy's raft sank.

In their smaller raft, Randy and Donna did indeed appear to be having a hard time. Randy was later to say he couldn't maneuver the raft very well with just one paddle, and Donna refused to help him. As a result, Randy said, he had a hard time controlling his raft, and Harvey and Judy shot ahead of them. Donna said that wasn't so; Randy knew just what he was doing.

In any event, soon Randy and Donna were fairly far behind Harvey and Judy—out of sight, anyway. Their raft was careening from bank to bank as Randy tried to keep it centered. Donna decided Randy wasn't trying nearly hard enough. In fact, it seemed to her that Randy was *deliberately* aiming for half-submerged rocks. "I kept telling Randy that he had to stay to the side of the river because it was so rocky, but he wouldn't," Donna said later.

As the raft rounded a bend, the river was separated into two branches by a sandbar. One channel was fairly shallow, with lots of rocks, while the other was deeper. The current—or Randy, depending on which story one accepts—swept the raft toward the shallower water. Donna kept telling him to go the other way. Randy denied aiming for the rocks and said he couldn't help it, because Donna wasn't helping him with the paddles.

"You couldn't propel yourself at the same time you were steering, and you were constantly changing from left to right to keep the raft as straight as possible, so in order to steer it you either had to drag on the oar or you had to change sides with it," Randy said afterward.

Pulled or paddled into the shallower branch, the raft almost immediately hung up on some dead tree snags along the bank. One branch hung out over the water, barring passage. Another branch punctured one of the raft's air chambers, then a second chamber. In seconds the raft was swamped, with only the inflated bottom to hold it up. Randy and Donna were wedged into the branches. She was in a panic and began screaming for her parents to help her, that she was going to die. Randy kept telling her to shut up. Harvey and Donna looked back and saw that the raft had almost completely deflated. They pulled up on a sandbar and called out to Donna and Randy to lie down in the raft to get under the overhanging branch, and somehow the remnant of the raft got through the narrow passage.

Randy now guided the semi-buoyant raft to the sandbar. As they pulled up, Donna was still screaming for her father. She leaped off the raft as fast as she could. To Judy, she seemed hysterical. Randy beached the raft while Judy tried to calm Donna. He and Harvey patched the raft and reinflated it. But Donna refused to ride any further with Randy and switched places with Greg. Greg and Randy had no difficulty getting down the rest of the river by themselves.

Meanwhile, Randy's time at Vitamilk was drawing to a close. Randy was unhappy at the number of hours of work he was getting and wasn't getting along too well with the management. Some of his supervisors began to suspect that Randy was pilfering things like gasoline and dairy products, but no one knew for sure.

Harvey Clift was also a mechanic. He worked for Cascade Ford, a dealership in Bellevue. As Randy began voicing more complaints about Vitamilk, Harvey got him a job interview at his Ford dealership.

Later, there would be a difference of opinion as to just why Randy left Vitamilk and his $14 hourly pay for a job that paid just over $11. Randy said he left Vitamilk by mutual agreement after a dispute with the management about gasoline. Randy had been using the company's gasoline in his own truck. He said he had just failed to get the proper authorization, because the person who usually did the authorizing was out sick one day. But Peters and Mullinax discovered that Randy was fired, and that people at Vitamilk believed Randy was stealing not only gasoline but milk products from the company. In any event, Randy started work at Cascade Ford in July of 1985.

By this time, Randy had become fairly close to the Clifts, particularly Harvey. Even after Donna decided to leave Randy in September of 1985, Randy and Harvey remained good friends, driving to work together with Judy, who worked nearby. Little was said about the end of the marriage.

For his part, Randy contended that the marriage hadn't worked because Donna was too much younger than he was. "She was immature," he later told Tim Brocato. And Randy was also discovering that Donna simply wasn't interested in being controlled by Randy; his efforts to limit her social contacts to those people he approved simply weren't working.

Donna, however, saw matters quite differently. The marriage wasn't working, she thought, because Randy wouldn't open up to her. Worse, Randy seemed often callously cruel. Once she went four-wheeling with Randy, and as the machine roared up a steep hill, Randy suddenly leapt off. The machine stalled and rolled backwards on Donna, causing a painful injury to her leg. While Donna lay on the ground crying, Randy ran up to her, giving her his nervous giggle that usually meant Randy was either lying or knew he had done something wrong.

The final straw, however, was the way Randy dealt with the kids. Donna's own daughter, four years old, was spanked hard by Randy. Ben Goodwin once saw him pinch the little child so hard in the cheek that he nearly lifted her off the ground. And once he'd gotten so mad at Greg that he'd thrown him in the shower in his underwear and beat him with the shower nozzle. Donna felt terribly sorry for Greg. She knew that he was scared to death of his father. But then, by September of 1985, so was she.

# 34

# For the Birds

For the first three or four months after Donna left, Randy seemed unwilling to accept the situation; at least, that's the way it seemed to Donna and her stepmother, Judy. They later remembered that Randy often drove by their house and made calls to Donna in an effort to induce her to come back to him. Yet Randy paid for the divorce, because Donna didn't have any money. Randy later contended none of what Donna and Judy said about this was true, and that he certainly didn't hang around the Clift house in any sort of attempt to woo Donna back. He was, he said later, just as fed up with Donna as Donna was of him.

Yet there is a similarity in this supposed behavior of Randy to his other relationships, namely, those with Terri McGuire in the 1970s, and later with Mary Jo Phillips in 1986, 1987 and 1988. Marilyn Brenneman later came to believe that Randy didn't want the women so much as he hated to lose power over someone or something that he had once had in his grasp.

Randy's stormy relationship with Mary Jo Phillips, which began in the spring of 1986, best illustrated this aspect of his character.

Mary Jo was separated from her husband in the spring of 1986. She had five children, three of whom sometimes stayed with their father. Late one evening, after Mary Jo and her children had returned from an outing to the beach, Mary Jo went to the grocery store to pick up some food for a late dinner.

"And I saw this man and boy in every other aisle I happened to go into," she remembered later. "And I was really windblown, and felt really, really silly. But they always managed to giggle and smile my way."

Randy the charmer was back.

At the checkstand, Mary Jo saw the man and his son in front of her. "And they kept turning around and looking at me and whispering in each other's ears and smiling," she said.

As Mary Jo went to her car with her groceries, the little boy came after her. "Hey lady," Greg said, "would you please go out with my dad?" And Greg gave Mary Jo their phone number.

Now, enlisting an eight-year-old boy to run interference in an approach to an unknown woman may seem a little unusual. But Mary Jo loved children, and in fact, she owned and managed a daycare center. Somehow, Randy had picked up the message that Greg would be the most effective emissary he could send on his behalf.

Mary Jo did call Randy about a week later. She talked to Greg. "He seemed like a fairly neat little boy," she said. Mary Jo called again about a week later, and this time Randy had primed his message machine with a personal message for Mary Jo:

"Mary Jo," the message said, "I've *got* to talk to you. Please leave your name and number." Mary Jo decided to call Randy back one more time, and finally a date was made.

Randy met Mary Jo at a restaurant. "And when I went out to get in his truck, he took a picture of me and said something to the effect that, 'I want some

proof that I have had such a beautiful lady out with
me.' Really made me feel silly, but at the same time it
was real flattering.''

Randy and Mary Jo drove into downtown Seattle.
They intended to go to a restaurant, but the place was
too crowded, so they took a romantic walk down the
beach at Edmonds, along the sound just north of
Seattle. The date lasted until about two or three in the
morning.

Mary Jo agreed to meet Randy for breakfast on the
following Saturday. Mary Jo put on nice clothes and
curled her hair to look nice for Randy, because she
thought "he was really a nice man."

"And I opened up the door and he was carrying
*motorcycle helmets*," Mary Jo said. "And I thought,
oh no, motorcycles. That means I've got to put this
thing on, squish my hair and everything.

"Anyhow, he said, 'Get your bathing suit.' It was
really a very dominant thing to say." Randy had
discovered a key to Mary Jo. She got her bathing suit.
Now Sir Randolph had arrived.

Mary Jo climbed on Randy's motorcycle and away
the couple went, roaring off north toward the town of
Bellingham, almost to the Canadian border. In the
early afternoon, they stopped at a waterslide amuse-
ment park.

As it happened, Mary Jo was terrified of water
because of a near-drowning experience as a child. "I
didn't know where we were going until we ultimately
ended up there," she said. "I thought, 'I've got to get
out of this.' I tried to make every excuse in the book."
But Randy insisted, and eventually Mary Jo did go
into the water. "He made me feel like I should really
trust him," she said.

After that, Mary Jo saw more and more of Randy.
"There was a real strong attraction. He was very, very
much the gentleman. Only kissed me. He wasn't all
hands or anything like that. It didn't matter to him

that I had five children at the time. He was very respectful. Utterly, completely courteous. Brought me flowers. Always had nice things to say. He was the only person in my whole life that I really felt like I didn't have to wear makeup around because he felt I was beautiful that way."

The flowers, at first, came every week, Mary Jo remembered.

Later, Randy's pursuers were to see in this court-ship many of the elements of Randy's pattern—some of the things that Randy did to first entice, then entrap women as his prey. Randy began each of his relation-ships with unfailing courtesy, romantic expressions, flowers, gifts—whatever it took to convince a woman that she was the only one in the world for him. And in each case, Randy found a hook, something that the woman needed or wanted or wished she had. Randy set the hook deep and began pulling, first gently, then harder.

"It was a very, very intense relationship," Mary Jo said later. "Incredibly romantic. He had become to me the kind of man that every woman would dream about. He did everything right. He rubbed my back. He combed my hair. He dressed so that he was coor-dinated with what I was wearing. He showed me off. Made me feel real good. Was always full of compli-ments."

With Janis, it had been security. With Donna Clift, it was stability and connection. With Mary Jo, it was romantic passion.

But Randy's pattern also showed other, less readily apparent aspects of his character; his hatred of makeup—seen later with Cindy, as well—evoked com-parisons to his earlier life with Lizabeth, who used makeup heavily, as well as his capacity to use wom-en's concern for their looks as a mechanism of emo-tional control.

Most importantly, however, the pattern followed by Randy seemed to indicate that Randy sought out women by some sort of test: what value would those women be to *him?* Janis, as things turned out, had been worth $107,500 in life insurance proceeds. Donna Clift, while not interested in life insurance, was useful for getting a new job. Now Mary Jo would be similarly useful to Randy. She would *give* him money because she was in love with him.

After several months of dates, in early July of 1986, Randy asked Mary Jo to move in with him. She agreed. She also started paying Randy $500 a month in rent. Soon Mary Jo brought over her furniture.

"There was," Mary Jo remembered, "too many of everything, and so it was suggested that—and I don't remember if it was him or if it was me—that we sell some of these things. I mean, obviously we can't use them, and if our relationship is going to be permanent, then we don't need them." So Mary Jo sold her things. The money went into remodeling Randy's recreation room and bunkbeds for the kids.

Much later, Randy was to say that he'd had no idea that Mary Jo had five children until the day he arrived to pick up her things.

"It was at a point when I arrived at her house with my truck and trailer to move her stuff that I discovered she had three more children," he said. "She had two girls and another son from another father, and she also had a very large bird collection. She had, I don't remember how many cages, but there was over one hundred birds, finches and canaries."

The kids and the birds, Randy said, were much more than he had expected. "It took a lot of adjusting," Randy said later in characteristic understatement.

But by early August, Randy and Mary Jo were ㅤking of marriage.

ㅤhen Randy in the past talked with women about

marriage, he seems to have favored a certain code phrase. "I want you to get me your ring size," he would say. Or, "Tell me your ring size." *Ring size*. It was as if Randy believed the words "ring size" was some sort of hypnotic chant capable of beguiling the prey, keeping them transfixed on the big prize: Randy.

But more subtly, it was also a constant test of the relationship temperature for Randy. When, for example, in the mid-1970s Terri McGuire expressed reluctance about rings and engagement and marriage—when she *wasn't* eager to engage with Randy in ring fantasies—it was a warning sign to Randy that control was slipping away.

So Randy urged Mary Jo to go to a jewelry store and *get measured* for a wedding ring. But about this same time, an event occurred which promised to throw off some of Randy's plans for Mary Jo.

As noted, Mary Jo was, with her estranged husband, part owner and operator of a daycare center. This was not a daycare facility such as that run by Jan, but a former school building with ninety children a day and thirty employees. It was a thriving business. In fact, Mary Jo was making $56,000 a year from her part of the business. That kind of money impressed Randy even more than the rent Mary Jo was willing to give him, Mary Jo realized later.

As her divorce proceeded, Mary Jo and her estranged husband got into a fight over the daycare center. Mary Jo decided to give in.

"Rather than fight over the daycare center through a divorce," she said, "I sold it to my husband, my ex-husband." Her ex-husband agreed to pay Mary Jo fifteen hundred dollars a month and provide daycare for the kids.

But when Mary Jo told Randy what she had done, Randy was furious.

"He was real upset that I hadn't discussed it with him, and I hadn't. I don't think he wanted me to get rid of it,'' Mary Jo recalled. Randy, she said, was quite aware of how much Mary Jo had been taking in from the daycare facility.

Unbeknownst to Randy, however, Mary Jo was becoming ill. About the time Randy was talking about *ring size*, Mary Jo went to the doctor and discovered that she had cancer. She didn't tell Randy very much about this, only that she had been feeling a little sick. But when Randy brought up the subject of life insurance, it all came out.

"At that point I just laughed," Mary Jo said later. "I said, 'I've got cancer. I'm not insurable.' ''

"What was his response?" Mary Jo was asked.

"He took it real well at that point in time," she said. "But from there on out, it's like we started seeing cold spots in our relationship, where for a couple of hours—I mean, this is the man that, you know, he would come home and come bounding up the stairs and say 'I missed you all day,' and give me the biggest hug and kiss and caress and make me feel so good— all of a sudden, for three or four or even two hours, it was like I didn't exist.

"Or he would come home and he wouldn't talk to me. I had made dinner, and he would go and make something else.

"And it started going so that more and more often as the days went by these cold spots, really cold, got colder and colder and longer and longer and the really warm, hot, passionate spots were less and less and less, until finally I just couldn't stand it anymore."

Mary Jo moved out, taking the birds and kids, but leaving almost all of her remaining furniture and other possessions behind. Later, her cancer went into remission. Randy took many of her belongings to a swap meet and sold them.

Having struck out with Mary Jo, Sir Randolph began ̄king for new worlds to conquer. It wasn't long before he decided to invade the world next door—at Ben and Marta Goodwin's.

For some time, beginning shortly after he met the Goodwins, the Goodwins' daughter had been babysitting Greg for Randy. She was eleven when Randy met her. Soon she developed a crush on Randy. By 1985, when Randy was married to Donna Clift, the crush was obvious to everyone, including Donna. "I mean, you could tell," Donna said later.

Now, in late 1986, the Goodwins' daughter was thirteen. With the departure of Mary Jo, Randy again turned to the teenager to babysit for Greg, who was now nine years old. It wasn't long before Randy seduced the impressionable young girl.

Years later, Randy's pursuers were to consider just why Randy did this. It was obvious that the Goodwins' daughter could provide no monetary incentive to explain Randy's attentions. She couldn't be insured, for example, nor could she give him any money.

But conducting a clandestine affair with the teen-aged daughter of his neighbors likely appealed to Randy's desire for power and status. Not only was he able to capture the undivided and uncritical adoration of their daughter, he was able to put one over on his neighbors. That probably made Randy feel clever, some thought.

Naturally, it didn't take long for the Goodwins to realize something was up.

Problems began cropping up in the Goodwin household, chiefly between Ben Goodwin and his step-daughter. Surreptitiously, Randy exacerbated those problems by telling the girl that Ben wasn't her *real* father and she didn't have to do whatever Ben told her to do. That blurred the always delicate relationships inside such second families. Dormant emotional problems began emerging.

Ben and Marta sat down to discuss the situtation with Randy. They believed the problem was that their daughter had developed a teenage crush on their next door neighbor. Randy continually assured them that he was doing nothing to lead their daughter on.

"Randy assured my wife and I . . . he sat right at our table and we confronted him and said, 'Randy, we need your help on this. This is a girl who is infatuated with you. And you, quite frankly, you're not helping matters. You really need to get this under hand.' And he swore to us that he wasn't doing anything. That he would take care of it. And it only got worse," Ben remembered later.

Despite his denials, Randy *was* making things worse. He had the girl come over to babysit on Saturday nights. Randy would drive away until Greg went to bed, then drive back to his own house, park several blocks away, and sneak back in to see the girl. In this manner, Randy continued to see the Goodwins' daughter secretly throughout late 1986, through 1987, and into 1988.

Matters grew worse in late 1987, when Randy began courting Mary Jo Phillips again. The Goodwins' daughter became very upset at this; Randy had promised to marry *her* when she was eighteen, yet here Randy was still seeing Mary Jo. Mary Jo was oblivious to Randy's affair with his babysitter.

By June of 1988, the Goodwins' daughter was emotionally unstable. Randy had made promises to her that he clearly had no intention of keeping. When the girl became upset with his behavior, Randy had the maturity and duplicity to smooth things over and keep her under his thumb. Randy convinced the girl that he was smart, in control, more clever than most men. In such a setting, it appeared, Randy felt comfortable boasting; in June of 1988, Randy confided to the Goodwins' daughter that if he ever got into new money problems, he would know exactly what to do. He ld, Randy said, burgle his own house and turn a claim into his homeowner's insurance company.

First, Randy said, he'd remove all the stuff that he would say had been stolen and put it in a rented storage locker, then he'd break the window in the rear of his garage, and then he would tear up his own carpet and toss his house to provide evidence of the nonexistent burglars' passage.

As it later turned out, that's exactly what happened.

# 35

## Burgled

**B**y late August of 1988, Randy was again in trouble at work. For some time he'd been feuding with several of his coworkers, including the parts manager and at least one dispatcher, the service representative who took the orders for car repairs from the customers. On one occasion, Randy challenged one of the dispatchers, a man in his sixties, to a fight. The frictions continued to build; as far as the parts manager was concerned, Randy was a know-it-all jerk who liked to act tough and cause everyone problems. Thus, in early September, Randy was fired.

Randy's initial reaction to his loss of income was to call Mary Jo and ask her for money. Mary Jo gave him $500. Randy applied for unemployment benefits, but they wouldn't be approved for a week. What to do? Randy called Mary Jo again, but now Mary Jo was tapped out. Randy asked her if he could sell the player piano she'd left at his house. When Mary Jo said no, Randy criticized her for being too materialistic.

Later, when reviewing Randy's life and his behavioral pattern, Peters and Mullinax noticed that Randy's dilection for breaking the law seemed to surface every time Randy ran into major financial difficulties: he robbed the tire store when it looked like he was going to have to become a teenage father in 1973; he burgled the Kirkbride residence after he'd lost his job at the gas station in 1974; he had Janis' car "stolen" in early 1981 to escape the car payments; he might have shoved Janis over the cliff in late 1981 when the house payments got to be too much; he advised Tim Brocato to break into his own house to establish an insurance claim in 1985; and he "invested" in Donna Clift in 1985 just as he was about to be fired at Vitamilk, an investment which paid off in a new job at Cascade Ford.

Now, in September 1988, Randy returned to the Brocato model, just as he had told the Goodwins' daughter he would do if things got tough.

On September 17, 1988, five days after Randy made his claim for unemployment benefits, the Snohomish County Sheriff's Department received a call reporting a burglary at Randy's house. Randy met the deputy sheriff and told him what he thought had happened.

Randy said he'd been away from home from about noon until eleven that night and had returned to find that someone had broken a rear window in the garage, then backed up a trailer to the rear of the garage by using the power line access road. Then the burglars had cleaned out the garage and the house, Randy said. He'd already contacted the neighbors, Randy said, but nobody saw anything.

The deputy sheriff looked over the scene, noticing numerous upended drawers and a depression in the backyard where it appeared someone could have backed up as many as several vehicles. Despite the vast amount of property that appeared to have been carted off, the burglary looked routine to the officer. Randy told the deputy that all of his extensive tool collection had been taken, but didn't say how much the tools were worth. He said two chain saws were gone, a safe, $960 in cash, a television, Greg's Nintendo game, and numerous other items. The carpet was torn up in two different places. It looked like it had been cut with a knife, then peeled back. The deputy filled out a routine report of the burglary, gave a copy to Randy and told him to file a detailed list of the items taken in the next few days. The deputy left without questioning any of the neighbors. Had he done so, he would have discovered that Marta Goodwin, living right next door, had never talked to Randy that night, despite Randy's assurances to the police that none of the neighbors heard a thing.

Randy's burglary was the talk of the neighborhood the following day. Marta Goodwin heard about it from Randy himself.

"He said he had gone down to Renton to help a friend work on a car, and that he had come home and found that his belongings were all gone," Marta recalled later. "And it scared me because—I said, 'Well, what time was this?' And he said, 'Well, it was between eleven and twelve o'clock.'

"And I said, 'Gosh, that's really bad because I was right in the bedroom the whole time and I didn't hear anything. That really scares me that these people were in my backyard and I didn't know it.' "

What also scared Marta Goodwin was that none of the Goodwins' three dogs barked, and neither did Randy's big German shepherd, Jackson, who usually barked all the time.

Marta asked Randy why Jackson hadn't barked. Randy told her that Jackson had been drugged by the burglars, and that he'd found Jackson passed out in the back of his house when he got home.

Several days later, the Goodwins' daughter—by this time fifteen years old and living elsewhere—stopped t the Goodwins' and was told about the burglary. didn't surprise her at all, she said; Randy had told her months ago that he intended to rob himself. Then the Goodwins' daughter told her family exactly what Randy had said he would do, right down to the broken window and the torn carpet.

But because of the girl's often emotional dealings with Randy, none of the Goodwins initially believed her. And in fact, Ben Goodwin advised her to say nothing to anyone about it; he was afraid that his stepdaughter's love-hate feelings for Randy were causing her to make up the entire story. If it got around that she was saying such things, Ben believed, it might be considered legal slander.

Thus, several months later, after Randy put in a claim for $57,000 in losses from the burglary, neither Ben nor Marta said anything about what their daughter believed to the insurance investigators, who had become suspicious that Randy was trying to cheat on his policy.

The insurance investigation, which was ultimately to result in a lengthy lawsuit between Randy and the insurance company, brought an end to the friendship between Randy and Ben Goodwin.

Ben had been visiting a relative in California when the burglary took place. Afterward, when Randy made his claim that nearly $40,000 in tools was taken from his garage, he listed Ben as a witness that he indeed had had an extensive tool collection.

The insurance investigator dropped in on the Goodwins to verify Randy's claim. Ben said he'd seen a lot of tools at Randy's house when they worked on cars together. The investigators accepted that, and then spent a fair amount of time talking to Marta about Marta's family in Nebraska. The investigator left about an hour later.

But Randy had been watching the Goodwins' house and clocking the time the investigator spent with the Goodwins. Doubtless he was worried that Ben and

Marta had repeated to the investigator what he had previously told the Goodwins' daughter about robbing himself. Later, Randy confronted Ben.

"Randy got real cold to me after he [the investigator] came to our house," Ben recalled later. "He got real vindictive to me one day out in the yard. About how the investigator was in my house for more than an hour, and what the hell did I have to talk to an investigator about him for over an hour?" Ben denied the investigator was in his house for so long. But Randy was sure Ben had cast suspicion on him, especially after the insurance company balked on paying off.

With his insurance scam temporarily derailed, Randy had to find a job. After about six weeks of unemployment, Randy found work as a truck driver in late December. When that job petered out, Randy went back on unemployment. Meanwhile, Ben Goodwin and the other Goodwins began noticing that some of the items they thought had been taken in Randy's burglary were starting to appear again in Randy's house. Over the next few months, as more and more of Randy's supposedly stolen possessions came filtering back, Ben and Marta began to conclude that perhaps their daughter had been telling the truth about Randy all the time—about everything.

In early March of 1989, Randy got a new mechanic's job at another Ford dealership, this one in Seattle. Suddenly, Randy had tools again, and at least an income. But Randy was by now looking for something better. He was looking for another mate.

# 36

## Hot August Nights

**R**andy easily settled into his new job at Bill Pierre Ford in Seattle. At thirty-five, he was by this time an excellent mechanic, a specialist in heavy engine repairs. He was assigned a service bay back toward the rear of the dealership's shop, not far from two large doors that were often kept open to catch the breeze, a choice spot.

As usual in a new situation, Randy quickly assumed his Quiet Deadly Veteran persona, and tried to let the other mechanics know he wasn't the sort of man to take any guff. On Memorial Day, in fact, Randy wore his Marine combat fatigues to work.

Meanwhile, Randy's homeowner's insurance company had become suspicious about his claimed burglary. An insurance investigator discovered that at least one item that Randy claimed had been stolen had actually been returned by him to the store, which gave him credit for the return. Later, when Randy asserted that he had spent two hundred hours compiling his claim, a lawyer hired by the insurance company calculated that from the hour of the burglary to the time he turned the statement in, Randy would have had to have spent eleven hours a day completing the claim forms. The attorney doubted that Randy had spent more than the few hours necessary to complete the forms.

Even more suspicious, Randy was saying that all of the tools taken in the burglary were his *home* tools, not business tools. The policy limited payment for business tools to only $2,500; suddenly *all* of the tools Randy had in his garage after having been fired at Cascade Ford were personal, used-only-at-home hobby tools, according to Randy. By early 1989, after Randy started work at Bill Pierre Ford, the insurance company was suing Randy in federal court to have the policy declared invalid because of fraud. Randy hired his own lawyer to contest the insurance company's contentions.

The battle with the insurance people thus inevitably became a subject of discussion among Randy's new coworkers. Randy told everyone about the burglary at his house, and how his tools had been taken. At the same time, Randy cited Mary Jo Phillips, Ben Goodwin and Tim Brocato as witnesses that Randy did own a lot of tools. All of them told the insurance company that Randy indeed kept a large tool collection in his garage. Still later, however, some of Randy's coworkers would remember the discussions about Randy's burglary, as well as what Randy told them had *really* occurred the night his dog had failed to bark.

Just why Randy became involved with Little League baseball isn't terribly clear. Ever since Greg had gotten old enough to play, Randy had been involved with coaching or otherwise supervising the kids.

It's likely that there were several motivations on Randy's part for his interest in kids' baseball. Randy ~~v~~ have felt that by being involved with Greg in this he was giving his own son something he hadn't n from Gordon; more likely, by being coach

Randy got the respect and obedience of the kids and was able to play the role of being an authority as far as the parents were concerned. Those reactions to Randy's "leadership" probably bolstered Randy's ego and appealed to his never-slackening desire to have control. Some of his fellow Little League parents later came to consider Randy a "superdad" because of his intense interest in Little League; Randy went to important lengths never to miss practices or games.

Thus, Randy "played," as he later put it, in the South Everett Little League as a coach or manager from 1985 forward, starting with T-ball and working his way up to regular baseball. By the spring of 1990, a year into his job at Bill Pierre Ford and with the insurance company still refusing to pay off his claim, Randy again was a manager of Greg's team in the South Everett Little League, and that was where he met Cynthia Baumgartner and her two sons for the first time. In late May, Randy volunteered to work in the concession stand with Cindy for a week, which gave him a chance to see up close what made Cindy tick.

To the mind of Marilyn Brenneman, Randy's pursuit of Cindy Baumgartner displayed all of the aspects of his previous, coldly calculated efforts to capture women: first, the sizing up, in which Randy measured the victim in terms of what she had to offer; followed by the assessment—deciding just what would it take to attract the woman's interest.

Then would come the implementation, in which Randy would attempt to project the image he had decided the woman *wanted* to see.

That was Randy's pattern, Brenneman would decide, and it was strikingly evident in the earlier marriages with Janis Miranda, Donna Clift, and the courtship of Mary Jo Phillips. For each of the earlier women, Randy had assumed false colors—at least lon⌐

enough to get control of them. In some ways, Randy's behavior resembled something out of a particularly gruesome nature movie, in which the secret predator lures the prey with an attractive disguise, until too late, when the unsuspecting victim is abruptly attacked and consumed.

It was well known in the South Everett Little League circles that Cindy Baumgartner was relatively well-off financially. As a widow, her previous husband Tom had left her with means, primarily through his life insurance.

For one thing, Cindy didn't have to work, unlike many other parents in the league. Attracting Cindy as a mate would give Randy access to a substantial pool of regular, guaranteed income—Cindy's saved assets, as well as about $1,700 a month in Social Security payments for Cindy's two boys. In addition, Cindy owned her own house free and clear. And Cindy had her own life insurance policy.

Randy, of course, was quite familiar with life insurance already. In Brenneman's mind, he likely saw Cindy as someone who would be far easier to convince of the value of still more life insurance than Donna Clift, for example.

Randy's years of experience in dealing with women—beginning with Lizabeth and continuing forward through three marriages and numerous girlfriends—gave him the tools he needed to assess Cindy's wants and desires, and to tailor his persona accordingly, Brenneman believed.

Cindy was a particularly feminine woman. Her preoccupation with her hair, her nails, her clothes, her makeup, indeed her intense interest in her appearance, all gave Randy clues as to what approach to take with Cindy, as did her house filled with dolls and similar ⁓ sh knickknacks.

ʾhile it would be inaccurate to say that Cindy was she was in many respects guileless. Married young to Tom, the product of a loving family, widowed at an early age, cared for by her family, her friends and members of her church, Cindy tended to have an idealized view of marriage—a view that was likely influenced by the bittersweet memories of Tom, as well as by her own strong Christian beliefs and her associated dedication to family values: going to church, doing things together in the family, expressing love for one another, adhering to clear standards of right and wrong.

In Cindy's worldview, a wife was someone to be cherished, appreciated and cared for, while a husband and father was someone who loved his wife and took responsibility for maintaining the integrity of the family unit, through his work, his role as head of the household, and through his behavioral example to the children.

Therefore, Cindy had fairly rigid standards in what she wanted in a man, and those standards were easily perceived by someone of Randy's experience in manipulating women and assuming poses. And while Cindy had come through the emotional pain associated with Tom's death, having independent financial means and a widespread support network had protected Cindy from some of the hard knocks that in others tends to temper such views or give them experience in detecting false behavior; thus, Cindy was more susceptible than others in accepting Randy's carefully crafted pose.

In Brenneman's view, Randy, searching through the toolbox of his psychic manipulators, selected some of the items he thought might be useful in gaining Cindy's affections.

The most powerful of these, Brenneman believed, was the use of the children. When Randy first asked Cindy on a date, he made sure all the boys, Greg included, went along. That made Randy seem like the family man Randy wanted Cindy to believe he was

On this and on subsequent dates, Randy portrayed himself as a man whose family life was most important. He buttressed this image by an earnest sincerity, leavened with sorrowful hints about the horrors of war, doubtless calculated to get Cindy's sympathy while also underscoring his masculinity.

Randy also engaged Cindy's attention on romantic dreams of the future together, which appealed to Cindy's romantic idealism; and finally, Randy projected the image of a strong, male father figure to Tyson and Rylie, which Cindy believed would be necessary to their growing up.

Some of the other familiar tools also began making their appearance: flowers, frequent telephone calls, fun dates in which Randy projected his best, chivalrous, I'm-in-love-with-you demeanor. Greg began spending more time at Cindy's house with Tyson and Rylie, and soon Randy made it a point to drop in after work. Cindy began cooking dinner for the whole group. Soon Randy and Cindy were going on weekend dates to movies and comedy shows or restaurants.

By June of 1990, Cindy was thinking seriously about a possible future with Randy. And when Cindy, Lori and the boys visited the family of Cindy's sister-in-law in California, Randy maintained his pursuit with long, intimate telephone calls and the dispatch of more flowers. "What do you think of him?" Cindy asked Tyson and Rylie. "He's great," the boys replied.

Meanwhile, Hazel and Merle Loucks watched this pursuit of Cindy with some degree of apprehension. Ever since Tom's death, the Loucks had been protective of their daughter. Merle saw Cindy's vulnerabilities as only a father could. He knew she was an attractive target for unscrupulous men. But Merle believed that Cindy had enough native shrewdness to out and detect the phonies, and as time passed Tom's death, Merle was gratified to see his daughter learn how to rebuff and discard unsuitable suitors.

Randy seemed to be different. Merle and Hazel thought he was quiet—maybe too quiet, the Loucks sometimes thought. On Father's Day in 1990, Cindy brought a picture of Randy and Greg over to her parents' house in Marysville, telling them she had just met Randy at Little League and was excited about their prospects.

A few days later, Cindy brought Randy and Greg in person to have dinner with Hazel and Merle. Cindy told her parents that Randy had been in Vietnam, and the Loucks put Randy's quiet nature down to natural shyness and his war experiences. They weren't sure about Randy, but Hazel and Merle knew that Cindy had been alone for five years after Tom's death, and that she wanted to be married again.

In mid-July, the Loucks went to visit relatives in North Dakota. While they were gone, Randy heard about a classic car show and parade in Reno scheduled for the week of August 1. "Hot August Nights" would include displays of cars from the fifties, along with musical acts like Little Richard and the Righteous Brothers. In late July, Randy asked Cindy if she would be willing to go with him. Cindy told Randy she couldn't go anyplace overnight with him if they weren't married.

"Well, maybe we could do that while we're down there, too," Randy told her. "Are you serious?" Cindy asked.

"Yeah," Randy said. "We seem to be getting along really well, and the boys all enjoy each other's company. I can't think of any reasons why we shouldn't get married."

"Well, if you're asking, my answer is yes," Cindy said.

* * *

Cindy quickly called Hazel and Merle in North Dakota to give them the news. Hazel and Merle tried to dissuade her. First Merle told her that she couldn't get married because they wouldn't be able to come to the wedding. But Cindy told them that she and Randy intended to get married in Reno, so Hazel and Merle wouldn't be able to come anyway. Then Cindy's parents suggested that she and Randy wait for awhile, arguing that Cindy hadn't known Randy long enough. "But her mind was made up," Hazel said later, "they were going."

Randy bought a ring and then took Cindy for a motorcycle ride. They went to Silver Lake—the place where Randy once claimed to have scattered the ashes of Jan Roth, and the place where his brother Davy had picked up the ill-fated hitchhiker in 1977. Later, Randy was asked to describe how he had popped the question.

"I presented her with the ring and re-asked her formally down at the lake that evening," he said.

"What did she say?" he was asked.

"She reinforced that she had desires to become my wife and that she knew that we were going to be happy," Randy said.

"Well, she certainly didn't say it quite like that, did she?"

"No, she didn't. I don't remember exactly what her words were. She expressed . . . she expressed her contentment with our relationship, and she was happy that we were, we were going to pursue this. And she was concerned that I would have enough time, or would not have enough time to be able to make all the arrangements that would be required on such a short notice in Nevada. And I tried to reassure her that I would do everything I could to make all the contacts and make it as memorable an occasion as it possibly could be."

Friday night, August 3, 1990, Randy and Cindy

went to the Chapel of the Bells in Reno and were married. The following two days were spent looking at the classic cars and listening to Little Richard and the Righteous Brothers. By Monday, Mr. and Mrs. Randy Roth were back in Seattle, and Randy, in Brenneman's later belief, was preparing to go on to phase two.

# 37 The Swamp

By the time Randy and Cindy returned from Reno, Lori Baker had moved out of Cindy's South Everett house. Randy and Greg moved in. Randy and Cindy decided to sell both of their houses and find another house with more room, hopefully one with four bedrooms and enough yard space so the boys could ride the four-wheelers.

In September, a real estate agent showed them a new house in Woodinville. The price was $275,000. Cindy and Randy both listed their houses for sale, and Cindy put down a deposit on the new house from her savings. Within two weeks, Cindy's house was sold, and all the proceeds, about $160,000, were used as a down payment on the new house. In late September, Cindy, Randy and all three boys moved in. The boys transferred to a new public school district, a big change for Tyson and Rylie, who had been attending the Christian school at Silver Lake Chapel.

Three weeks after the move, Randy and the insurance company finally settled their dispute over his "    glary," when the insurance company agreed to     st over $28,500 for the claim. About $10,000 of the settlement went to Randy's lawyer, leaving Randy with a bit over $17,000.

On the day the settlement came through, Randy spent nearly $4,400 on three more used four-wheelers for Tyson and Rylie and one of Greg's friends; the rest of the money went into a separate savings account maintained by Randy. But in early December, Randy withdrew most of the remaining money to make a down payment on a used pickup truck with an extended cab. Randy wrote another $5,000 check to cover the balance and asked the dealer to hold on to the check until his house closed escrow.

Two weeks later, Randy's house closed, and Randy received a check for $49,000. Randy put $30,000 into the joint Randy-Cindy checking account and the remaining $19,000 in his own savings account. A day later, Randy bought a four-wheeler for Cindy as a Christmas present; it wasn't exactly Cindy's idea of a romantic gift, but she had made up her mind to try to adjust to Randy. Randy also spent some money for a small Caterpillar-like tractor, which he said he would use to cut four-wheeler trails through the backyard.

Later, Brenneman was to consider just why Randy went through this spending spree, which had some similarities to the time after Jan's death, when the life insurance had come through. In her view, Randy liked to spend money to show off; as with Tim Brocato earlier, and with the previous women, buying things for people made Randy feel like he was Mr. Big, the man in control, that his largesse would more firmly cement people to him.

Brenneman likewise pointed out that with Cindy providing the enormous down payment on the new house, and Tyson and Rylie's Social Security covering the mortgage, Randy had no need to use any of his newfound funds for anything other than the sort of manipulative "gifts" he liked to provide.

As the winter unfolded, problems cropped up between Randy and Rylie. Randy made it plain to Rylie that he thought the nine-year-old wasn't tough enough. Rylie was taking piano lessons; Randy thought that was sissy stuff. Rylie was less than satisfactory, in Randy's view, in riding the four-wheelers; the nine-year-old couldn't manage the gearshifting the way Randy thought he should. Randy also didn't think Rylie was sufficiently aggressive. Soon fourteen-year-old Greg was "wrestling" with Rylie.

"Sometimes we'd go a little too far than just having fun," Rylie said later. "We'd get mad at each other, and it would get to the point where we would try to hurt each other, but by then someone would come and break up the fight."

By mid-winter, Rylie was looking for ways to steer clear of Randy and Greg.

"Whenever he was angry—'cause if he was angry and you did anything wrong—you did not want to do anything wrong, because then you're bound to get punished even if it wasn't bad at all," Rylie later recalled of Randy.

"If he was angry, you didn't even want to go around him. I would run up to my room and I would stay in there. The only reason I would come out was to go down for dinner, and I would be right back in my room, because if you do one thing wrong you're going to get punished just because he's in a bad mood."

By now Randy had extended his Marine-style punishment to Tyson and Rylie as well as Greg. One night, in fact, Randy got mad at all three boys. He made them strip down to their underwear and go out into the backyard. The temperature was just above freezing. Randy ordered the boys to perform two hundred squat-thrusts, vigorous exercises requiring the boys to drop to their hands, shove back their feet, then leap to a standing position, over and over. When Tyson and didn't move fast enough, Randy sprayed them ater from the hose.

* * *

In early January of 1991, Randy and Cindy decided to buy some life insurance. Cindy called Bruce Timm, who had handled all of her insurance, and asked him to come by. Timm arrived that night. After asking Randy some questions about his income and his debts, Timm worked up two different proposals: one for $250,000 in life insurance on both Cindy and Randy, and a second one for $350,000.

Cindy thought the second alternative was too expensive, and Randy agreed. By this time, Randy already had his own $100,000 policy. He told Timm he intended to change the beneficiary on the policy to Cindy. Timm had Randy and Cindy fill out the application. A few days later, he put the paperwork through his New York office. Arrangements were made to pay the premium through automatic withdrawals from the joint Randy-Cindy checking account.

About a month later, Cindy called Timm. She wanted Timm to the change the beneficiary on an earlier $100,000 policy she had purchased. The money was to have gone to a trust benefitting Tyson and Rylie in the event of her death, but Cindy wanted the new beneficiary to be Randy. Timm got the impression that Randy had been pressuring Cindy to make the change, and that Cindy had delayed doing so; she didn't want Randy to know that she hadn't made the change already. Timm suggested that Cindy leave the policy as it was.

Later, Timm was asked why he made that recommendation. "Well," he said, "I told her that you're applying for the additional [$250,000] policy, [but] the first policy is for the benefit of your children. Money can change people sometimes, and with the proceeds payable all to your husband, you know, there is no absolute guarantee that he would always . . . use that benefit for your children. So if you want to be certain, I would leave that benefit to your kids."

But Cindy was insistent on the change, saying that Randy had changed *his* policy to name her and she wanted to reciprocate. But, as Sue Peters and Randy Mullinax were later to discover, Randy had made no such change in his own $100,000 policy, despite what he had told Cindy. That coverage continued to name Randy's father, Gordon, as the trustee for Greg Roth, and for Greg Roth alone, even up to the day that Randy became a suspect in his wife's murder.

By the spring of 1991, the bloom had worn off Randy's latest marriage. By this time, Randy was into his usual withdrawal pattern. His moods darkened easily, and he had little tolerance for Cindy's more feminine behavior. He had taken control of Cindy's checkbook, complaining about her spending for such things as hair appointments, her fingernail fun and similar casual items. Randy's income was far short of the amount needed to pay the family's $1,300 monthly mortgage payment, and Randy was acutely sensitive to the fact that Cindy had a substantial amount of resources in her own name.

As usual in such situations, Brenneman believed, Randy struck back by trying to belittle Cindy or lashing out at the boys. Another major argument unfolded over the new house. Because the property didn't drain adequately, Randy began referring to the house sarcastically as "the Swamp," and berated Cindy for her role in the choice. Randy wanted Cindy to spend some of her money to fix the drainage, while Cindy thought Randy should be able to do the job himself.

At work, Randy was overheard complaining about Cindy. Actually, some at the dealership later recalled, the complaints had begun even before the New Year. Once, a woman dispatcher at the shop overheard ıl of the mechanics complaining about their Then she heard Randy tell the others that he ly a one-year contract with Cindy.

"Yeah," Randy said, "my contract's up in August and [after that] the bitch is gone." That overheard remark, in fact, was where the rumor began at the dealership that Randy had only a one-year marriage agreement with Cindy. Others heard Randy complaining about Cindy's behavior. His one-year wife was too much of a whiner, Randy told others; she was restricting his freedom too much. A source of anger was Cindy's objection to Randy's purchase of a $100 membership in a health club. "The bitch" was jealous of him, Randy told others.

By late spring, several months after the new life insurance had gone into effect, the marriage had deteriorated so badly that Cindy was thinking about leaving. Randy was still complaining about money and criticizing her spending. But that wasn't all: it suddenly seemed to Cindy that there was *nothing* she could do to please her new husband. Randy sneered at her whenever he got the chance, Cindy realized, even while assuring her that he loved her. Randy complained about her makeup, her perfume, her fingernails; her cooking, her food shopping; her activities outside of the house; her driving; her doll collection; indeed, Randy's criticism of Cindy seemed incessant and was wearing Cindy down.

In late May, Randy made a stab at taking another job, this time applying and being hired as a mechanic for the Seattle area's mass transit utility, Metro. The job paid much better than Bill Pierre Ford, and the fringe benefits were great. One of the Pierre mechanics had already gone to work there and urged all of his former friends to do the same.

In mid-June of 1991, Randy was asked to attend an orientation meeting at Metro for new bus mechanics. The program was scheduled to last for two days. Randy showed up for the first day but never came for the second session the next day. Instead, Randy called the supervisor of the orientation and left a message on a phone recorder.

His wife had been in an accident in Idaho, Randy said. She was in critical condition, he added, and it "looked like she wasn't going to make it." That's why he hadn't come in for the second day's orientation, he said.

In fact, Cindy *had* been in an accident—a minor fender-bender at the Silver Lake Chapel parking lot. Later, Randy was to say that it was this accident he had been talking about when he called Metro. Because Cindy's car was damaged, he needed to take it someplace to get an estimate on repairs, and that's why he hadn't come to the orientation. He said nothing, Randy claimed, about Cindy's supposed "critical condition," nor Idaho. The Metro supervisor had simply misunderstood him.

But Randy later admitted that he had fibbed to Metro; the real reason he didn't want to complete his orientation was that he no longer wanted the job. At the first session, Randy said, he learned that his seniority in the shop would be the lowest, which meant he would have to work nights. That would interfere with his family life, he said, and his Little League responsibilities.

Several weeks later, a Metro official—a woman who was the shop supervisor, which may also have played a role in Randy's decision—mailed Randy a registered letter expressing her condolences about his wife's serious accident "in Idaho." The woman wrote Randy that he needed to decide by July 23, 1991, whether he would accept the Metro job. That, of course, was the same date Randy, Cindy, Tyson and Rylie went to Lake Sammamish on the hottest day of the year.

# 38

## Randy Is Not Like Us

The day after Cindy drowned, the Loucks returned from their trip to North Dakota. As they reached their house in Marysville, they found their son Leon and his wife Arletta waiting for them. Arletta saw them drive up. The Loucks thought she looked very serious. The Loucks wondered what had happened.

"Arletta," said Hazel, "what's the matter?"

"We lost Cindy yesterday afternoon," their daughter-in-law told them. At first, the Loucks weren't sure what she was talking about. But then it became all too clear.

The Loucks family immediately drove over to the Woodinville house. Lori Baker was there, along with Cindy's cousin. The boys seemed strained, but the Loucks put it down to the tragedy. Randy told the Loucks his version of what happened at the lake: the swimming, the cramp, the passing motorboat, the inability of the medical people to save her. Then he told Cindy's family that she would be cremated the following day, and if they wanted to see her before that they should call the funeral home and tell them to hold off for a bit.

Randy advised the Loucks not to visit Cindy's remains in the funeral home. "She doesn't look very good," he said. "She's kind of swollen up in the face and everything."

Randy stayed home from work the day after Cindy died. He turned on his answering machine and again let it screen the calls. By this time, Cindy's death had been on the news, and one by one, Cindy's friends called to see if the Cindy Roth who had drowned was the Cindy Roth they knew. Randy ignored most of the inquiries.

Instead, he, Tyson and Rylie began packing up Cindy's makeup, perfume and clothes. Randy stuffed most of the clothes in several plastic garbage sacks and put them in the three-car garage. He took down most of Cindy's photographs and other knickknacks and put them on the floor of an unused closet. That afternoon, Randy took the two boys out to shop for new four-wheelers. He used Cindy's money to buy them.

On Saturday, Randy and the boys took Cindy's bicycle to a nearby swap meet, along with some other odds and ends, including Randy's old stereo and a couch. Randy sold the stuff, and on the way out encountered an old friend. Tim Brocato nodded to Randy. Randy said nothing about Cindy. It was only two days later, when Tim read Cindy's obituary in the newspaper, that Tim discovered another wife of Randy Roth's was dead.

On Sunday Terri McGuire, her husband Bob, and their three children went to church. In one of the strange twists of the Randy Roth case, Terri and her happened to be members of Silver Lake . They had known Cindy slightly before her e to Randy, when she had coached a children's

T-ball team. Terri and her family knew Cindy Baumgartner as Coach Cindy, but they were completely
unaware of Randy's involvement with her. As far as
they knew, Randy Roth was someone who had fallen
out of their lives more than a decade before.

One of Terri's children asked Lori Baker how Coach
Cindy was, and Lori had to tell her Cindy had just
died in a swimming accident. How awful, Terri
thought.

On Monday, as Sue Peters was still making her first
telephone calls, Randy and the boys went to Silver
Lake Chapel for Cindy's memorial service.

Nearly five hundred people attended the memorial.
Randy, dressed somberly in a black suit and tie,
arrived with Tyson and Rylie. Both boys were pale.
Some in the church thought the boys looked scared to
death. Randy quietly told the boys to sit down and
keep out of the way. Scores of people approached
Randy to offer their condolences. Randy seemed dis-
interested, even cold. The Loucks thought he was
nervous. A pastor who had known Cindy when she
had been married to Tom gave the eulogy.

After the service, the boys' aunt and uncle on the
Baumgartner side of the family offered to take care of
Tyson and Rylie for a few days, to give Randy a
chance to sort things out. Randy agreed, and the boys
left with the Baumgartners and the Loucks.

As the crowd dissipated, a number of people noticed
Randy talking quietly to an older, sharp-featured
woman wearing a leather mini-skirt. The woman
seemed nervous, high-strung, ready to lash out. Who
was *that?* people whispered to each other, struck by
the oddity of the woman's attire in such a setting.
That's Randy's mother, others answered, and in that
short time, those who remained in the church swiftly
came to the realization: *Randy is not like us.*

Later, the Loucks accompanied the boys to the

Woodinville house to pick up some of their clothes.
Randy came in about a half-hour later. The Loucks
thought he was very jovial, under the circumstances.

The next day, Randy returned to work at the car
dealership for the first time since Cindy's death. The
people there collected some money and enclosed it in
a sympathy card for him. Randy took the card, opened
it, and walked away without a word.

Later that morning, he called the cashiers' office.
He told Stacey Reese he had two tickets to Reno that
weren't refundable. Would she be interested in going
with him?

Stacey couldn't believe what she was hearing.
Randy was embarrassing her. "I don't think it's a
good idea," Stacey told him. "Well, I'll just have to
give the tickets away, then," Randy said. Stacey told
her fellow cashier about Randy's invitation, and by
early afternoon the story was all over the dealership.

That same afternoon, Terri McGuire was scanning a
local newspaper when she came across the obituary
for Cindy. Terri read that Cindy was survived by her
husband, Randy G. Roth.

Terri's blood ran cold. Could this Randy Roth be
*her* Randy? She hadn't seen her Randy Roth for more
than ten years—not since Greg was a small child, and
that was by sheer coincidence. Suddenly she had to
know.

Terri called Silver Lake Chapel and asked to talk to
Lori Baker. It took her several days to reach Lori, but
when Terri was finally able to talk to her, Terri asked
Lori to describe Randy. Lori described Randy as
short, muscular, with dark hair, and told her that
Randy had grown up in Mountlake Terrace. *That has
[to be] him,* Terri thought numbly as she hung up. *The
[descrip]tion is perfect.* She looked down at her arm. It
[was cov]ered with goosebumps. She called the police.

\* \* \*

At just about that same moment, Randy Roth was ending his first extended interview with the police, on August 1, by telling Peters and Mullinax he wanted to talk to a lawyer.

# 39

## "I Had a Damn Good Idea"

By the end of the first week of August, 1991, the lines were clearly drawn between Randy and the police.

Randy had talked to his lawyer, George Cody, and Cody wasn't at all surprised that the police were interested in Randy in connection with Cindy's death.

"I had a damn good idea of why they wanted to talk to him," Cody later said. Cody advised Randy to let him handle all the contacts with the police from then on. Cody then talked to Mullinax and began negotiations for the lie detector test. According to Cody, Mullinax told him nothing would happen in the immediate future, so Cody took a short vacation. While he was gone, he read a 19th-century British case about a man who was charged with killing one wife, although evidence had been permitted to show that three others had died in similar circumstances. Cody had an idea the case might be relevant. Randy went back to work. He talked to Stacey Reese.

"Do they think you killed her?" Stacey asked.

"__'s all a matter of interpretation," Randy told her.

__ her forces were about to be brought into play.

\* \* \*

Just about the time that Peters and Mullinax were driving to Marysville to see Tim Brocato for the first time, the police department issued a request to the public for any information about the events at the lake.

Distributing the request was tantamount to a declaration of war between the police and Randy. Once the police revealed that they were seeking new witnesses, the news media jumped to the not unnatural conclusion that if the police were unsatisfied with the previous explanation of Cindy's death, there must be something *suspicious* about it.

Within hours, reporters were calling the Woodinville house demanding to talk to Randy; one television station actually drove to the house and parked out front in a classic news media stakeout. Greg took the calls and immediately phoned Randy at work to tell him the reporters wanted to talk to him about Cindy's death.

Randy quickly called Cody to ask him what to do, only to learn that Cody was on vacation. Cody's office was able to reach him later in the afternoon, and after talking with Randy, Cody tried to figure out how to handle this latest development. But Cody, for his part, was furious with Mullinax. He figured the detective had conned him.

That night, Lori Baker called Randy at the Woodinville house and told him about the will, and that she would be the executor as well as guardian for the boys. That meant the boys wouldn't be coming back, she said. Randy was very silent. They would be over to pick up the boys' belongings on the following Saturday, Lori added.

The following day, while Cody was rushing back to Seattle from his aborted vacation, Peters and Mullinax met with Brenneman for the first time to discuss the case.

The most important thing, Brenneman said, was to concentrate on the crime itself, the murder. What were the facts of the crime? Would the facts be sufficient to justify a criminal charge, and would the charge stand up in front of a jury?

The raft, Brenneman said, was probably the key. Could the raft have flipped over, as Randy said? Was there anything about the raft itself that might be useful to prove that Randy was lying?

"We'll need to have a reenactment," Brenneman told Peters and Mullinax.

"We already have," they said. The only way *they* could flip the raft over, the detectives continued, was by very nearly climbing into the craft while violently jerking it with the pure intent to turn it over.

Well, said Brenneman, what about the sacks? Weren't they substantial evidence that the raft had never flipped? How did Randy manage to gather them all up? Was Cindy lying in the raft choking to death while Randy was swimming around in the lake gathering up all of his precious towels? Could he even physically do that without the towels sinking before he could get to them? And if that *hadn't* happened, how did the towels get wet? Did Randy cause them to get wet on purpose? Was that inferential evidence that Randy was lying, an implication that he was already preparing a cover story even while Cindy was dying?

By resolving the central questions about the raft and the drowning, Brenneman told the detectives, it would be possible to move outward to other questions. If Randy was lying, *why* was he lying? What was in it for him if Cindy drowned? Were there any parallels between the death of Cindy and the death ten years earlier of Janis? Brenneman thought there probably be.

*the man is clever, but he's not smart*, Brenne-
ught to herself. *Once he's established a pat-*

*tern that works, he's going to follow it to the degree
that it makes it clear that this is what happened.*

Early that afternoon, Cody called Mullinax. What
were the police trying to *do* to his client? The request
to the public for information had caused Randy to be
besieged by reporters. A television crew was camped
outside his house, for Pete's sake.

Mullinax was cool toward Cody. They'd only asked
for any witnesses who might have seen what happened
at the lake to come forward, he said. If the news media
read too much into that simple request, well, that was
their doing, not the fault of the police.

And by the way, Mullinax continued: while we're
talking, what's all this about *Randy* holding a press
conference? The media is calling us to ask what we
know about what *you're* doing.

It wasn't going to be a press conference, Cody told
Mullinax. Because all the reporters had been hounding
Randy for statements, Cody told the detective, he'd
decided to let Randy answer everyone's questions
once and for all in public. After that, Cody said, the
media could take a hike.

Mullinax immediately called Brenneman. Would it
be legal, he asked, if the police attended Randy's press
conference? Would it be okay if they taped it? Absolutely, said Brenneman, intrigued with the idea of
having a videotape of a raw, uncut Randy Roth to
study.

Brenneman had already realized that one of the
major keys to the case would be Randy's personality,
and seeing Randy as he really was rather than as he
might appear on the nightly news would give her a
substantial assist. Mullinax arranged for two detectives in the department's intelligence unit to pose as
Canadian newsmen to tape the event.

Shortly after three that afternoon, a crowd of r

porters swarmed into Cody's law office. Among them were two undercover detectives. Cody realized that the news media was already suspicious of Randy.

The questions came pouring forth. Had Randy sought help? How could his wife have drowned so quickly? Had he tried to give her CPR? Was it true he'd been married before, and that an earlier wife had also died? Was there insurance? Cody began to regret inviting the press and grew surly. When one reporter persisted in asking Randy about his previous marriages, Cody advised Randy not to answer and then invited all the reporters to discuss *their* marital histories first.

There was nothing suspicious about Cindy's death, Cody insisted. "Then why are we all here, then?" one reporter asked.

"Hey," said Cody, "my office called you and said we were going to be here. Why you're all here is your own business."

After extended discussion about the events at the lake, someone asked Randy how he felt.

"Will you ever recover, obviously not, you probably don't think so," said the reporter. "But do you think life will ever return to normal for you?"

"It's hard to say," Randy said. "I could be optimistic and hope so."

"Will you remarry?"

"That's impossible to deal with, that idea at this time."

"You've lost two wives, under tragic circumstances, how are you dealing with that emotionally?"

"I'm putting my trust in the Lord, I guess," Randy said. "I'm hoping that He'll guide me."

ᶠollowing day, August 10, was Saturday. Lori Tyson and Rylie, Lori's mother, her brother-
d one of Cindy's cousins arrived at the Wood-

inville house in a rented truck to pick up the boys' things. Randy was alone.

"At first he was cordial," Lori said later. "Like, 'No problem.' " But when they went into the house, Lori and the boys saw that Randy had gathered up all of Tyson and Rylie's belongings and had crammed them into plastic garbage sacks, just as he had with Cindy's stuff the week before.

"Everything was just thrown into the big plastic garbage bags," Baker recalled. "Rylie had a great big picture, color glossy, it was all crumpled. All of his Ken Griffey Jr. baseball cards were missing. You know, one of them was worth quite a bit, as collector's cards go. All that was gone and all the stuff was just thrown into the bags."

Rylie was very upset about this. Randy said he didn't know anything about the Griffey cards. Then Randy began making a list of the things the kids were taking. But he wouldn't let the boys take the four-wheeled motorcycles he had bought for them two days after Cindy's death with Cindy's money, or their crash helmets, and he wouldn't let them take Rylie's piano. Randy told Lori he intended to sell them to make the house payment.

"You can't sell them, they're community property," Lori told Randy. Randy got mad at her.

"You come in and ruin my whole scenario," Randy told her heatedly. He calmed down a bit and tried to explain.

The house payment was more than he could afford by himself, Randy continued; he'd been counting on the boys' Social Security checks to make the mortgage payment.

But now that the boys were going to live with Lori, it would be *Lori* who would be getting the Social Security money, not him, Randy complained, getting mad again. He'd intended to quit his job and take care of the boys, Randy told Lori, but Lori's assumption of custody had wrecked all of his plans. Now it would be *Lori* who would get to quit work, he said. Randy accused her of only wanting the boys for the money they could bring in. Lori and her helpers loaded the stuff as fast as they could and got out of there.

# 40 | The Case

As August turned into September of 1991, Detectives Peters and Mullinax found themselves scrambling to assemble all the leads that Randy's past offered them, while at the same time working to interview the more current witnesses of Randy's behavior at the beach following Cindy's drowning.

Meanwhile, they maintained clandestine contact with Stacey Reese.

Later, Mullinax was to remember Stacey's assistance as invaluable—at least as far as giving the detectives some clue as to what Randy was thinking and doing as the investigation proceeded. For one thing, Stacey told them that Randy had insisted he'd never be taken alive, that he might kill himself first. "Think of the children," Stacey told him.

"We wanted to maintain contact with Stacey to see what she could tell us about Randy's movements, his behavior," Mullinax said later, "in case anything out of the ordinary was happening." The detectives thought it was possible that Randy might decide to make a run for it if he felt too much heat. So, Stacey kept them updated on Randy's moods.

"It was good to have some eyes inside the place," Mullinax said. Randy, still out to impress Stacey, apparently never suspected that Stacey was also talking to the detectives.

What was also striking about digging into Randy's past was the number of people who remembered him—usually for the same things. Scores of people told the detectives about Randy's war record; many said they were afraid of him. Others talked about Randy's constant desire for money, his attitude toward women, his need to dominate and control others. Whatever else he might be, the detectives thought, Randy Roth was not someone who tended to fade into the background as far as people's recollections were concerned.

Much of August and early September was devoted to tracking down the witnesses of both the lake and the Beacon Rock incidents and taking their recorded statements. Soon Peters and Mullinax had made contact with Maureen Devinck, the nurse on the beach who had felt so sickened by Randy's behavior toward the dying Cindy, and Alicia Tracy, who first thought Randy was in shock and then was horrified at Randy's indifference toward Tyson and Rylie.

Then, in late August, the detectives were contacted by Kristina Baker.

Kristina Baker said she'd also been at the beach the day of the drowning, with her husband and children. She'd watched the raft pretty closely, Kristina continued, because she feared it might be run over by the powerboats.

Kristina told them she'd watched the raft for a long time—maybe forty minutes or so, because she was sure the fools in the raft would be hit by one of the spe̶e̶d̶i̶n̶g boats. At one point, she said, she'd seen ̶ ̶ ̶upants of the raft jump into the water.

̶ ̶ ̶ oman had jumped first and seemed to be ̶ ̶ away from the raft. The man had followed her, and about twenty or thirty feet away, caught up with her. Then Kristina saw the woman waving her arms. When she looked next, the couple was swimming back to the raft, and a few minutes later, Kristina saw the man pull the woman into the raft. The raft had *never* flipped over; Kristina was positive.

Peters, Mullinax and Brenneman were very interested in Kristina's story. Brenneman, for one, came to believe that what Kristina Baker actually saw was an attempt by Cindy to escape from Randy just before she was drowned. Kristina seemed to recall that Cindy had been swimming in the direction of an idling ski boat when she first noticed Cindy waving her arms; Brenneman theorized that Cindy was trying to signal the ski boat for help, but the boat pulled away without noticing her.

At that point, Brenneman guessed, Randy caught up with Cindy and convinced her to return with him to the raft. Cindy did go back, where Randy drowned her by holding her under the water, concealed from observation from the shore by the shape of the blue-gray inflatable.

The Beacon Rock witnesses were harder to find; after all, the events in Skamania County had taken place nearly a decade before. Even when witnesses could be located, memories were hazy. But slowly the events at Beacon Rock came into focus, aided by the reports compiled by Blaisdale and Grossie years earlier.

Eventually, Mullinax and Peters talked to Louise Mitchell, Janis Roth's best friend, Shirley Lenz at the pediatric clinic, Jalina and Joe Miranda, Janis' mother Billie Ray, and finally, Steve and Shelly Anderson. This time, significance of the Andersons' recounting of Randy's initial statements about Janis' "disappearing" were recognized as evidence that Randy h? probably lied about Jan's death.

By mid-August, the detectives talked to Terri Mc-Guire and recovered the letters Randy had sent her while in the Marines. Together, Peters and Mullinax read the letters, with all of the stories of battles and violent encounters; they concluded they were dealing with a pathological liar. Randy's military service records, obtained by Peters from the Marines, showed the true story.

The detectives also contacted Randy's insurance company and obtained all of the records about the supposed burglary at his house in 1988, along with the information that he had received a $28,500 settlement of the claim. Peters interviewed Donna Sanchez Roth and conducted the follow-up on Tim Brocato, in which Tim confessed to the phony burglary at his house. Debbie, Tim's now-divorced wife, confirmed his story. They talked to the Goodwins' daughter and learned directly from her about Randy's seduction and his boast about the as-yet-uncommitted burglary in 1988.

The detectives conducted another reenactment on the lake, this time after asking Lori Baker to find out from Tyson and Rylie about the sacks. They found similar bags and put them in the raft, timing how long it would be before the bags might sink. The test showed the bags started filling with water almost immediately, and that someone intent on preventing their sinking would have to grab all of them within forty seconds before they would be irretrievably lost.

In mid-September, Brenneman, Peters, Mullinax and another detective, Joe Lewis, drove down to Beacon Rock to look over that scene. Brenneman stayed at the Skamania County authorities' office to discuss the case, while the three detectives went to the top of the windswept volcanic rock. That was when Peters 
̄ ̄ ̄ e theory that Randy had led Janis far off the
̄ ̄ ̄ rder to kill her; she couldn't see how Jan
̄ ̄ ̄ e fallen from the place Randy said she did
̄ ̄ ̄ nd up so far away.

Meanwhile, Stacey Reese continued to report in. Randy, she said, was growing more upbeat by the day. "No news is good news," Randy told her. He said he'd taken a private polygraph test. Stacey didn't know what the results of the test were, but Randy implied that he'd passed.

The lie detector test was a piece of outstanding business between Mullinax and Cody. Stacey's information about Randy and the private test was no surprise to Mullinax; defense lawyers often ask their clients to take such private tests before agreeing to subject their client to the official police examination. If the client passes the private test, that may give the defense lawyer confidence that the client can pass the police test as well. If the client fails, then the defense lawyer can figure out a way to turn down the police test.

In late August, however, Cody had finally agreed to let Randy take the police test. A week later, Randy and Cody showed up at the detectives' offices for the police lie detector test.

As Cody later told the story, the police examiner wanted Randy to tell his whole story about the lake all over again. Cody objected. The examiner explained that he needed to hear the details from Randy before he could decide what the questions should be. Cody said he thought the questions had already been agreed to between he and Mullinax. The police examiner was insistent. In that case, Cody said, anything Randy said should not be available to be used against him at a later date. Mullinax refused to agree.

At that point, Cody advised Randy not to take the test, and they left. Much later, Cody was asked whether he indeed had Randy take a private polygraph test before the police examination. "No comment," he said.

\* \* \*

Meanwhile, Joe Lewis cased the Woodinville house preparatory to asking a judge to approve a search warrant.

By this time, Randy had listed the house for sale, after a sharp albeit brief dispute with Lori Baker about the property's ownership and disposition. Posing as a would-be homebuyer, Lewis had a real estate agent show him the house, inside and out. That gave Lewis a good idea of the places to search if and when the time came.

Thus, after numerous interviews and extensive meetings, by early October of 1991 the detectives and Brenneman decided they were ready. They had a score of witnesses about the events at the beach; another group from Beacon Rock was rounding into shape; they'd had two reenactments that seemed to show Randy was not telling the truth about what happened to the raft; they had boxes filled with documents, including copies of Randy's insurance files, records of his burglary, and records from the joint checking account with Cindy. They had a theory: Randy, the habitual insurance scammer and inveterate liar, had murdered for money; and most of all, they had a hope that they would be able to prove it to a jury.

On October 9, 1991, just after nine in the morning, Peters and Mullinax, along with Joe Lewis, Sergeant Frank Kinney and several other officers, pulled up in front of Bill Pierre Ford. Peters and Mullinax walked directly past Stacey Reese without giving her a glance and went into the shop area. Mullinax walked toward Randy's workstation. Peters stopped and looked at the parts counter. Randy Roth stood there. He hadn't yet seen her.

For months, Peters had been working with one ⸺Mullinax—to develop a murder case against ⸺ndy—Roth.

⸺'' Peters called, and in that instant, like ⸺of reversed mirror image, the Randys both

Mullinax and Roth turned to face her. Peters walked up to Randy Roth.

"You're under arrest," she said, "for investigation of first degree murder."

Randy the Bad immediately put his hands out in front of him for the handcuffs. "That's not the way we do it," Peters told him, and turned him around while pulling his arms behind him. The cuffs went on in back, and Randy Roth, putative war hero and master manipulator, the man who hated to be told what to do by women, was on his way to jail, collared by a woman detective who wasn't fooled at all.

# 41 Woodinville

**R**andy's arrest happened so quickly almost no one in the shop noticed his departure. On the way out to the detectives' car, Randy asked Mullinax to go back into the shop and get his clothes and contact lenses. Mullinax did that.

A few minutes later, driving toward the jail in downtown Seattle, Mullinax noticed that someone seemed to be following them in a pickup truck. The man was talking into a cellular telephone. Mullinax sped up and slowed down; he tried several other evasive maneuvers, but the man in the truck stayed with them. Mullinax was pretty sure the other car held a friend of Randy's.

What was he up to? Was some sort of attempt to rescue Randy in the works? After all the talk Mullinax had heard about Randy's *Mission Impossible* boasts, and his claims that he would never be jailed, the detective knew that nothing could be ruled out. Mullinax drove onto the freeway onramp, then pulled over. The pursuing driver slowed down, stopped then, apparently deciding that he had been shot forward past Mullinax and into the freeway traffic. Mullinax, Peters and Randy then drove to the county jail without further incident, and on reflection, Mullinax thought he had a pretty good idea of the purpose of the unexpected shadowing.

Sure enough, no sooner had Peters and Mullinax booked Randy into the King County Jail than Mullinax was hearing from George Cody about Randy's arrest. Randy had to have prepped someone to let Cody know just as soon as he was arrested, Mullinax thought; he had obviously expected it, never mind that "no news is good news."

But Mullinax had no intention of calling Cody right away; instead, he and Peters started for Randy's house in Woodinville, where Joe Lewis and Frank Kinney were waiting for them with a warrant to search Randy's house.

But the unknown man in the pickup truck had no connection to Cody. Instead, Randy's lawyer found out about his client's arrest from the news media.

For weeks, the newspapers and television stations had been waiting for something to happen. After his press conference on August 9, the news media was sure something was up. Soon stories appeared about Randy and Janis and the events in Skamania County a decade earlier. In mid-August, the media helped goose the investigation a bit by reporting that police were still looking for witnesses to Cindy's drowning. In the last week of August, the papers reported that the Skamania County authorities were thinking of reopening their investigation into Jan's death, as well.

Now, on October 9, 1991, the police announced Randy's arrest on a recorded news media information line—five minutes before Randy was actually in custody. A reporter from the *Seattle Times* had been tipped that the arrest was imminent and happened t
call the information line just after nine A.M. Th

porter immediately called George Cody and asked him to comment. "I'm surprised," Cody told the reporter.

Much later, however, Cody said he really wasn't surprised that Randy was arrested, only that the reporters knew about it before he did. The reporter told Cody about the police information line; Cody called the hotline and listened to the announcement himself.

Next, Cody called the police and was told that neither Peters nor Mullinax was available to take his call. He called the jail and was told no one named Randy Roth had been booked. Repeated calls yielded no information at all on Randy's whereabouts. Cody figured the police were trying to keep Randy from talking to him; he knew that in the shock of arrest, criminal defendants often made admissions to police, and he wanted to get to Randy as quickly as he could.

"Screw this," Cody told his secretary. "I'll go down to the jail. The booking process may take them forever to get him in. If Randy calls, call me in the car, we can conference-call the thing." As Cody was approaching downtown Seattle, Randy finally called. Cody told Randy he'd be there in twenty minutes and to say nothing to the police. Randy assured him that he wouldn't.

A police search is one of the more dangerous activities the police can perform. In Randy's case, the search wasn't physically dangerous; by that time, Lewis and Kinney were certain the house was unoccupied. But searches also carry myriad potential legal pitfalls.

An improper search—one ineptly conducted, or one without adequate attention to procedural rules—can cause an otherwise solid criminal case to go right down As a result, the best police searches are with an elaborate, almost myopic attention tails.

and Lewis had indeed already determined

that the house was unoccupied. They did so by knocking on the door and announcing themselves as police. When no one answered, they sat down on the front porch to wait for Peters and Mullinax and other police officers to arrive. Kinney watered Randy's potted plants and Lewis played with Randy's dog, Jackson.

About an hour after they booked Randy into the jail, Peters and Mullinax arrived at Randy's house. Together with Lewis and Kinney, the four detectives approached the front door. Lewis had Randy's door keys. He opened the door, calling out, "King County Police with a warrant," and the four detectives fanned through the house to make sure no one was inside.

Unfortunately, no one bothered to knock on the door when it was unlocked. Over such a trivial omission—the law required police to "*knock* and announce" at the time of the presentation of the warrant, not an hour before—several days of courtroom wrangling were later to ensue, as lawyers for Randy and the prosecutor's office haggled over whether the search was legal.

One of the most important steps in conducting a police search is the documentation of exactly where and when something is found, along with a specific description of the item seized. In Randy's case, the detectives were searching for records relating to Randy's marriages and insurance; clothing, footwear or towels that might have been in the sacks in the raft, which the detectives considered important for the accuracy of any new reenactments; and any tools or other articles Randy had reported stolen in his 1988 burglary.

After Joe Lewis videotaped each of the rooms, the detectives went into separate areas of the house to conduct the search. Lewis meanwhile maintained a log; as each detective discovered something of possible relevance, the item was brought to Lewis for listir before going into a bag with Lewis' log number the discovering detective's initials on it. That way, the police could make sure of precisely where the item was found, by whom, and when.

Peters began in the family room, where she found miscellaneous papers, including newspaper articles about Cindy's death, and books on Vietnam. A search of Randy's desk yielded tax records, bank records and an address book. Peters went on to the kitchen and found more papers and telephone records.

Mullinax started in the master bedroom, where he found another article on Cindy's death and Cindy's wallet and checkbook. Mullinax found some pornographic material under the bed along with some condoms.

In a closet, Mullinax found two pairs of rubber flip-flop sandals, footwear that might have been in the sacks in the raft. Tyson and Rylie's bedrooms were completely empty. In the bedroom occupied by Greg, Mullinax found the nail-studded baseball club that Randy used to impress the boys; in an upstairs recreation room, Mullinax found a collection of brand new Marine Corps patches, along with photo albums containing pictures of Janis, Jalina, Cindy, Greg and Lori.

Next the detectives turned their attention to the three-car garage. Mullinax located many of Cindy's financial and tax records on a shelf. Another detective with professional experience as a car mechanic went through Randy's tool box, listing most of the tools separately; it appeared that many of the tools were the same type and manufacturer that Randy had claimed were stolen in 1988.

Meanwhile, Peters found a four-drawer file cabinet in another corner of the garage which yielded still more papers, some going back to the marriage of d Janis. In the back of the second drawer of t, Peters found a torn, four-page note that wadded into a ball. Peters unfolded the l noticed that it appeared to be a letter in

Cindy's handwriting. *That will probably be worth looking at more closely,* she thought, and dropped the wadded papers into the sack for later review.

By mid-afternoon, the detectives had completed the garage search and a search of Randy's backyard storage shed. The shed yielded two chainsaws—apparently the same saws Randy reported taken in the 1988 burglary.

Next, Mullinax and Peters located a locked door leading to a crawl space beneath the house. Mullinax found the keys in the kitchen, and he and Peters bent down and made their way inside. The hidden area was crammed with cases of Ford Company motor oil and numerous Ford parts and tools, including an expensive jack. Mullinax and Peters felt sure the stuff had been stolen by Randy from Bill Pierre Ford. Peters and Mullinax removed all the items and stacked them on the floor of the garage. A call was made to Randy's boss at Bill Pierre.

Just before seven P.M. Randy's boss arrived and looked over the Ford items. The oil, tools and parts, he said, appeared to have come from his dealership. He made a list of all the items to compare them to the dealership's inventory.

Back in the house, Peters removed Randy's Marine wall shrine, including his "Iron Man" plaque. The relics of a past that never was, she thought, would do Randy precious little good where he was headed.

Just after eight P.M., the detectives returned to the courthouse with a truckload of items taken in the search, including scores of sacks crammed with papers and most of Randy's tool collection. The detectives carted all the stuff into the police department evidence room and locked it up for the night. A closer examination, with Marilyn Brenneman in attendance, was set for the following day.

# 42

## A Message from Cindy

The following morning, Brenneman and the detectives began poring over all the papers and other items seized from Randy the day before. The detectives and the prosecutor hoped that the paperwork taken in the search would document their theory that Randy was a habitual defrauder of insurance companies. But Peters was interested in the letter she had seen with Cindy's handwriting on it. She retrieved it from the sack and sat down next to Brenneman.

"Look at this," she began, and together she and Brenneman attempted to fit the torn pieces together. It was like assembling a jigsaw puzzle. It appeared to be a note that Cindy had written to herself. As the words on the ripped pages fell together, both Peters and Mullinax felt a chill. It was, as Brenneman said later, as if in death Cindy were trying to send them a message.

*Randy does not "love" Cindy*, the note began. *Randy hates Cindy . . .*

*Randy hates Cindy's face make-up.*
*Randy hates Cindy's blush*

*Randy hates Cindy's lipstick.*

*Randy hates Cindy's blonde hair*

*Randy hates Cindy's ugly toes—they're the ugliest toes he's ever seen.*

*Randy hates all of Cindy's 5 or 6 different perfumes.*

*Randy hates Cindy's cold feet*

*Randy hates Cindy's cold hands.*

*Randy hates Cindy's fingernails.*

*Randy hates Cindy's dolls in every room.*

*Randy hates Cindy's pink feminine things in every room.*

*Randy hates Cindy's peach feminine things in every room.*

*Randy hates Cindy's pictures.*

*Randy hates Cindy's furniture.*

*Randy hates Cindy's drawers because they aren't real drawers.*

*Randy hates the way Cindy drives because she'll wreck the cars and trucks.*

*Randy hates the way Cindy cooks most of the time.*

*Randy hates the way Cindy buys groceries too many times every week and spends too much money.*

*Randy hates the swamp that Cindy made him move to.*

*Randy hates Cindy's house.*

*Randy hates Cindy's things.*

*Randy hates Cindy's money.*

*Randy hates Cindy's independent nature.*

*Randy hates the way Cindy grinds her teeth.*

*Randy hates the way Cindy picks up his papers all the time.*

*Randy hates the way Cindy uses all the hot water to fill the huge tub for a bath.*

*Randy hates that Cindy drinks coffee.*

*Randy hates that Cindy eats more than all the boys.*

*Randy hates how Cindy decorates a house.*

*Randy hates Cindy shopping.*

*Randy hates leaving Cindy leaving the house at all.*

*Randy hates Cindy driving the Trooper.*

*Randy hates Cindy's pants.*

*Randy hates that Cindy likes to eat because she'll get fat.*

*Randy hates that Cindy made a cookie for Valentine's Day & not a cake.*

*Randy hates if Cindy wants to help or volunteer anywhere.*

*Randy hates Cindy having Lori over to our house.*

*Randy hates coming home from work instead of shopping or doing other things.*

*Randy hates not being able to go shopping alone all the time.*

*Randy hates telling Cindy where he goes.*

*Randy hates Cindy's monthly thing and putting up with her each month.*

*Holy cow!* Peters thought as she and Brenneman finished reading the note. The list of "Randy hates" was obviously written by Cindy not long before her death. It provided a picture of a desperately unhappy woman. Even the handwriting had indications of severe emotional stress. While the first few lines appeared neatly printed, letters calmly formed and kept within the lines of the notepaper, by the end the letters were nearly frantic, weaving between the lines as if Cindy had been writing in furious haste as the thoughts roiled through her mind.

And what of Cindy's view of Randy? Based on the note, it seemed that Randy was constantly criticizing her, belittling her appearance, her capacities, her very nature. And with spiteful vitriol. "Randy doesn't 'love' Cindy, Randy hates Cindy . . ." *Randy hates, indeed,* thought Peters.

# THE TRIAL

# 43 | Nothing There

The same morning, the day after Randy's arrest, the prosecutor's office filed its information formally charging Randy with first degree murder. Brenneman attached a nineteen-page affidavit of probable cause to the official charge. The affidavit outlined the facts of the state's case against Randy and included the background of Randy's marriages to Donna Sanchez Roth, Janis Miranda Roth, Donna Clift Roth, as well as his courtship of Mary Jo Phillips, his seduction of the Goodwins' underage daughter, and his approaches to Stacey Reese, including the invitation to Reno less than a week after Cindy's death.

The facts about Jan's death at Beacon Rock in 1981 were recounted. The witnesses to Randy's behavior at Lake Sammamish were quoted, as were the observations of paramedics and hospital workers. But Brenneman didn't specifically spell out how all these events tended to show Randy's guilt in the death of Cindy; instead, Brenneman's recitation of Randy's history was meant to be taken together as powerful circumstantial evidence that Randy had indeed murdered his last wife. Brenneman asked that bail for Randy be set at one million dollars.

As George Cody read over Brenneman's affidavit, he was almost instantly aware of what his strategy would have to be. Cody believed that the whole case against Randy was based on fate, on circumstances, most prominently the death of Jan Roth a decade earlier.

Just as Lee Yates had predicted months earlier, Cody concluded that much of that evidence, maybe all of it, would never be allowed to come before a jury.

How could *Jan's* death be proof of what happened to *Cindy?* Randy hadn't even known Cindy when Jan died, Cody reasoned; he would have had no way of foreseeing what would happen a decade in the future, so the two events were completely unconnected. And if they were unconnected, the first event couldn't be included in a trial on the second.

What, after all, was the *relevance* of Janis Roth's death to the death of Cindy Roth? Just because a man had two wives die in tragic accidents didn't mean that he had killed either one of them, Cody knew he would argue.

The state, Cody concluded, was attempting to boot-strap its case by circular reasoning: we *know Randy killed Cindy because Jan is dead, and we know he killed Jan because Cindy is dead*. That just wasn't allowed.

Cody thought the prosecution's case would therefore collapse. This was the purpose the "prior bad acts" rules of the evidence code, Cody thought: to prevent a prosecutor from using unrelated facts that might tend to make a defendant look bad as a means of convicting in a completely separate case.

Furthermore, thought Cody, where was the proof that Cindy had actually been *murdered?* Hadn't the medical examiner already ruled that Cindy's death was the result of an accidental drowning? The law compelled the prosecutor to present evidence that a murder had in fact taken place.

This was the so-called *corpus delicti* rule—requiring that not only that a dead body must exist, but evidence that the dead person has died from obviously criminal means.

In the case of Cindy, that simply wasn't available, Cody concluded. No one was saying, for example, that they *saw* Randy hold Cindy under the water until she was dead. Nor was there any physical evidence to show the drowning had been anything other than a tragic accident.

Nor would the observations of Randy's emotionless behavior at the beach and at the hospital be admissible. As Yates had predicted, Cody believed those accounts would be ruled out as "opinion testimony." What relevance did those accounts have, anyway? Since when was it a crime to show no emotion?

Still other portions of the story of Randy as proposed by Brenneman would similarly have to be withheld from a jury, Cody believed. The best thing to do, he reasoned, would be to force the state to put its case on trial before they were completely ready, then fall upon its disparate, hard-to-connect facts and attack them one by one until the whole thing fell apart.

"There's nothing there," Cody told others.

Meanwhile, Lori Baker was hearing some disturbing stories about Randy's activities immediately prior to his arrest. As the personal representative of Cindy's estate and the guardian of Tyson and Rylie, Lori had a duty to prevent Randy from selling the estate's assets and keeping all of the money for himself.

Randy had already listed the Woodinville house for sale, even though he hadn't put any money into it. Lori discovered that Randy had listed the house for $225,000—fully $50,000 less than what Cindy and he had paid for it a year earlier. Lori had a sharp dispute with Randy over the telephone about the sale before his arrest; Randy told Lori again that with Tyson and Rylie and their Social Security payments gone, he couldn't afford to make the payments by himself. He wanted to sell the house and buy another one, he said.

As September unfolded, Lori learned that Randy had been selling other items, as well: the Isuzu Trooper, the four four-wheelers, the small bulldozer, and the $15,000 pickup truck Randy had bought the prior December. All of these vehicles were community property, Lori believed. Randy, she thought, had to be stopped before he completely gutted the value of the estate.

She consulted a lawyer, and four days after Randy was arrested, she sued Randy to have all the property declared community property, to force an accounting from Randy on what he had already sold, and to force him to disgorge any money he'd obtained from the sale of any items.

A few days later, Lori obtained the keys to the safe deposit box she had once rented with Cindy. She'd been curious for weeks about the box, ever since Randy had insisted to her in early August that there was no such box.

Lori *knew* there was a box, because she'd been there with Cindy and had even signed papers relinquishing her interest in the box over to Randy. After Cindy died and Randy began insisting there was no box, Lori had checked with the bank. Yes, the box *did* exist, but the bank refused to allow her to open it without Randy also being present. Randy, of course, said the box didn't exist. It was a frustrating Catch 22.

The last time she'd been to the box with Cindy, it had contained a copy of Cindy's will, wedding rings from Cindy's marriage to Tom, a valuable pocket watch, some investment papers, and several other items Cindy wanted to give to Tyson and Rylie when they were older.

Now, with Randy in jail and Lori officially Cindy's personal representative, Lori finally got permission from the bank to open the box to see if Cindy's will was in it. On October 18, 1991, Lori went to the bank. Accompanied by two bank officials, Lori unlocked the box and looked inside. There was nothing there; it was completely empty.

Lori asked the bank people to find out the name of the last person who opened the box. The officials checked. The last person to open the box had been Randy Roth, on July 25, 1991—two days after Cindy's death, and about two weeks before Randy insisted to Lori that the box did not exist. Lori now concluded that Randy had rushed to the bank after Cindy's death to destroy the will.

# 44

## For the Defense

**R**andy came to court for the first time a few days after his arrest. Cody argued that Randy should be released on a reasonable bail. The charge of murder, he said, was ludicrous.

Even if one took the most suspicious view of Randy's behavior, Cody argued, the facts presented by Marilyn Brenneman could at most only warrant a charge of manslaughter, not murder.

And that was the *worst* case, he said; the facts assembled by the police were certainly ambiguous as to whether a crime had even occurred, let alone cold-blooded homicide. The county medical examiner, Cody pointed out, continued to say Cindy's death had been *an accident*.

Listening to Cody denigrate her case against Randy made Brenneman wonder: *was Cody sending signals that Randy might be willing to plead guilty to manslaughter instead of standing trial for murder?*

While that might save the state the large expense of a jury trial, if that was what Cody was up to, Brenneman thought, it was laughable. Even as she listened to Cody talk, she was sure she could convince a jury that

286

Randy had killed Cindy deliberately, not accidentally, as Cody seemed to be suggesting.

The only real question was whether she could prove that Randy killed Cindy with *premeditation*, which was the difference between first degree murder and second degree murder. Brenneman might be prepared to consider Cindy's death as the result of an outburst of rage on Randy's part, which might conceivably have been unpremeditated, but manslaughter was a nonstarter.

But if Cody was suggesting to Brenneman that his client was willing to enter a plea to a lesser charge, nothing ever came of the signal. After that one possible hint, Cody gave no sign of wanting to dispose of the case with a guilty plea. Instead, he told Brenneman that Randy would not waive his right to a trial within sixty days from the day of his arraignment.

That would mean Randy's trial would have to begin by the middle of December. Brenneman happily agreed to the short time schedule.

But the following month, Cody discovered the vast amount of investigation of Randy that had been done by Peters and Mullinax—literally hundreds of interviews and thousands of documents, among them the "Randy hates" note written by Cindy before her death.

Cody said nothing as he carted the first installment of all this material out of the prosecutor's office. But Mullinax, for one, formed the impression that Cody was shocked at the amount of work that had already been done to prove his client guilty.

As October turned into November, Cody realized that a second lawyer would be needed to help him prepare Randy's defense. Brenneman and the police just kept churning out paper, thousands upon thousands of pages of the stuff.

All of it would have to be read and evaluated, Cody

realized, and it was more than one person could possibly hope to do before the start of the trial. Suddenly, it seemed that the prosecution intended to overwhelm *him* rather than the other way around, Cody thought.

About the time Cody was reaching that conclusion, Brenneman returned to court with two new charges against Randy. In addition to murdering Cindy, Brenneman contended in the new charges, Randy had also stolen $28,500 by fraud from his insurance company in his 1988 burglary, which Brenneman and the police were convinced was faked; in addition, Bill Pierre Ford officials had identified the stuff found in the crawlspace under Randy's house—the tools and car parts—as having been stolen from them. So, by the end of October, Cody was pretty sure his insistence on a trial within sixty days would have to be abandoned.

Early in November, Cody contacted another lawyer for help. John Muenster was, like Cody, forty-two years old. A graduate of Yale University and Harvard Law School, Muenster had defended nearly fifteen murder cases, including some of the most publicized cases ever heard in the Seattle area.

Muenster also had a reputation in Seattle as one of the brightest lawyers in the city. He saw his job as defending the Constitution. He was meticulous in the preparation of his cases, prolific in assembling briefs and arguments, painstaking in his efforts to force the prosecution to prove each and every segment required; for Muenster, a criminal trial was a form of mind combat in which no quarter was asked or given, and in which the stakes were the sanctity of the legal process as well as a person's life. And as Cody and Muenster together looked over the state's proposed evidence against Randy, Muenster was convinced that state was about to seriously break the rules.

* * *

As Cody and Muenster sorted through the thousands of pages of reports and interviews provided by the prosecutor's office in November and early December, they began to develop a series of defensive entrenchments Brenneman would have to surmount before Randy could be convicted.

Almost all of these efforts would require fairly arcane legal arguments before a judge; but if the judge agreed with Cody and Muenster, Randy's chances of walking free would be greatly enhanced.

The overall strategy of the two defense attorneys, as in most cases where there is no clear alternative guilty party, involved reducing the case to its minimum possible size, if not finding a way to make it disappear altogether.

The first defense by Randy's lawyers centered on whether a murder had actually occurred. Muenster was convinced that under the so-called *corpus delicti* rule, the law required two things before a murder charge could go forward: that Cindy was dead, and second, that she had been murdered.

That Cindy was dead was beyond all dispute; but whether her death was a murder or an accident was very much in dispute.

Without an undisputed finding that murder had in fact happened, the court would have no choice but to dismiss the murder charge, the defenders reasoned. If that happened, Randy would be home free—possibly even able to collect at least half of the $385,000 in insurance on Cindy.

Cody and Muenster also knew, however, that Brenneman and the prosecutor's office would point to Jan's death as powerful circumstantial evidence that murder *did* occur with Cindy, that Jan's death showed a pattern of Randy's behavior making it more likely than not that Cindy was murdered.

To deal with this, they decided to erect a second

barrier behind the first: *all* discussion about Jan Roth should be ruled irrelevant and therefore excluded.

Cody and Muenster knew this was where the most serious battle would be fought. If Jan's death could be kept out, Randy's chances of being found innocent would be greatly improved; but if it was allowed, Randy would probably be convicted. Jurors, they thought, would probably conclude that once might have been an accident, but twice was too suspicious.

How to keep Jan out? Muenster and Cody were convinced that Jan's death, legally speaking, would have to be considered an inadmissible "prior bad act." And if it *was* nevertheless allowed and Randy was then convicted, higher courts would require the conviction to be thrown out, and a new trial granted.

The "prior bad act" rule seemed clear: *"Evidence of other crimes, wrongs or acts is not admissible to prove the character of a person in order to show that he acted in conformity therewith."* In other words, just because Randy had acted like a creep many times in the past—and even if he *had* been the only person present when Jan fell to her death—it couldn't fairly be used to prove he had killed Cindy.

The same objections could be applied to Randy's fraudulent military career, his disciplining of the boys, the raft trip with Donna Clift, the murder committed by Randy's brother Davy, the supposed faked burglary at Tim Brocato's, the later one at Randy's, the stolen Bill Pierre goods found at Randy's house during the search, even the "Randy hates" note written by Cindy. All of this stuff should be ruled irrelevant by the judge, or if not irrelevant, more prejudicial than should be permitted.

Cody and Muenster now put a third barricade behind the Jan Roth issue, as well: even if Cindy's death *was* legally a murder, and even if Jan's death *was* admissible, all testimony about Randy's *behavior* at the beach and at the hospital should be suppressed as opinion testimony.

The defense lawyers knew that all the descriptions of Randy unconcernedly deflating his raft while Cindy was dying would be dynamite, and also prejudicial, so all witness opinions about the propriety of Randy's behavior should be kept out.

The major problem with allowing all this material, Cody and Muenster believed, was that *taken* together it might convince a jury that Randy was guilty of the murder of Cindy even if she *had* died by accident. That was the very definition of prejudice, they agreed. It would be a miscarriage of justice, Muenster later said publicly, if this evidence were allowed in the trial and Randy were thereby convicted of a crime that had really been an accident.

As a final obstacle, the defense lawyers wanted to have separate trials on the three charges so far filed by Brenneman; such "severance" of the charges each into their own trial would reduce the possibility that Randy would be found guilty of murder merely because of his possible guilt in defrauding his homeowners insurance company in the faked burglary, or his possession of the items allegedly stolen from Bill Pierre Ford.

Separate trials on each charge would also increase pressure on the prosecutors to plea bargain, because of the cost of bringing the separated cases to court.

To achieve these varied objectives, Cody and Muenster on December 19, 1991, filed a series of motions in King County Superior Court: first, a motion to dismiss the murder charge because there was no proof that murder had actually occurred; a motion to declare the search of the Woodinville house legally invalid; a motion to have separate trials on the three different charges; and numerous other motions to exclude testimony about the death of Janis Roth, Randy's harsh disciplinary methods, his true military record, and anything to do with Davy Roth and his 1979 murder conviction.

If the motions weren't granted, and if all that stuff came out at the trial, Cody and Muenster knew Randy would probably be sunk.

But there was an additional part to the "prior bad acts" rule, one which created an exception *allowing* such evidence. Even as Cody and Muenster were focusing on the first part of the rule, Brenneman was thinking about the second: prior bad acts were admissible *"for other purposes, such as proof of motive, opportunity, intent, preparation, plan, knowledge, identity or absence of mistake or accident."*

That meant if Brenneman could prove to the judge that there was some connection between the two deaths—indeed, to Randy's other bad behavior—there was a possibility of getting the Jan Roth material into the trial. Randy and his lawyers were contending Cindy's death was an accident; the law allowed Brenneman to present evidence to show that "absence of mistake or accident." Jan's death was just such evidence, Brenneman reasoned.

Where Cody and Muenster wanted to limit the allowable evidence, Brenneman, of course, wanted to get as much of the material before the jury as she could.

Her case depended on the jury's understanding that Randy's behavior constituted a discernible pattern—a continuing plan or scheme, as she saw it, to get money by cheating insurance companies—not accident, but a plan or motive for insurance fraud that had origins at least as far back as the "theft" of Jan's Pinto.

To that end, the facts of Jan's death were vital, as was the information about the faked burglary—burglaries, if one included the Tim Brocato caper, as Brenneman intended—as well as the various aspects of Randy's behavior and demeanor, which Brenneman believed would demonstrate Randy's calculating nature. Altogether, Brenneman believed the detectives had found nine different cases of insurance fraud or attempted fraud by Randy. It was the pattern of fraud that would tie all the issues together, she thought, and allow her to bring in the Jan Roth evidence.

Moreover, Brenneman guessed that Randy would be a witness on his own behalf. While defendants have the constitutional right not to testify in their own defense, and while juries are routinely instructed not to draw conclusions about guilt or innocence because of a defendant's refusal to testify, Brenneman knew as well as Cody and Muenster that Randy's refusal to give testimony would be seen by the jury as suspicious, particularly since Randy was claiming Cindy's death had been an accident.

In Brenneman's mind, virtually *all* of Randy's prior bad acts were admissible as evidence of his "motive . . . plan . . . [and] absence of mistake or accident," with the possible exception of his disciplining of children and his military lies. But even there, Brenneman thought, if the defense opened the door to those questions by presenting testimony about Randy's character, she would be ready.

# 45

## The Whole Truth, Nothing But . . .

**J**udge Frank Sullivan was a sixty-five-year-old, eleven-year veteran of the King County Superior Court, and in a week of hearings on the Randy Roth case in January of 1992, Sullivan disappointed Randy's defenders over and over again.

In his career as a lawyer before becoming a judge, Sullivan had been a deputy county prosecutor as well as a defense attorney. He had, in fact, created the first felony public defender's office in the county and was widely regarded by both prosecutors and defenders as one of the county's most neutral judges, a close listener and a diligent reader of the voluminous briefs and precedent cases often generated by complex legal issues.

That the case against Randy Roth was complex was beyond dispute; already, Brenneman planned to call nearly one hundred fifty witnesses against Randy, including some who had known him only for brief moments more than a decade earlier. There would also be hundreds of documents and photographs, along with charts, videotapes and physical items of evidence.

Because much of the case against Randy was based on circumstantial evidence, it would be necessary to lead the jury through a forest of subtle facts. As a result, the case was placed on a fast track through the legal system, which allowed it the highest priority for courtroom time and resources.

Like Cody, Brenneman had realized early that the case against Randy required a second attorney. In December, she obtained the services of another senior deputy prosecutor in the fraud division, Susan Storey.

Together, Brenneman and Storey pored over all the evidence and worked out their strategies to deal with the defense; they also divided up the witnesses, each prosecutor concentrating on what their respective witnesses were expected to say once they reached the stand.

By late January, both sides were ready, and Sullivan set aside a week to consider the motions brought by Randy's lawyers in their efforts to derail the case against him. For their part, Cody and Muenster knew that if they prevailed before the trial began, Randy stood a good chance of going free; but if they failed in their motions, they would be reduced to their last line of defense: Randy himself.

Randy sat quietly at the defense lawyers' table in Sullivan's courtroom, dressed in the red jail coverall uniform worn by accused felons, the center of the storm but otherwise uninvolved. It had been impossible for him to raise the $100,000 necessary to make the million-dollar bail, and indeed, virtually all of his remaining money, as well as his tool collection, had gone to Cody and Muenster to pay their legal fees.

All through the week, the lawyers for both sides marshaled their arguments, citing old cases and previous court decisions; so voluminous were all the legal papers that both sides distributed bound books of photocopies, hundreds of pages, marked by scores of colored index tabs to help everyone keep at the same page at the same time.

As both sides had foreseen, the arguments were convoluted, even arcane. Both sides also knew, however, what the stakes were: if Randy's side prevailed, he would likely go free, and maybe even collect at least half of the $385,000 in total life insurance police had by now discovered Randy had on his last wife.

But if the prosecutors' side won out, there was every chance a new rule of law might be developed. There had never been a case decided with the exact circumstances of the Roth situation: while others had committed multiple murders over the years, the crimes contained elements which indicated a particular *modus operandi,* or method in committing the murders; others included several crimes that were related to a single scheme; but none, it seemed, fit the Roth situation perfectly, where there were some aspects of *modus operandi,* but not clearcut, and other aspects of motive, albeit not a single scheme.

In the end, the question of whether Jan's death might be presented as evidence to the jury as a sort of trial-within-a-trial, even though her death had not been charged, came down to an obscure British case—the very one Cody had been reading on his vacation when Randy called to tell him the news media was after him.

Brenneman found the case for the prosecution. It was titled *Smith v. The King,* but was more popularly known as the "Wives in the Bath Case." The decision dated from the nineteenth century.

In the old case, a man named Smith was accused of murdering his wife by drowning her in the bathtub. There was no evidence to indicate any foul play.

But when the British police looked a bit deeper, it turned out that Mr. Smith had been married *four times,* and that three of his previous wives had similarly died in the bathtub in different parts of England. The British courts had allowed the testimony about the earlier wives to be heard—"to shew the design" of Mr. Smith—in killing his last wife, and Mr. Smith was convicted of the final death.

Sullivan easily decided the defense argument that there was no proof that murder had taken place—no *corpus delicti,* as Muenster kept insisting—was wrong. It was true there was no physical evidence of murder, he said, but the circumstantial evidence was strong, and it was just as good as physical evidence—at least, in terms of permitting the issue to be submitted to a jury.

As for the Jan Roth evidence, *that* was a bit more complicated. After reading all of the cases cited by both sides, including *Smith v. The King,* Sullivan ruled that the evidence about Jan would be admitted.

"Well," said Sullivan, "I spent a great deal of time last night re-reading several of the cases. And the more you read, why, the more double your vision gets on these issues. But, as to the relevance of the Janis Roth evidence, I think it is *highly* relevant. I can't see any other solution to it."

The Jan Roth testimony *was* prejudicial to Randy's right to a fair trial, Sullivan acknowledged, but the law allowed for prejudicial testimony if its necessity for the state to prove its case outweighed the prejudice.

"I think," said Sullivan, "in reading the cases that it is clear the Janis Roth events would certainly tend to make the latter one [Cindy] more probable, which is the test for relevance."

The defense had one more major line of attack on the prosecution's case against Randy—the one foreseen months earlier by the prosecutor's own Lee Yates. That was the area of Randy's demeanor in the immediate aftermath of Cindy's drowning.

The law, Cody and Muenster contended, forbade the state to present any evidence that Randy failed to show emotion or act appropriately while the paramedics were working to save her life. Different people act differently when loved ones die, the defense lawyers said. Evaluating someone's reaction to a death was a matter of opinion by the witness. Prior cases had clearly established that such opinions were inappropriate as evidence before a jury. The prosecution should not be allowed to introduce any testimony in which witnesses would be asked to characterize Randy's behavior.

But Sullivan quickly drew a distinction between witnesses' *opinion* of Randy's behavior and mere observations of outward manifestations of Randy's behavior.

In other words, a witness would not be allowed to say that Randy *had* no emotion, only that he did not *display* any emotion. The difference was subtle but distinct.

With that last ruling, Sullivan cleared the way for the trial to begin.

But the defense would take one more shot at keeping the Jan Roth information away from the jurors.

In early February of 1992, Cody and Muenster asked the state's Court of Appeals to decide whether Sullivan's most important decisions on the defense motions were right. The law permitted such pre-trial appeals if it appeared that the Superior Court had made an obvious error that would make a fair trial impossible.

The defense lawyers were convinced that the murder charge against Randy should have been dismissed by Sullivan because there was no overt showing that criminal means had been used to cause Cindy's death, that Sullivan's ruling allowing the testimony about Jan Roth was wrong, and that testimony about the fake burglary was likewise admissible.

In mid-Feburary, two weeks before the jury was to be selected, the appeals court rejected those arguments. There was no obvious or even probable error in Sullivan's rulings, the court's commissioner held. Besides, Randy could still appeal after the trial was over and the actual record was established.

As they walked out of the Court of Appeals, it was clear to Brenneman, at least, that the prosecution now had a very good chance of winning a conviction. She turned to Muenster.

"Why don't you talk to your client, John?" she suggested. Brenneman was suggesting that Randy might avoid a harsher sentence by entering a guilty plea. Muenster indicated that the defense might be interested in a deal to avoid trial and said he would talk to Cody.

But neither defense lawyer later called, and Brenneman formed the impression that even if Randy's lawyers advised him to make a deal, Randy himself would never go for it. *He still thinks he can get away with it*, Brenneman thought. The trial would go forward.

# 46

## "A Bad, Bad Time for Anybody"

**"H**e married for greed, not for love or companionship. And he murdered for money, not for hate or fear or even passion. This man stole to feed his hunger for money. Nine separate times in the past ten years, this defendant has either committed or schemed to commit insurance fraud."

With those words, deputy prosecutor Susan Storey opened the case against Randy Roth on March 10, 1992.

After nearly five months in jail, Randy seemed to have lost a considerable amount of weight. He sat impassively at the defense lawyers' table, his mustache neat, pale from incarceration, dressed in a conservative suit, wearing his thick glasses. All in all, on the surface he hardly appeared to be the type of man who would have murdered two wives. He fiddled with a yellow legal pad as Storey outlined the evidence the state intended to present.

Storey's opening statement lasted naerly seventy-five minutes as she took the jury through the events of Randy's life, starting with his marriage to Cindy and the insurance policies, the events at the lake, then going back to his earlier marriage to Jan and her death, the subsequent marriage to Donna Clift, the courtship of Mary Jo Phillips, the seduction of the Goodwins' daughter, and finally, the events after Cindy's drowning.

Three times Storey told the jury that witnesses would say that Randy displayed no emotion as two of his wives were dying. "That, ladies and gentlemen, is but a summary of the evidence you will hear in this case. And as you will see, all of these insurance frauds or schemes to commit insurance fraud point to the defendant's greed, and explain Cynthia Baumgartner Roth's death."

Sullivan called for the regularly scheduled morning recess. As soon as the jury was out of the room, Muenster jumped to his feet and demanded a mistrial based on Storey's opening statement—chiefly, because of Storey's discussion of Randy's demeanor.

"For the record," he said, "the defense would move the court for an order granting a mistrial in this case based upon what I believe was the prosecutor's cold, calculated and premeditated violation of the court's orders . . . to exclude opinion testimony regarding Mr. Roth's demeanor."

The trial was only an hour old, and already the defense was saying the jury was so tainted by improper information that a fair trial was impossible. The mistrial was the first of what ultimately would become more than a dozen such motions by the defense before the trial ended.

Brenneman responded to Muenster by saying that no one had offered any *opinions* about Randy's behavior, only that the evidence would include the witnesses' *observations* of Randy's behavior, not their beliefs about it. Sullivan agreed with Brenneman.

"Physical descriptions of what they observed or did not observe are perfectly appropriate. The motion for a mistrial will be denied."

The jury returned to the courtroom, oblivious of the earlier maneuvering. Now Cody gave the opening statement for the defense, retelling the same facts described by Storey but with a benign interpretation. After saying the state was making too much of a series of perfectly understandable events, Cody went on the attack during his conclusion.

"Now," he said, "the question that will be before you in examining the evidence is . . . Is the state correct in its theory that Randy Roth chose the hottest day of the year, the most crowded time anybody can remember out on Lake Sammamish, the date where there were powerboats and other people all over the place, to suddenly, premeditatedly, drown his wife in a manner that is yet unclear? Or did she die by accident?

"And under the circumstances, did he do what he could to respond to those circumstnaces as they struck him on that day as those events unfolded around him?

"I think the evidence is going to show you, when you listen to all of it, that the physical signs at the autopsy, the evidence at the scene, that any questions you have about how it occurred could [have been] rectified [if the police had] asked Randy exactly what happened. . . .

"It was an accident, a terrible accident, to strike anybody," said Cody. "And when you look at how people respond to death, when they have been through it before, well, it was a bad, bad time for anybody."

# 47

## "I Was Very Glad"

Randy's trial had opened amidst a huge amount of news media coverage. Ever since his press conference in early August, the news people had been waiting for his arrest; now, with the trial underway, the coverage exploded.

At long last, Randy was at the center of the attention Brenneman believed he had always craved. Television stations flooded the courthouse hallway with bright lights whenever he appeared wearing his suit with hands shackled behind him, escorted by two uniformed jail guards. Photographers from the newspapers popped their strobes in his face.

From the news organizations' point of view, the trial of Randy represented exactly the sort of story guaranteed to push ratings and circulation up: a white, neatly groomed, photogenic defendant, accused of coldbloodedly killing two pretty wives a decade apart to cash in on lucrative insurance policies, in the process turning two winsome boys into tragic orphans. It was a real-life made-for-television movie, fraught with opportunities for dramatic visuals.

As the boundary between drama and reality thus

blurred, the case of *State v. Roth* began to assume the dimensions of a modern morality play, thirty seconds of good versus evil, where gray subtleties of character were washed out in the harsher light of the nightly news summaries, in which the worst that Randy had ever done was the order of the day.

In Washington State, trials may be televised. To exert some control over the circus, Sullivan permitted only a single video camera in the courtroom, which provided a feed to a monitor set up in the hallway outside. Each television station recorded the feed and edited it for later rebroadcast.

As a result, Seattleites would get a near-daily dose of Randy's trial for almost seven weeks—usually, encapsulations of the day's most sensational testimony, pared down to a handful of pithy seconds, backed by a standup summary from the on-camera reporter. However else he might feel about what was happening, at least Randy was the star of the show.

To protect both witnesses and jurors from the media, Brenneman and the defense agreed that their home addresses and telephone numbers would be kept secret. Additionally, Brenneman and Storey asked each witness whether they objected to being photographed while in the courtroom; if witnesses did object, Brenneman so informed the news people, who then removed the witness' face from their broadcast tapes. The same procedure was followed for the seven-woman, five-man jury.

Organizing a trial expected to last for weeks, with more than one hundred witnesses and well over two hundred exhibits, obviously represented a logistical challenge. Brenneman and Storey had to estimate how long each witness might testify and make sure that the right witnesses appeared on the right day. It was a constant juggling act, made more uncertain by the difficulty of determining how long the defense might wish to cross-examine the witnesses. Brenneman and

Storey moved to a temporary office in the courthouse with all their files and kept in near-constant contact with Peters and Mullinax, along with a paralegal and a victim/witness advocate, all of whom worked diligently to keep the witness list up-to-date. Meanwhile, both detectives continued following up leads even while the trial was underway.

Brenneman's plan for the trial, despite the dimensions involved, was relatively simple. She wanted to establish the identity of the victims on the first day in order to acquaint the jury with what the trial was really all about.

Then, over the next five weeks, Brenneman would summon witnesses in near-chronological fashion, telling the story of Randy and his life in clear, almost visual terms. Presenting such a case was, she thought, somewhat akin to directing a movie, with the witnesses as the actors.

On the first day, for example, Brenneman called Hazel Loucks as a witness; she wanted Cindy's mother to identify Cindy from her photograph, as well as to describe Cindy's relationship with Randy. That way, Brenneman thought, the jury would know from the outset that there was a real person who had been murdered. She did the same with Louise Mitchell, Jan Roth's best friend.

Then Brenneman began calling witnesses who had been at Beacon Rock on the day Jan was killed, starting with Shelly and Steve Anderson, the couple who had encountered a "crazy" Randy in the minutes immediately after Jan's death.

Virtually all of the first two days were taken up with testimony of the Beacon Rock witnesses, including the rescue worker Bill Wylie and others who had looked for Jan's body. The next day, Brenneman took the testimony of former undersheriff, now Sheriff Ray

Blaisdale, followed by two critical witnesses: Jalina
Miranda and Jan's mother, Billie Ray.

Thus, by the end of the week, as Tim Brocato was
taking the stand, Brenneman had been able to establish the contradictory facts about Randy's story of
Jan's death, the insurance policy and Randy's surprising call to the insurance agent the day after Jan died,
Randy's apparent heartlessness in taking the envelope
from Jalina, and Jan's second thoughts about the marriage to Randy.

By showing that Randy *could* have murdered Jan—
indeed, that he had a motive to murder—Brenneman
and Storey hoped to lead the jury to the conclusion
that Randy had similarly killed Cindy, that he had a
track record for just such a thing.

As Peters and Mullinax had foreseen, Tim Brocato
emerged as one of the key witnesses against Randy.
Brocato was on the stand for two days. He seemed
nervous and soft-spoken the first day, particularly
when it came time to admit that he had committed a
crime with Randy.

But Brocato stuck to his story and was particularly
devastating to Randy in recounting the Halloween
night conversation he'd had with Randy about whether
he could kill his wife and in telling about his talk with
Jan on the weekend before the trip to Washougal, the
time when Jan told him about her dream that she was
going to die.

While Brenneman's objective was to get the evidence of the witnesses before the jury in a chronological fashion in order to show the scope of Randy's
decade-long activities, the defense goal was to mitigate
as much as possible the more damaging testimony.

This was a difficult maneuver, in that most of the
witnesses summoned by Brenneman were ordinary
people, well-intentioned, and certainly not imbued
with any desire to even an old score with Randy.

Attacking that type of witness on cross-examination was dangerous; the jury might perceive the defense as being unfair to people who were, for the most part, just like them.

The defense strategy thus required close examination of the witnesses' testimony in an effort to develop alternative, more innocent interpretations of the events. On cross-examination, the witness had to be asked to retell the story that had just been given to Brenneman, but with an eye toward inducing, as gently as possible, admissions from the witness that he or she might have been mistaken about certain facts, or that they might have reached unwarranted conclusions.

If uncertainty could thus be introduced, so possibly could reasonable doubt; but the downside of the strategy was that it allowed the witness to reiterate the salient facts all over again, which had the effect of reinforcing them in the jurors' minds.

Worse, on some occasions, the defense lawyers inadvertently stumbled into areas they would rather have avoided.

In cross-examining Hazel Loucks, for example—an area fraught with potential for irritating the jury, if the questioning was seen as too harsh—Cody tried to have Hazel acknowledge that Randy had been "fairly emotional" about Cindy's death while visiting the Loucks the day after the police had interviewed him on August 1.

"You indicated that at some point he did get fairly emotional about this whole situation; is that right?" Cody asked.

"Not real emotional," Hazel said. "Maybe a couple of tears." In trying to get Cindy's mother to confirm that Randy was a caring person, Cody had instead obtained testimony that showed Randy in the opposite light.

And Cody's question gave Brenneman a chance to

next ask Hazel why Randy had been driving around all night before he came to visit.

"Well, yeah, he did talk about that," Hazel testified. "For just dodging the police." Thus, Brenneman was able to use Cody's own question to bring out a new item of suspicious behavior on the part of Randy.

Later, in questioning Tim Brocato, Cody tried to suggest that Tim was lying when he testified that he had repaid Randy the money he owed him because he was afraid of Randy.

"Let me get this straight, Mr. Brocato," Cody said. "You hadn't had any contact with Randy Roth in at least a year going back to 1991. You called him up out of the blue. You had been remarried by that time to another person. You called him up out of the blue, said you wanted to get together with him and pay him some money, and that was done because all of a sudden, you got up that morning *afraid?*"

"No," Brocato said. "I was fearing Randy for years."

All that did, of course, was reinforce the image of Randy as a violent intimidator.

Then Cody, trying to recover, asked Brocato sarcastically, "Were you perhaps in some kind of counseling at that time for these phobias of yours?" Brenneman objected to Cody's argumentative question, but she needn't have bothered, because the jury well understood how Cody had damaged his own case.

Even worse for the defense, this exchange now allowed Brenneman to get into the area of *why* Tim was afraid of Randy—his boasts about his "war record."

"Counsel's questions," she said to Brocato, "suggest you have no reason to be fearful of the defendant. Did you have a reason to be fearful of the defendant?"

"Yes, I did," Tim said.

"What was that reason?"

"There are a few reasons. Do you want them all?"

Brenneman had already told Brocato no questions would be allowed about Randy's military career unless the defense opened the door to the subject. Brenneman believed that Cody had just done so, and wanted to have Tim testify to what he believed about Randy's war record. "Go ahead," she said.

"Randy had told me that I should never turn my back because . . ."

"Go ahead," Brenneman encouraged.

". . . that he would . . . he said you don't—first of all, Randy said that he had killed somebody, okay, in the service."

"Okay," said Brenneman.

"Okay. And also he had talked . . . about his brother."

Too late, Cody realized where Brenneman was headed. Now the jury had reason to believe, based on Tim's testimony, that Randy had killed before he ever met Jan. Additionally, there was this mysterious reference to Randy's brother, which obviously had something to do with violence or killing. Further questions along the same lines were sure to elicit even more damaging information.

"Your Honor, I'm going to object to this," Cody said. And while Sullivan sustained the objection, which had the effect of foreclosing further questions from Brenneman on the subject, there was no way of retrieving the black eye Tim had just given Randy.

Throughout the second week, Brenneman and Storey tried to build up a picture of Randy's life and personality, relying on the testimony of his neighbors Ben and Marta Goodwin, his coworkers, and most telling, the stories of Donna and Judy Clift, and Mary Jo Phillips.

Donna Clift told about finding Jan's ashes in the closet and about the raft trip that had almost ended in disaster.

Asked why she didn't want to ride any further with Randy in the raft, Donna said, simply and directly, "I was afraid of him." Asked why she had divorced Randy—over repeated objections from Muenster—Donna said, "I just was not happy. I just had to get away from him. I didn't feel safe."

Judy Clift gave her version of the raft trip and added that she had told her husband Harvey not to let Randy's raft out of sight.

"Why did you do that?" Storey asked her.

"Because I was afraid my daughter would not come off the trip alive," Judy said.

That question and answer outraged Muenster. Later, during a recess, he once more asked Sullivan to declare a mistrial. The testimony from Judy Clift, he said, far exceeded the rules of evidence because it allowed the jury to improperly hear an opinion about Randy's character.

"I believe that the testimony had the effect of introducing the witness's opinion that the raft trip was a case of an attempt to cause her daughter Donna's death," Muenster said. "And I believe the witness's opinion in that regard is of extreme prejudice in this trial, as the state is alleging that Mr. Roth caused Cynthia Roth's death in Lake Sammamish."

Indeed, said Muenster, much of the testimony that had so far come in was prejudicial to Randy's right to a fair trial.

"I must say that I believe the prior rulings in this case in which this man, while on trial for something that happened in 1991, is being run through the wringer regarding allegations over the past ten years that very few of these people saw fit to complain about until, all of a sudden, he finds himself charged with Cynthia Roth's death.

"And frankly, from their point of view, one wonders how they spent *any* time with him. And yet they all liked him and spent time with him, but miraculously, attitudes have changed.''

Sullivan denied Muenster's mistrial motion. The state, he said, was entitled to have Judy Clift testify as to why she had told her husband not to let the raft out of his sight.

Much of the next few days was taken up with testimony about Randy's 1988 burglary; Brenneman and Storey wanted to establish that Randy had faked the break-in to collect on his insurance. The Goodwins testified about seeing things in Randy's house and garage that had supposedly been taken in the burglary months after the burglary had taken place; even more damaging to Randy, his coworkers testified that he had previously bragged to them about staging the burglary himself.

By the middle of the second week, the prosecutors were up to the relationship between Randy and Cindy. Stacey Reese took the stand and testified about her conversations with Randy before and after Cindy's death; the prosecutors wanted to establish that Randy was eager for Cindy to be out of his life.

Then Stacey told how Randy had invited her to go to Reno with him the week after Cindy's death—on the tickets Cindy had paid for. Cody tried to blunt the effect of Stacey's testimony by suggesting that she had been a police plant and therefore capable of making up stories about Randy. But the more Cody tried to shake Stacey from the details of her story, the more vivid the details became.

Later in the week, Brenneman began to set the stage for the lake witnesses. She called Kristina Baker, the woman at Lake Sammamish who had been watching Randy and Cindy in the raft because she was worried that it might get run over by all the powerboats.

Kristina Baker was the closest to an eyewitness of Cindy's drowning that the prosecution could produce. Brenneman, in fact, had come to believe that when

Kristina Baker saw arms flailing as Cindy swam away from the raft, what she was actually seeing was Cindy waving for help as she tried to get away from Randy.

"Something was going on out there," Brenneman said later. "She didn't want to be near him." Possibly Randy had already tried once to drown Cindy and Cindy was trying to escape. But somehow Randy had convinced Cindy to go back to the raft, and that was when the drowning occurred, Brenneman believed.

Now, at the trial, Brenneman had Kirstina tell her story to the jury. Kristina's version of the events was detailed and seemed to indicate that she had indeed been closely watching the raft for some time.

Most importantly, Kristina said she never saw the raft flip over. Nor, she said, did she ever see Randy motion to any other boats for help. It took Randy, she said, about twenty minutes to row into shore.

To counter this damaging testimony, Cody tried to shake Kristina's insistence that she had watched the raft as closely as she claimed.

Just exactly *when* had she first seen the raft? What direction was it going? Had she really watched it steadily for over an *hour*, as her testimony seemed to indicate? Cody wanted to show that Kristina Baker might not have seen the raft flip over because she wasn't watching it all the time.

But the more Cody tried to find inconsistencies in Kristina's account, the more details emerged to buttress it.

By week's end, the state had reached Randy's actions on the beach. For the next four days, a parade of witnesses came forward to descibe Randy's behavior, including Alicia Tracy, who had marveled at Randy's cool demeanor but then was sick to her stomach over his behavior toward the boys; the paramedic Patti Schultz, who had tried to save Cindy's life, and who then rode to the hospital with Randy, Tyson and Rylie; the Redmond police and firefighters who had taken

Randy's initial statements; and the hospital social worker, D'Vorah Kost, who had believed Randy was uptight and sullen after Cindy's death.

Kost provided more damaging details about Randy's behavior while at the hospital. "Do you remember," Storey asked her, "whether he shed any tears?"

"No," said Kost.

"He definitely did not?"

"I don't remember any tears."

Had she observed Randy trying to comfort Tyson and Rylie after the doctors had pronounced Cindy dead?

"I didn't observe any comforting behavior. I didn't observe any sense of reassurance, or I don't remember any physical contact between the defendant and the boys. It was more like the three of them [were] sort of moving in their own little spaces, not a lot of interaction." Randy's behavior, she said, was unemotional, controlled and constricted.

By the fourth week of testimony, Brenneman and Storey were ready to go into the twin questions of whether the raft had flipped over, and if it hadn't, just how Cindy might have been drowned instead.

To do this, the prosecutors and police had hired two expert witnesses to assist them with two more video-taped reenactments.

The first expert, a man who had once worked as a consultant on drowning deaths to former Los Angeles County Coroner Dr. Thomas Noguchi, testified that the Roth raft—actually, an inflatable boat, the expert pointed out—was designed to maximize its stability even in the open ocean. The raft was like a leaf, he said, bonding to the water as it rode over swells; it was impossible for the raft to have flipped over as Randy maintained.

Nor was it possible for a wave to have hit Cindy in the mouth from fifty to one hundred yards away; by the time the wave arrived, the expert said, it would have been nearly flat and far more likely to have buoyed Cindy higher in the water instead. There was little the defense could do to counteract the first expert's testimony, other than point out that Randy was never very clear in his initial statements about the proximity and direction of the speedboat that supposedly had created the wake.

The second expert was a professor and swimming coach at the University of Oregon. It was very unlikely that a cramp could have caused Cindy to drown by herself, the expert said, at least in the time and under the circumstances as described by Randy. The only way Cindy could have drowned so quickly was if she had panicked, and the most likely explanation for the panic was because someone was holding her under the water.

The expert brought a videotape of an experiment by two students, in which a male student about Randy's size and weight attempted to keep a female student close to Cindy's size and weight under water until panic set in. Cody and Muenster vehemently objected to the introduction of the tape, saying it was a powerful suggestion to the jury that Randy had done the very thing depicted.

While Sullivan ruled that the expert would not be allowed to say that he believed Randy had killed Cindy in that manner, the judge did allow the tape to be played for the jury. The impact of the tape was obvious: it *was* possible that Randy could have drowned Cindy suddenly and without sustaining a scratch to either himself or her.

Brenneman and Storey had saved some of their most powerful testimony for the end of their case. On Thursday, April 2, they called Lori Baker, who told the jury about her conversation with Randy, in which Randy had complained that Lori's claim of the boys had ruined his "scenario" and about the empty safe deposit box. Lori's mother confirmed the scenario statement. Then Brenneman called her two star witnesses—Tyson and Rylie.

Brenneman's motive in calling the two boys was more than just their appeal to the sympathetic instincts of the jury. Granted, the two little boys were spectacular witnesses in terms of their emotional impact. In addition, the boys were capable of providing graphic testimony about what happened on the beach the day their mother died.

But Brenneman also knew that both boys had vital evidence.

Tyson, for example, validated the contents of the sacks that had been in the raft, as well as others' observations about Randy's behavior in the immediate aftermath of the drowning.

But it was Rylie who applied the crusher on Randy. In a way, it was only fitting.

For the better part of a year, Randy had derided and abused Rylie, calling him "dummy," sneering at his piano lessons, generally making life miserable for him, to the point where Rylie tried to spend hours alone in his room to keep away from his new stepfather. Now it was Rylie's turn.

Brenneman, trying to draw on her own experience of raising four boys, tried to reassure Rylie by being warm and supportive. Bit by bit, gently, she took Rylie through his story about the events at the beach.

Rylie responded with vivid descriptions that had the courtroom transfixed and on the edge of tears. Rylie told of seeing his mother lying blue in the bottom of the raft, and Randy's indifferent behavior, then the ride to the hospital.

"When you got to the hospital, where did you go?"

"We went to the . . . I don't know what type of room it was. It was just a room," Rylie said. "Then there was another room. It was really small. And the lady took us and was talking to us. And then the doctor came in and told us that she wasn't alive anymore.''

"Well, what did you and Tyson do when you heard your mother wasn't alive anymore?"

"Cried harder.''

"What did the lady do?"

"She tried to comfort us a little, but there wasn't much she could do.''

"What did the defendant do?"

"He just stood there. Same look. Sat there. Same look on his face. And the detective came in and he was talking to him and he said . . .''

Rylie's voice began trailing off. Brenneman encouraged him. "I need for you to speak up, Rylie.''

"Okay. And he was wearing really dark glasses, sunglasses. And he said, 'I'm not wearing these sunglasses to hide anything from you,' and the detective didn't remark or anything like that.''

Rylie went on to describe the trip home, and Randy's telling him to be quiet. "I tried my hardest," he said, "but—I tried not to be loud, but tears still fell down my face.''

"What did the defendant say then?"

"He said, 'Where do you guys want to go eat?'''

Now Cody committed a serious tactical error. Rylie's testimony had been so devastating that Cody resolved to try to show that Rylie had a motive to be angry with Randy. It was a dangerous gambit and had to be done skillfully so the jury didn't form the impression that Cody was being abusive toward the boy.

After a preliminary question about Rylie's relationship with Greg, Cody turned to the subject of Randy.

"How did you get along with Randy?" he asked.

"Not very well," Rylie said. "Not very well at all.''

Cody asked several other questions that implied Rylie didn't like Randy because he had married Rylie's mother. He also implied that Rylie liked Lori much better than Randy, and that by describing Randy in unfavorable terms, Rylie was trying to please his guardian.

But in Brenneman's mind, Cody's question opened the door to further inquiry as to why Rylie and Randy didn't get along.

"Were there some reasons for that, Rylie?" she asked.

"Yes."

Cody, guessing what was coming, objected. Sullivan sustained the objection, but Brenneman asked to be allowed to argue why she should be allowed to pursue the matter. In the end, despite Cody's objections, Sullivan changed his mind and agreed with Brenneman.

"Rylie," she said, "can you tell us why you didn't get along with the defendant? You can tell us."

"I was afraid of him," Rylie said, and in so saying, echoed Tim Brocato, Donna Clift and a long string of others who had previously testified to their fear of Randy.

"Why were you afraid of him?"

"The things that Greg had told us, the stories and—"

Cody objected again. "Just tell me what you personally observed, Rylie," Brenneman persisted. "What made you afraid of him?"

"Just what I had seen."

"The way he treated you?"

"Yes."

"And the way he treated Tyson?"

"Yes."

"And the way he treated your—"

Cody objected once more. "Your Honor, this is leading [the witness]." It was, Sullivan agreed.

"And what were some of the things that happened that made you afraid?"

Rylie told the story about the boys being made to do squat-thrusts at night in the winter under the hose.

"I never got under the hose," Rylie added, "but Greg and Tyson had."

"And you watched that?"

"Yeah. Well, I didn't watch, because I was looking at the ground, doing mine as fast as I could."

"So you didn't have the hose on you?"

"Because if you did them slow, you would get the hose on you, so I was doing them as fast as I could."

Brenneman now turned to the subject of Lori Baker. "When Lori told you that you could live with her instead of going back to live with the defendant, what was your reaction?"

"I was very excited," Rylie said. "I was very glad."

Brenneman rested her case.

# 48 | Band-Aids

**T**he sheer size and length of the prosecution's case—
Brenneman and Storey had called one hundred and
thirty-one witnesses over nearly four weeks of testimony—presented Randy's defenders with grave problems.

If nothing else, the cumulative weight of all those
testifying against Randy showed *something;* but when
coupled to the oft-expressed negative views of Randy
from so many different people from as long ago as a
decade past, it was clear to Cody and Muenster that
saving Randy would require a major rehabilitative
effort.

The portrait of Randy that had emerged from the
weeks of testimony was that of a cold, calculating,
greedy and boastful liar, a self-absorbed man who was
mean, petty, churlish and often cruel. Somehow the
defenders had to rehumanize Randy, make him seem
a figure to be sympathized with rather than reviled.
But, in comparison with the prosecution's case, the
defense lawyers had woefully little to work with; in
effect, they were being asked to apply Band-Aids to a
patient in desperate need of major surgery.

* * *

In contrast to the state's two busloads of witnesses, the defense had two minivans. In general, Cody and Muenster hoped that Randy's witnesses could create doubt in the minds of the jury about the state witnesses' descriptions of the same events.

One, a man who had been hiking with Steve and Shelly Anderson at Beacon Rock on the day Jan died, gave a slightly different description of Randy's actions and behavior. Randy ran past the hikers, disappeared, and about ten minutes later, ran past them again going in the opposite direction. Ten minutes after that, the witness said, Randy came by again, and this time the Anderson group stopped him to ask him what was wrong.

"He was kind of pale, sweaty, looked like he might have been in shock," the witness said, "and really looked confused." Cody's interest here was in trying to counteract the Andersons' previous testimony that Randy wasn't confused, only "crazy."

Another witness, the owner of a local newspaper in Skamania County, testified about photographs he had taken the day Jan fell. The photographs seemed to indicate that the rescue helicopter was much closer to rescue climber Bill Wylie's rope position than previous testimony had indicated. Cody wanted to undercut Wylie's earlier estimate that Jan had fallen much further away from the place Randy had first told him. Wylie's testimony had been powerful evidence that Randy had lied about how Jan fell, and Cody hoped to introduce doubts about the accuracy of Wylie's recollection.

The following day, Cody put several Little League acquaintances of Randy and Cindy on the stand, who testified that they believed Randy and Cindy got along exceptionally well together.

Randy, they said, was a "superdad," always willing to pitch in and help with the kids. But the prosecutors undercut that testimony by demonstrating that those observations were made in the summer of 1990, when Randy was courting Cindy, not after they were married.

Other witnesses likewise testified about Randy and Cindy, or Randy's behavior at the shop, all as part of a defense effort to depict Randy as far less than the monster the prosecution witnesses had described.

But the differences in perception were over matters so minor and inconsequential that the defense witnesses actually tended to accentuate the earlier negative portrayals; it was almost as if the poverty of Randy's defense was powerful validation of what everyone else had said about him.

The major defense effort was invested in a counter-reenactment of the lake events. Cody and Muenster had hired a local aquatics instructor and pool manager to try to prove that the raft *could* be capsized, given the right conditions. The defense video showed the raft going over as a woman in a wetsuit—it was wintertime, after all—tried to get into the raft.

But on cross-examination, the prosecutors were able to establish that the raft had failed to capsize thirty-seven times as opposed to the four when it had, and that the woman playing Cindy's role was substantially taller and heavier than Cindy—especially wearing the wetsuit. The prosecutors also pointed out that in flipping the raft, the woman playing the role of Cindy had repeatedly grabbed the raft's oarlock to give her the necessary leverage. The oarlock would later come back to haunt Randy in a way no one could have foreseen.

Thus, by the end of a week of defense testimony, it was clear to everyone, as it had been to Cody and Muenster almost from the outset, that the only person capable of saving Randy would be Randy himself.

The defendant would have to take the stand and, by his own testimony, convince the jury that he was nothing like the person so many others said he was, that he was really a kind, generous, open-minded, loving husband and father who was only the pitiable sufferer of two tragedies, and the target of a misguided, vindictive prosecution by the state.

# 49

# Badly Damaged

Cody's major goal in putting Randy on the stand was to show that Randy was a far different person than the way he had been depicted by the state and its witnesses. It was the only reasonable defense under the circumstances, but it was severely handicapped by Randy's own innate personality.

Ideally, the best impression Randy could have made on the jury would have been to burst early and easily into tears about the awful events that had happened.

If Randy had been able to cry and portray himself as a man caught up in a maelstrom of tragedy that was beyond his control, he might have been able to create reasonable doubt in the face of all the circumstantial evidence accumulated by the state.

Better yet, such demeanor would have cast the state in the role of the heavy, the persecutor of a man widowed twice by tragic and unforeseeable circumstances; thereby, in his closing argument, Cody could have effectively appealed to the jury to put themselves in Randy's place: There but for fortune might you have gone instead of Randy.

But Randy apparently wasn't capable of filling that

role. After all, as Donna Sanchez, Donna Clift and numerous others had remarked, Randy *never* cried. Probably, in his own mind, for so long, Randy had been the hardbitten hero, the Billy Jack who was tough, who fought back when challenged, and who never showed a moment's weakness.

Moreover, Randy appeared to have a compulsion to present himself as in control of the situation; it seemed to be so much a part of his adult persona that he could not possibly shed it in a convincing manner. Even in his answers to friendly questioning by Cody, Randy seemed to feel as if he had to appear intellectually sharp and emotionally in command.

His words thus struck most in the audience as formalistic, his demeanor rigid, even slightly condescending. Most pointedly, it left the impression, when Randy was describing what should have been the most emotion-laden moments of his life, that he had practiced his speeches in front of a mirror.

Cody began by having Randy provide some of his vital statistics: his age, his birthplace, his early life in Snohomish County and his work history. Cody quickly took Randy through his marriage to Donna Sanchez, his first acquaintance with Tim Brocato, and meeting Janis at the Parents-Without-Partners dance. Randy described life with Jan as fairly typical of other young marrieds. As for Jan's Pinto, Randy said he only knew that the car had been stolen; if an insurance claim had been put in on it, it would have been Jan's doing, he said.

After more questions and answers about life with Jan, Cody asked Randy about the first trip to Beacon Rock—the one that Randy claimed he and Jan had first taken the shortcut while with Jalina and Greg. Randy said he probably held Greg's hand on the way up the trail; he insisted that they *had* taken the shortcut.

"Now," said Cody, "to get to this shortcut, how

did you identify [it], other than the party ahead of you [that] took this route?"

"Well, this particular section did have railings on both sides, handrailings on both sides of the trail, so we had to actually go through the railing," Randy said. "Some of the people went between the two rails and some people went over the top."

Cody continued, taking Randy rapidly through the other events of his life with Jan, before broaching the subject of the Halloween conversation with Tim Brocato.

"Do you recall the discussion that Mr. Brocato related in which he indicated you talked to him about whether he could under some kind of circumstances kill his wife?"

"I don't recall that conversation having ever taken place, much less on Halloween," Randy said.

Brenneman noted to herself that Randy hadn't actually denied the conversation, only said that he couldn't recall it.

Cody moved up to the events after Thanksgiving at Beacon Rock. Randy said Jan suggested returning to the rock. They walked up the rock, Randy said, and then took the same shortcut they had on the earlier visit. He went over the rail and Jan went under it, he said. They began climbing up the shortcut.

What happened next? Cody asked.

"She stepped down with her left foot and her traction broke away and she fell almost at a forty-five degree angle. Her tracks fell off to the left-hand side and she fell to the left and to the back, but it was basically away from me."

"What happened then?"

"Well, she did what I had earlier mentioned, that she had actually looked like a cartwheel because the first contact she had with the ground was almost on her head and shoulders, and at that point she did another roll similar to that, but as she was falling, she was falling away from me and it was downhill, and at that point she rolled on her side and disappeared over the edge.''

"Did she make any sound?"

"She hollered when she went over."

Brenneman was making notes furiously. *"Her tracks fell off,"* she scribbled. Brenneman thought Randy sounded as if he were describing Jan as some sort of piece of machinery, a malfunctioning tracked vehicle rather than a human being, let alone a wife.

Randy went on to describe his efforts to find a way down to where he thought Jan had fallen. He remembered meeting the Andersons.

"All I can remember saying was, 'Will somebody come up and help me find my wife? She fell,' " Randy said, adding words the Andersons were positive he never said.

After more questions and answers about the rescue effort, Cody raised the subject of Randy's role in identifying Jan's body.

"Well, I can remember not really accepting that she couldn't be helped, that she was dead yet," Randy said as Brenneman continued her notetaking. "So I asked that I be allowed to have access to her to actually see her to be with her."

"And were you allowed to take a look at her?"

"Yes. I don't recall if Sheriff Blaisdale escorted me all the way to the aid truck or whether there was one of the drivers or the paramedics that was with me when I saw her."

"And what did you see?"

"She didn't look as badly damaged as one of the individuals had communciated to me. Her hair was matted down on the side from being bloody, but other than that her face wasn't damaged."

*First, tracks falling off, now "badly damaged,"* Brenneman thought. Randy *was* talking about Jan as if she had been a machine. Brenneman was surprised he hadn't used the word "unit" to describe Jan; as in, "the tracked unit was not as badly damaged." *So cold,* Brenneman thought.

Randy testified for the rest of the day under Cody's open-ended questioning, covering the events at the pizza parlor, how Jalina was told about Jan's fall, the insurance discussions—here Randy likened calling the agent to reporting a car accident—and finally, his conversations with Louise Mitchell about notifying Jan's family.

The rest of Randy's recollection of the events immediately after Jan's death was hazy, with Randy frequently saying he could not recall exactly what had happened. Randy said he didn't recall taking any envelope from Jalina. He didn't recall telling Tim Brocato not to ask any more questions, or saying that he didn't want to have to lie to him. He denied offering to buy the Brocatos' mobile home and denied helping Tim burgle his own house for insurance proceeds.

Randy's first day of testimony created a major media stir. Randy refused to be photographed in the courtroom, and Sullivan upheld his request.

Randy's testimony, Sullivan said, would probably be "the most important hours of his life." If Randy got nervous or distracted because of the camera, he might have been denied a fair trial, Sullivan added. A lawyer for a television station argued against the ban to no avail, and a photographer for a newspaper who somehow failed to get the word snapped a shot of Randy in front of the now-infamous raft, leading Sullivan to threaten the paper with contempt if it published the photo.

But Randy's choice of words in describing Jan's death had caught more than the attention of just Brenneman. One newspaper reported Randy's remarks about Jan's cartwheeling and hollering, and quoted his observation that she had not looked "badly damaged." Both remarks added to the public impression of Randy as a cold, almost robotic personality.

The same paper hunted up Lizabeth, who said that Randy had been raised by his father not to show emotion. "The prosecutors are presenting him as cold-hearted and cruel, but he's not," Lizabeth said.

The following day, a Friday, Cody resumed his questioning of Randy. Randy described his marriage to Donna Clift and the incident over Jan's ashes.

"She didn't understand why I would have continued to keep it all the years and not have done something with it, with the box, and she didn't feel that it was proper that I would continue to keep it now that I was remarried," Randy said. "She didn't seem to understand that I was unwilling or unable to deal with finding a proper way to dispose of it, as she referred to it."

Randy said he put the box with Jan's ashes in the attic and told Donna a fib about what he had done with them.

Later, Randy testified that the problem with the ashes was one reason his marriage with Donna Clift had broken up.

"There always seemed to be some sort of a gray cloud hanging over us about the remains that she had discovered of Janis," Randy said. "She had strong feelings about that, and I believed that she had carried them over. I was still in an emotional state that I really couldn't explain or understand at that point on how I was going to deal with it and the fact that I wasn't allowed to be able to explain why I couldn't part with those, and she had demanded that I not have them in the house, so I think that probably stayed with the both of us the entire time."

Also, Randy said, he once saw Donna socializing with some people he didn't know. He later discovered that the people were planning a marijuana party that Donna intended to go to. Randy said he confronted Donna about this, and Donna acted "a little different."

"When I say different, she was acting different than I had normally seen her acting while we were together. I asked her who the people were that she was down there with, and she informed me that I didn't need to control every aspect of her life and there was some socializing that I shouldn't be restricting her from, and as long as it didn't bother our home life, I should let her do what she was doing because it wasn't hurting me."

Randy gave his version of the raft trip with Donna, Harvey and Judy, saying that Donna had become hysterical for no reason.

Later in the afternoon, Cody began an interminable discussion with Randy over the tools he owned.

While Cody wanted to establish that Randy owned a large set of tools which he often used at home—in order to undercut the insurance fraud count relating to the faked burglary—one effect of the tool discussion was that for the first time Randy seemed animated during his testimony. For many in the courtroom, it appeared that Randy was far more in love with his tools than any of his wives; he spoke lovingly of screwdrivers, socket wrenches, pliers, chainsaws and other tools.

As for the burglary, in lengthy testimony Randy asserted that the burglary was real, and that his dog Jackson had in fact been drugged the night it took place.

Next, Cody turned to the subject of Mary Jo Phillips. Randy described meeting Mary Jo at the grocery store and later dating her. Soon Cody had him discussing Mary Jo's decision to move in with Randy and Greg.

"It was at a point when I arrived at her house with

my truck and trailer to move her stuff that I discovered she had three more children,'' Randy said. ''She had two girls and another son from another father, and she also had a very large bird collection. She had, I don't remember how many cages, but there was over one hundred birds, finches and canaries.''

''And you moved all of that over to your house?''

''I was apprehensive at that point because this was something—it took me kind of by shock at this point, but we were extremely compatible so I decided that I would be able to make a compromise and somehow find a way to make it work.'' Randy seemed to be trying to imply that Mary Jo was a bit flakey.

Later, Randy returned to the subject of Jan's ashes once more, this time asserting that Mary Jo too had found the box in a closet. But Mary Jo had thrown them out with some trash, Randy said. ''I was very upset about that,'' he added.

Near the end of the day, Cody had Randy describe his Little League activities in an effort to portray Randy as a community-minded person and a devoted father.

But the testimony dragged on and on, and in the end, Randy's stiff responses to Cody's questions robbed the whole subject of any mitigating value. In short, Randy seemed more like a self-important bore than a helpful molder of growing chidren. On that note, Sullivan recessed the trial for the weekend. Randy would return to the stand the following Monday to discuss the most important question: just how his fourth wife, the woman insured for $385,000, had come to drown in Lake Sammamish.

# 50

## "Sick to My Stomach"

Cody wasn't happy with the first two days of testimony from his client. He knew that Randy wasn't winning any hearts and minds. Randy's stiffness, his seeming effort to sound authoritative, his use of words more suited to writing than speaking, all was working against him. It was hard to have sympathy for someone who talked about his wives' deaths as if he were reciting a technical manual for motor overhaul.

But there was nothing for it, Cody thought, but to plow on and hope that the jury understood that this was just the type of personality Randy really was, and that it didn't mean he was a murderer.

After more discussion about Little League when testimony resumed on Monday morning, Cody finally took up the subject of Cindy's death. He began by asking Randy about the water conditions on the lake and then led into the events around the raft and the swimming. Randy said he guessed they might have been twenty or thirty feet from the raft when they decided to climb back in.

"She started back to the raft," Cody said. "Did she actually get back to the side of the raft?"

"Yes, she did. She would have gotten back to the raft," Randy said. "And her initial contact with the raft, she reached up and hung onto the oarlock on the back and to the rope. The rope just had a little bit of slack in it, so it doesn't support your weight out of, your face out of the water very well. She had to use the oarlock, holding onto it, for a previous weekend when we were in the river, for stability, because the both of us just had to sit up against the pontoons because of the number of people we had in the raft."

Cody was taken aback by Randy's remark about the oarlock but tried not to show it. This was the first time Randy had mentioned *that*. In all of his previous statements, Randy said that Cindy had been hanging onto the rope when the accident occurred.

*Why did he say that?* Cody wondered to himself. It must have been all the videotapes of the reenactments, which showed clearly that the best way to capsize the raft was by grabbing the oarlock. Somehow the idea was planted in Randy's mind. *We're gonna be in trouble over that during cross-examination,* Cody thought.

He tried to work through Randy's remark, paper it over by giving him some room to explain that he hadn't mentioned the oarlock originally because he hadn't actually *seen* Cindy grab it, he was just inferring that she had.

Cody showed Randy a drawing of the raft and asked him what it was.

"The picture on the front would be a diagram of the particular raft that we had at the lake that day."

"And you indicated that you had the oars in oarlocks closest to the bow?"

"Yes, they would have been on the forward oarlocks. And they have some rubber grommets that you slide on over the oars, handles, to hold them in the oarlocks so they don't fall out when you take your hands off them."

"Were there actually oarlocks in the back part of the raft where there are oarlocks shown in that photograph?"

"I'm pretty sure I remember there being four oarlocks in my raft."

"When you said that she went back toward the side of the raft, would you describe again how she first took hold of the raft as she approached the side?"

"Well, her initial contact would have been to hold on. That is the most predominant thing on the raft is the oarlock. And she grabbed the oarlock with one of her hands and held onto the rope with the other one." Randy was persisting in saying he actually *saw* Cindy grab the oarlock. Cody tried again to get Randy off the hook.

"Which oarlock are we speaking of: the one that's in the front with the oar in it or the one in the back?"

"Well, if in fact I had four of them in there, and I believe I did have four in the raft—it's not here to look at, but I think I had four of them in there—it would have been the back one. I wasn't, didn't have a reason to really think about what she was doing. I just remember her holding one hand higher than the other, and what she would have been grabbing would be the oarlock." Randy seemed to be waking up to the danger. He was now using the conditional tense, "what she would have" grabbed.

"And at that point, what did she do? She grabbed hold of the raft as you described. What did she do?"

"She reached the raft before I did. She was about ten feet closer than I was in the water. And as soon as she made contact with the raft, she tried to pull herself up into it. And we, neither one of us, had ever gotten into the raft in deep water, and the raft seemed unstable. It kept bobbing up on the side.

"So when I finally reached the side of it, I told her it didn't look like she was going to climb in there, that

I would swim around to the, on the other side and hold it down so that she could climb in.''

"Now did she seem to be, as far as you could see, able to use her legs to assist her in getting up on the side, or did you make any observation of that kind?''

"I didn't pay attention to her legs in the water, but she told me that she wasn't able to use her leg to kick with. I didn't know what fashion, I didn't know where the cramp was, whether it was in her, a cramp in her foot or upper leg. I just knew she had a cramp and she wanted to get out of the water.''

"So you came to the area of the raft where she was located, told her that you would go around and hold the other side. Is that what you proceeded to do?''

"Yes, I did. I—she was still holding onto the side at that point. I don't know what her grip was on the side of the raft, whether she had an arm inside or still on the rope or still on the oarlock. All I know is she had one hand higher than the other.'' Randy appeared to have gotten it now.

"Had she actually been trying to pull herself up and in?''

"She was continuing to bob on it, trying to be ready so when I got to the other side she could pull herself immediately into it.''

"And what did you do then?''

"I started swimming around the same side of the raft towards the front so I could go to the opposite side and stabilize it.''

"And how far around the raft did you actually get?''

"On that particular diagram there that the detective drew, I would have been in that position where the X is indicating myself at the bow. I was just short of being at the actual bow itself.''

"You're talking about this X that's marked next to the word 'bow'?''

"Yes.''

"And is this a reasonably accurate representation of where Cindy had been when you last saw her?"

"Yes, that was the end that she was hanging onto. She was climbing in that end, because the oar was in the other oarlock and it would have been hanging on the side, and that's the end of the boat that she was riding in, so she was attempting to climb in to the same end that she had exited from."

"And as you approached the bow of the raft, were you facing her so you could look back and see what she was doing, or were you facing in some other direction?"

"No, my back was towards her. I was facing away from her, swimming away from where she was at on my way to the, on the other side. So I wouldn't have been able to make visual contact until I actually turned and was up high enough to look at her or was on the other side and had pulled myself up to see her, because when you're in the water on the raft, you either have to pull yourself up to the side of the raft or you actually float in the water where your head is at the same level as the raft pontoons." So Randy hadn't been looking at Cindy just before the accident, that's why he hadn't said anything about the oarlock originally. Cody hoped that would protect Randy when Brenneman's onslaught about the oarlock came.

Cody continued to take Randy through his story about the events on the lake, trying to show that Randy *had* been able to both get Cindy into the raft and gather up all the sacks before they sank. He *had* tried to give Cindy two rescue breaths, but wasn't able to get any air into her.

"Now when you put on your glasses, you were there in the raft, what else did you see or what generally did you observe when you tried to figure out what was going on around you?"

"I observed the boat activity that we had observed

earlier, but the predominant feature in my mind was the three lifeguard towers on the beach. And I focused my attention on the lifeguard tower and just paddled there. I didn't look at anything anywhere else other than directly straight ahead to that lifeguard tower.''

"How long do you think it took to get to the beach?"

"I have no way of knowing how long it took. When I started rowing, all I had in my mind was that it would only take a few minutes, just a few minutes, just a few minutes to get to that lifeguard.''

"And what did you do when you got to the beach?''

"I was turned around facing the beach, facing the guy who came down to the beach and met me when I hit the sand. I grabbed hold of Tyson and said, 'Run over to the lifeguard as quick as you can without creating any panic so everybody comes down here and gets in the way. Tell the lifeguard we have an emergency over here.' And he ran.

"I stayed with Cynthia in the raft. And Rylie and Tyson ran to the lifeguard and attempted to get some help from him. And he came back to me running and said the lifeguard can't leave his chair. And at that time I started standing up. I was going to holler at him. And in the meantime, the lifeguard must hvae changed position or somebody else saw something, but he came running to me before I actually came running back to him.''

"What happened then?''

"The lady, the lifeguard, started working on her giving her mouth-to-mouth. A lady paramedic came running through the crowd, and identified herself as being an off-duty paramedic, and she worked with the lifeguard. I don't remember which one was doing which part of the resuscitation on her, but they both started working on her at that point. I stayed at her feet. And I lost track of where the boys were at. I was aware of a crowd that was growing around us, but I assumed they had been absorbed in it. I was focused primarily on Cindy.''

''Was she conscious? Did she ever seem to stir?''

''She was unconscious. They were able to get water out of her. Once they were able to begin resuscitation on the beach surface, they were able to start getting water out of her. So I had in my mind they were going to be able to help her.''

''And how long did they continue CPR before anybody else arrived, do you know?''

''I don't have any idea. I had stayed with her until they started pushing very hard on her stomach area and started getting goop to come out of her. And it was at that point I left her and went over past the boys and went to the raft and sat on the edge of the raft and watched from there. And sometime very shortly after that, I don't remember if it was a red and white truck or yellow and white truck came from either Redmond or someplace like that. A medic truck came down. They interrupted people and started working on her.''

''What did you do? Did you stay and watch? Did you talk to somebody?''

''I felt sick to my stomach at that point, so I pulled all the air vents out of the raft. And I knew I wanted to be ready to go as soon as they were. The truck had got finished doing whatever they had to do. They were working on her and putting her into the aid truck.

''I wanted to be ready to go as soon as they were ready to go to the hospital, so I deflated the raft and rolled it up, put the wet items I had pulled out of the sacks into the plastic sack. And there was another lady there that was helping me gather things and put them in the sacks, helped me roll up the raft.

''At that point, when that was done, I went back over to the paramedics who were working on Cindy, and I continued to stand there until someone directed somebody else to take me to the side and get some information as to who she was.''

\* \* \*

As the afternoon wore on, Cody tried to cover with Randy all of the allegations raised against him—both the crimes that were charged, as well as the situations which, if not crimes, tended to show Randy in a bad light.

He and the boys were tired and emotionally upset after the events at the lake, Randy said, and that's why he hadn't called anybody about Cindy's death. He was upset when he was left alone in the house because he knew he couldn't afford the payments by himself without the boys' Social Security, and he didn't want to ruin his credit.

It was true that he applied for Social Security benefits from Cindy's death for Greg, but that was at the suggestion of the Social Security people. If there were misstatements on the Social Security application, it was the fault of the Social Security people, not him, Randy insisted; besides, he hadn't actually received any of the money before he was arrested.

He had *not* invited Stacey Reese to go to Reno with him; instead he had only offered her the tickets to use, since he wouldn't be going himself.

And if there was confusion on the part of the detectives about what he had told them about Cindy's drowning, he said, it was because the police simply had failed to ask the right questions.

But one question that Cody did not ask that day was whether Randy had killed either of his wives. As the end of the afternoon approached, Brenneman's turn to question Randy was drawing ever closer, and from then on, there would be no place to hide.

# 51  On the Cross

"**M**r. Roth, have we heard the *final* version of what happened to your wife, Cynthia, on the day she drowned?" Marilyn Brenneman asked, the sarcasm in her voice obvious.

"You have, you have heard the version as specifically asked for," Randy stammered.

Well, said Brenneman, did Randy remember the written statement he had given to the Redmond Police detective, Larry Conrad, on the day Cindy died? Yes, Randy said, he remembered.

"Mr. Roth, is there any place in that written statement where you *ever* say that Cynthia Roth, your wife, had hold of the oarlocks?"

"No, I don't believe that the detective questioned me for, specifically as to—"

Brenneman interrupted. "You were given the opportunity to write your own statement, weren't you?"

Yes, Randy agreed. "Did you ever use the word 'oarlock,' yes or no?" Brenneman asked. Randy said he hadn't.

Did Randy mention the oarlocks to the medical examiner's office? Randy said he couldn't recall. Did he tell Sue Peters about the oarlock over the telephone in the first interview, on July 29?

"No," Randy said. He tried to put the responsibility on Peters. "They were asking the question in general in relationship to her position on the side of the raft," he said.

Well, did he tell Peters and Mullinax during the long interview two days later that Cindy had been holding on to the oarlock?

"No, I did not, but the reason for that would be—"

"You didn't?"

"—they were general, they were [asking] general questions."

What about during his press conference on August 9? Did he use the word "oarlock" then?

Having watched the videotape of the press conference played before the jury earlier, Randy knew he hadn't said anything about oarlocks, and that in fact he had said then that Cindy was holding on to the raft's rope when the incident took place.

"In fact, isn't it true, the *only* thing you ever said specifically up until the time you testified in front of this jury was that your wife Cynthia was holding onto the *rope* on the side of the raft when the boat went by that caused it to flip?"

"No," said Randy. "There are a couple different statements that were taken, and the general reference was either to the side of the raft or to the rope."

"You never once mentioned the word 'oarlock' until you took the stand in your own defense in this trial," Brenneman said.

Randy fumbled to explain. "At this particular time, in this questioning, this is the first opportunity that I have had to address that specifically as it was questioned," he said. Brenneman again thought Randy's attempt to sound authoritative was making him only seem stiff and badly rehearsed. That's what she wanted.

Well, said Brenneman, he'd been present throughout the trial as witnesses testified, hadn't he? And he'd watched as his own expert witness had shown in a videotape how it was possible to flip the raft by pulling on the oarlock, wasn't that true? He'd had a chance to prepare his testimony after seeing all that, right?

"In a manner of speaking," Randy said.

"And *only* after you watched [the defense expert] testify, *only* after you had an opportunity to watch the video presentation given by him, where the young woman was able to flip the raft by holding onto the oarlocks, only *then* did you mention the word 'oarlock' in describing what Cynthia was holding onto in that raft. Isn't that accurate?"

"No," said Randy. "No one has asked me specifically until this point in time."

Done well, the art of cross-examination requires a lawyer to have an iron grip on the facts of the case, an agile ability to recall the testimony that has just been given—particularly where it differs from previous testimony—and a good "third ear" to take advantage of slips of the tongue or unhappy phrasing by the person being cross-examined.

Speed is an essential weapon of the cross-examining lawyer. Quickly following one question with another demonstrates to a jury that the cross-examiner is supremely confident of her version of the facts. It also gives no respite to the witness, no time to think of possible alternative answers, thus leading to a greater likelihood of unexpected admissions. Being pounded by a rapid drumbeat of hostile questions can rattle even the most sophisticated witness, even those telling the truth.

A second major tool of cross-examination is the abrupt change of subject. Hopping quickly from one topic to another reduces the ability of the witness to anticipate questions and increases the likelihood of unrehearsed statements.

By the rules of evidence, cross-examination is generally limited only to matters testified about on direct examination, as well as matters relating to a witness' credibility. But that disadvantage is often more than outweighed by the cross-examiner's right to ask questions predicated on previous statements, often called leading questions.

Randy had been on the witness stand for nearly two days answering questions from his own attorney, Cody. As a result, by that Monday afternoon Brenneman had a wealth of material to use to probe both Randy's testimony and his truthfulness.

But even more important, Brenneman had been hearing and thinking about Randy Roth for nearly eight months. She believed she understood his personality. Mostly, she was sure she could get under his skin.

"I had a game plan," she said later. "I wanted to keep him in front of the jury long enough for the jury to get to know him, to see how he reacted to me, and how he reacted to stress."

Randy, Brenneman thought, was a man who did not like women. Most of all, he did not like women who had authority *over him*. And what was cross-examination, if not authority? Where else is someone locked in place, unable to move, to escape, literally forced to respond to every question, no matter how tiresome or excruciating or odious?

For the first time in his adult life, Randy would be under the power of a woman impervious to his implied threats, beyond his belittlement and sarcasm. It was a page out of Randy's childhood, when he'd been disciplined by being made to stay on his knees in the kitchen, under the domination of his mother.

Moreover, like Lizabeth in the kitchen, Brenneman had the advantage of being free to move around the courtroom, whereas Randy was stuck in the witness chair; when questioning Randy, Brenneman consciously moved toward him, advancing on him, threatening his space, as if he were pinned in the corner on his knees.

But by the time Randy began to answer her question, Brenneman would have her back turned to him, moving away, already discounting his response in her own visual body language. It was calculated to drive Randy, a man who had to have control, completely nuts. And it ultimately did.

Just as Cody had Randy go over all the points of testimony raised by the state's one hundred thirty-one witnesses, now Brenneman intended to do the same with Randy's version of the same events.

Normally, lawyers don't like to give witnesses the opportunity to repeat lies. But in Randy's case, Brenneman decided the opposite tack would be far more beneficial.

"A cardinal rule of cross-examination is to prevent a witness from repeating his lies," Brenneman said afterward.

"I decided to break it. I wanted Randy to keep repeating his transparent and unbelievable excuses for the things that had happened to his wives. He was happy to oblige, even embellishing his direct testimony with even *more* unbelievable details."

In short, Brenneman intended to put most of Randy's adult life on trial, make him defend himself, and give him every opportunity to expand his earlier testimony, so that the jury could see him for what he was.

But this would be no *This Is Your Life*, because Brenneman had not the slightest intention to proceed in chronological order. Indeed, she intended to deal her questions like a professional cardsharp in order to keep Randy off-balance.

* * *

Altogether, Randy was on the witness stand six days, including the two of direct testimony under Cody's questioning. Anyone who has ever been on a witness stand knows that even one full day of testimony can be exhausting. Six is torture.

Brenneman, in fact, was worried that the jury might begin to feel sympathy for Randy under her hammering. She kept glancing at the jurors with her peripheral vision, trying to judge whether the jurors thought she was pouring it on, going too far. But never once in the six days did Brenneman pick up signals that the jury felt she was being unfair to Randy.

So Brenneman continued to use all the verbal tricks at her command: sarcasm, obvious disbelief, repetition of Randy's own words, anything and everything to break down Randy's wall of denial and what she believed was his deceit.

Randy battled back. *Good,* thought Brenneman. *The more he fights with me, the more of his personality comes out for the jury to see.* Where Randy tended under Cody's questions to be calm and even, in responding to Brenneman, Randy's defenses rose. He fenced with Brenneman over words, dodging and weaving, occasionally attacking, trying to slip her punches with verbal tricks. It was a game he could not win.

Brenneman concentrated on areas where she was sure she could demonstrate to the jury that Randy was lying. Thus, one area that became a battle was over the lease-option of the house Randy lived in when he first met Jan—after all, he had told Jan he *owned* the house, which was one of the main reasons Jan had married him.

"So in fact, there was no real agreement that you were renting that home with a purchase option?" Brenneman asked.

"There was no contract, as I stated earlier."

"Merely casual conversation?"

"Yes."

"On that basis, you led Jan Miranda to believe you owned that house?"

"I did no such thing."

"She *didn't* think you owned the home?" Brenneman's tone implied incredulity.

"I don't know what she thought," Randy said.

Over the first two days, Brenneman made Randy go over and over his relationship with Jan and the events at Beacon Rock. She scored a telling point against Randy over his previous testimony about the railings on the Beacon Rock trail the first time he, Jan, Jalina and Greg had been to the rock.

"Now, you indicate that you needed to go through the railing to get onto the shortcut," Brenneman said. "How did you get through the railing?"

"Well," said Randy, "some of the people went over the top railing, because it's fairly low, and some people went between the top and second railing. I believe I probably climbed over the top of it."

"And what did Jan do?"

"I believe she more than likely would have gone between the two rails." That was what Randy had also told Cody only two days earlier.

But later, after more questions, Brenneman suddenly veered back to the railing issue. She showed Randy a picture of the shortcut.

"You would agree with me, would you not, in looking at the picture, Mr. Roth, that there is no necessity for going under a rail or over a rail to get to the shortcut you say you and Jan were taking when she fell to her death?" Brenneman was absolutely right: the photograph showed there was no railing whatsoever.

Randy stuttered for a minute, trying to reconcile the photographic evidence with his previous testimony.

"This, this would not indicate, this doesn't show

where the main trail would be or whether, where the shortcut would have been," he said. "This, if this were in fact the same spot, it would not be necessary to go through a railing. Here you could walk straight onto the shortcut. It's unclear to me where the shortcut would actually be on this particular portion."

Brenneman kept pressing the issue, and Randy said he couldn't be sure that the photographs represented the area where he and Jan actually had been on the day of her death. But with the testimony of rescue worker Wylie, the Skamania County sheriff's deputies, and even Randy himself earlier, Randy's protestations sounded obstructionistic and weakly evasive. If there never had been a railing at the shortcut, that meant Randy was almost certainly making up the whole story of Jan's death, a fact certainly not lost on the jury.

As Brenneman's cross-examination continued, she paid particular attention to Randy's choice of words, especially those used during his own direct testimony to Cody. She believed that Randy's language was so extraordinary a clue to his inner nature that the jury deserved to hear it several times.

One of Randy's most unhappy phrasings had been "badly damaged," in connection with Jan's fall.

"Your indication that she didn't look as 'badly damaged' as someone had indicated reflects that someone had told you she wasn't looking real good," Brenneman suggested.

"Yes, but I don't remember who that might have been, if I had the conversation, or if they would have been actually talking to someone else and I overheard it."

"And you found yourself surprised that her face wasn't more damaged?"

"Yes, considering that she had fallen off the side of the rock," Randy said.

"And the reason that you insisted on having the opportunity to look at Jan was to make sure she was dead; is that fair?"

"That's not fair."

"Well, you indicated that you wanted to look at her just to make sure she was dead, beyond help, is how you put it."

"I don't believe that I used the terminology, dead beyond help. It was my interest in verifying the fact that she was still not alive."

"You needed to verify that she was still not alive?"

"Yes."

Brenneman paused to let that implication sink in.

Brenneman also scored heavily against Randy with the "Randy hates" letter. She used Randy's own admission that he had discussed his "differences" with Cindy with Stacey Reese.

"Would you tell us about some of those differences?" Brenneman asked.

"Well, it seemed—"

"Your Honor, I'm going to object to this line of questioning," Cody said, attempting to head off inquiry into this perilous area. "As indicated, I'm sure that everybody who has been married has had differences of one kind or another, and I don't think that is, in and of itself, relevant to this case."

"I think it's quite relevant," said Sullivan. A better wake-up call to the jury could not have been delivered by Brenneman herself. "Overruled."

Randy tried again for the high ground and only succeeded in looking stiff once more.

"Our individual differences would have involved specifically the way she might have handled the boys or the things that she would have been involved in, activities, versus the way that I would have lived as a single male parent," he said.

Brenneman asked Randy what other differences he

had with Cindy. Randy said he had disagreed with Cindy on several mundane matters. Well, said Brenneman, wasn't it true that Cindy had been mad at Randy about his joining the weight-lifting club? Randy admitted Cindy had been unhappy with him about that. Did he ever disable her car? Brenneman asked. No, Randy said. The car had mechanical problems, that's all. He had fixed it.

"Did you and Cynthia have arguments about other things than the things you have talked about?"

"I don't recall. I wouldn't even call those arguments. They were differences of individual opinions. I don't recall anything other than that."

Now Brenneman, having established that Randy was claiming he and Cindy got along well, was ready to spring the trap.

"Do you recall telling Cynthia that you hated her makeup, her blush, her lipstick, her blond hair and her perfumes?" Brenneman asked.

"No. There might have been one incident where she wore a perfume that I suffered allergic reaction to and the sneezing."

"Do you recall telling Cynthia that you hated her fingernails, her doll collection, her pink feminine things, her peach feminine things—"

"No," Randy interrupted.

"—in every room of your house?"

"No."

"Do you recall telling Cynthia that you hated her perfume, her pictures, her furniture, and the way she drove the cars and trucks?"

"No."

"Do you recall telling Cynthia you hated the way that she cooked?"

"Cynthia's cooking was one of the most outstanding aspects about her," Randy said, trying to struggle free.

"Do you recall telling Cynthia that you hated the

way she bought groceries too many times every week and spent too much of your money?"

"No."

"Do you recall telling Cynthia that you hated the swamp that she made you move to?"

"I recall complaining about the water problem we had on the property."

"Do you recall telling Cynthia you hated her house, her things, her money and her independent nature?"

"I don't believe I've ever used the word 'hate' in any of our conversations," Randy said.

"Did you tell her you didn't *like* her things, her money, her house and her independent nature?"

"I didn't know anything about her money or her financial situation. And her house was our house. I'm not sure what house you are referring to."

"Any house."

"I would have no reason to hate them. She had a nicer home where she lived previously than what I did, so it was very acceptable. And the house we moved into was one we both wanted."

"Do you recall telling Cynthia that you hated the way she grinds her teeth, the way she picks up your papers all the time and the way she uses all the hot water to fill up the huge bathtub for a bath?"

"The only conversation we've ever had about any teeth grinding was the fact she would do it in her sleep. And I was concerned that it would cause a dental problem. That was the only conversation we ever had regarding her teeth."

"You don't recall saying you hated the other things?"

"I'm a sound sleeper. Teeth grinding in her sleep wouldn't have bothered me."

"I see. Do you recall telling Cynthia you hated her going shopping, you hated her leaving the house at all, and you hated her driving the Isuzu Trooper?"

"No. The Trooper was hers to drive."

"How about leaving the house?"

"She was in and out of the house all day long when I was at work."

"The question I asked you, Mr. Roth, is did you tell Cynthia that you hated her leaving the house?"

"I had no control over Cindy. I never attempted to keep her in the house. She had reactions—free access to coming in the house throughout the day."

"Basically your testimony is, then, that you and Cynthia had some minor disagreements about various things, but overall your relationship was going well?"

"That was my impression of it."

"Is that the impression you conveyed to Stacey Reese when you had lunch with her before Cynthia died?"

# 52

## "Isn't It True, Mr. Roth..."

The following day was Randy's sixth day on the witness stand, and both he and Cody were getting tired. Brenneman, however, was showing no signs of letting up.

"Mr. Roth, when we recessed yesterday, I just asked you about your statements regarding the relocation of Tyson and Rylie during the press conference that you called on August 9th, 1991. Do you recall?"

"Yes, I do," Randy said.

"Isn't it true at that press conference that you misstated to the press the reason for the relocation of Tyson and Rylie?"

"I had been in control of the boys up until I believe one or two days prior to the press conference, and I had allowed them to go with relatives at the point in time where they were still staying when I received a phone call that they would not be coming back."

"You allowed them to go with relatives because relatives wanted them. But you told the press, did you not, that it was because of the media coverage that the children had been, quote, relocated. Isn't that accurate?"

"I can't have a total recollection of what I would have stated. I do recall stating to the media that I had relocated the boys."

Would it help his recollection if they replayed the tape? asked Brenneman. "Yes it would," said Randy.

"Let's see if we can't locate it, Mr. Roth," Brenneman said, and she asked Peters to find the place on the tape of Randy's press conference.

Peters found the place on the tape of Randy's press conference about the boys. The news reporter's question followed by Randy's answer came out of the television set:

" *'How did you feel about that?'*

" *'I had to relocate the kids to prevent them from being exposed to the elements of the media on my telephone and in my driveway and it's not fair—'* "

Peters stopped the tape.

"Mr. Roth, when you made that statements that you just heard, that was a lie, wasn't it?" asked Brenneman.

"I don't believe so," Randy said.

"In fact, Tyson and Rylie had been relocated, as you put it, because their mother's will gave their custody to her best friend, Lori Baker, *and you knew it,* didn't you?"

Randy insisted he was only trying to protect the boys.

"I believed it to be in the best interests of the boys to stay at relatives' homes visiting as long as possible until the media lost interest in mass publishing their exposure, which they did from the very first day of the accident."

"Actually, Mr. Roth, isn't it a fact that you answered that question in that way to attempt to gain *sympathy* for how you were being treated in this whole matter and to use the boys to get that sympathy?"

Cody objected. Sullivan agreed. Brenneman returned to the safe deposit box.

"Let's go back to the safe deposit box, Mr. Roth. You entered Cynthia's safe deposit box on July 25th, 1991. You heard Lori Baker's testimony, did you not, that the last time she saw that box it contained an original of Cynthia's will and jewelry Cynthia was saving that had belonged to her husband Tom for her sons, Tyson and Rylie? Do you recall that testimony?"

"I do. I also recall the bank representative stating that Cynthia had been in the box two times after that," said Randy.

"Mr. Roth, do you recall that Lori Baker stated very emphatically that it was Cynthia's desire to keep the jewelry that was in that box for her sons, Tyson and Rylie?"

"I recall Lori making that statement," Randy said, referring to Lori Baker's testimony.

"Well, Mr. Roth," said Brenneman, "do you have that jewelry?"

"No, I don't," said Randy.

"Did you ever see it?"

"No, I didn't."

"Is it in your possession?"

No, said Randy, he would have no use for it.

"The last person other than Cynthia, who is dead, and Lori, who testified the box was empty when she got there, the only other person to have access to that box was you, was it not, Mr. Roth?"

Cody objected again. "Overruled," said Sullivan.

"I was the last person," Randy said, "but as I stated earlier, Cynthia was in the box on two occasions between Lori having been in it and when I made my first and last visit." Randy said he thought Cindy might have removed the items from the box to spare Randy any uncomfortable feelings in case the two of them visited the box in the future.

"I see," said Brenneman drily.

Cody objected. "Your Honor, I ask that that remark be stricken."

Sullivan agreed. "It will be stricken. The jury will disregard."

But Brenneman's disbelief of Randy was a bell that could not be unrung. She returned to the custody of the boys.

"Mr. Roth, you testified that you were upset because Lori advised you that Cynthia's will placed the custody of her sons, Tyson and Rylie, with Lori Baker. Do you recall that testimony?"

"I don't believe that Lori would have stated that the will stipulated the boys were supposed to go with her," said Randy. "She told me that the boys would not be returning to the home."

"I'm more concerned about your reaction, Mr. Roth. You were upset, weren't you?" Brenneman was planting a seed here that she would soon use with devastating effect.

"I was upset that I was not involved in the decision-making process," said Randy.

"In fact, on August 1st, when you talked to Detectives Peters and Mullinax, you specifically advised them that your wife Cynthia had no will, didn't you?"

"In reference to the will, that Cynthia and I were never, [we never] reached a level where we would have obtained one," Randy said. "That would have been the answer I provided."

"You told Detectives Peters and Mullinax, [to] the best of your knowledge, [that] Cynthia had no will, yes or no?"

"She had no will between the two of us. I had never seen, I had never seen a will."

'I'm asking you what *you told* Detectives Peters and Mullinax on August the 1st, 1991, shortly after Cynthia's death," Brenneman persisted. "Did you or did you not, yes or no, tell those two detectives that Cynthia, your wife, had no will?"

"I did not believe that she had a will."

"Is that a yes, Mr. Roth?"

"I told them she didn't have a will that I was aware of."

"Isn't it a fact, Mr. Roth, that she did have a will, you found the original in the box on July 25th, and you thought that was the sole copy of the will?"

"I have never seen a will. I wouldn't know what an original or independent will would look like."

"Is that a yes or a no, Mr. Roth?"

"Will you re-ask your question?"

"Isn't it a fact that on July 25th, two days after Cynthia died, you went into the safety deposit box, you found the original of Cynthia's will, you thought you'd found the only copy, [and] you destroyed it? Isn't that a fact?"

"There was nothing in the safety deposit box when I went to the bank."

"I take it your answer is no, Mr. Roth. Is that your answer?"

"There was no will," Randy again insisted.

"No; is that your answer?"

"No, there was no will."

After a few more questions, Brenneman returned to the trap she had set earlier.

"You testified when Lori advised you that she was going to take custody, the boys were going to stay with her, Tyson and Rylie, you were upset. And isn't it true that you testified you were upset because they took control of the boys away from you without your input?"

"That was my impression, that they—she called me and told me the family had gotten together and decided the boys won't be coming back. Those were her words."

"And *your* words were, it was *the control* of the boys being removed from you that upset you. Those were your words, weren't they, Mr. Roth?"

"They took control of the boys. They took the control of any input that I might have been able to contribute to where the boys would like to stay," answered Randy.

"And *control* over Cynthia and the boys and other people in your life is very important to you, is it not?" Brenneman shot back.

Cody objected. "Overruled," said Sullivan.

"I don't believe that I'm a control-type individual," Randy said. "I allow everyone around me to have whatever input they would like to contribute to whatever we are doing."

Brenneman pressed ahead. Wasn't it true that Randy was upset mostly because if Tyson and Rylie lived with Lori Baker, he would no longer have access to their Social Security benefits?

"In fact, you were very well aware of that Social Security income, and it was *you* who was counting on that money. Isn't that a fact?" asked Brenneman.

No, said Randy.

Wasn't it true that Cindy had filed a joint income tax return with Randy for 1990, and that the return showed $6,000 in interest income, almost all of it from Cindy's investments? Yes, Randy admitted.

"In fact, the year before you met Cynthia, isn't it true that you filed an income tax return that showed that your total taxable interest income was $43?"

"That's probably true in regards to interest income, yes."

"Did you have any dividend income?"

"No, I don't."

"Did you have any investments of any kind that you reported to the IRS?"

"No, I've never had any stocks or bonds or anything along that line."

"So when you married Cynthia Roth, you certainly didn't have the big savings account, did you, Mr. Roth?" No, said Randy.

Wasn't it true that Randy applied for Social Security benefits for Greg after Cynthia's death, even though Greg was already collecting them from Jan's death? And wasn't it true that Randy told the Social Security people that Cindy and her first husband had been divorced, not that Tom was dead? In fact, wasn't it true that Randy somehow couldn't even recall Tom's name?

It was the fault of the Social Security people, Randy answered. They had sent him the forms, told him what to put on them, he said. He hadn't read them, just filled them out. It was the Social Security people who listed Cindy as having been divorced from Tom; he had nothing to do with it.

"Mr. Roth, isn't it true that what you *really* were attempting to do was to recover Social Security benefits for your son Greg, and that in fact you had intended to do that from the time that you wrote your list that we went over yesterday, your list that puts SSI right under going to the attorney and right above dealing with insurance and right above going to the bank and checking on the bank account? Isn't it a fact that you had been planning that right after Cynthia's death?"

"No, that's not a fact."

"And the reason that you did it was the same reason that you went after Social Security benefits for Jalina, it's because you *wanted the money*. Isn't that a fact?"

"I did not attempt to apply for money for Tyson and Rylie. It was my express desire to communicate where the boys were at and their status. And as a result of that, the Social Security department asked me questions as to the status of any other children that existed in the marriage."

But Brenneman was hardly interested in Randy's explanation. She was closing in for the kill.

"And isn't it a fact, Mr. Roth, that *money* is why you married Cynthia Roth?"

"No."

"And isn't it a fact, Mr. Roth, that money, insurance proceeds, is why you murdered your wife Janis?"

"That's not true at all."

"Why you murdered Cynthia, your fourth wife?"

"That's—"

"Isn't that a fact?"

"That is *not* a fact." Randy was starting to break down.

"And in fact, money has been at the root of every insurance fraud scheme that you've committed that's been testified to in front of this jury."

"That's—"

*"Isn't that a fact?"*

"That's totally incorrect. My lifestyle has never been indicative of having or controlling any large amounts of money."

"Controlling people and controlling money is what your lifestyle is all about, Mr. Roth, based on this testimony that we've heard here. Isn't that a fact?"

"No." By now, Randy was biting his words off, on the edge of tears.

"I object, Your Honor," Cody said. "That's simply argumentative."

"Well, the record will stand," said Sullivan.

"No further questions at this time," said Brenneman. Six days after Randy had first taken the stand, Brenneman was, for the moment, done with him. Now it would be up to Cody to try to rehabilitate Randy in the eyes of the jury.

"Redirect?" Sullivan asked Cody.

"Yes, Your Honor." But Cody knew it was going to be an uphill fight.

Randy was finally weeping.

# 53

## No Blueberry Pie

As the trial neared the end of its second month, fatigue was starting to get to Marilyn Brenneman, along with everyone else. After each day's session concluded, Brenneman returned to the trial team's fifth-floor conference room to prepare for the following day. In addition to preparing questions for witnesses, Brenneman and Storey had to anticipate the roadblocks the defense was still attempting to erect.

The prosecutors spent hours in the office after work, poring over witnesses' statements, formulating questions and trying to line up new witnesses to rebut Randy's testimony. Well after normal closing hours, Brenneman found herself walking down to the Seattle ferry terminal to catch the late boat back to the Puget Sound island where she lived with her husband and youngest son.

At home, Brenneman's husband cooked all the meals and kept care of the house, while Brenneman closeted herself in her study with a yellow legal pad, trying to plan ahead. On one occasion when Brenneman returned a bit earlier than expected, her husband turned to their son and asked him wryly, "Who is that strange woman?"

On the weekend before closing arguments were scheduled, Brenneman decided enough was enough. Outside, a party in progress was suddenly enlivened by a boisterous water balloon fight. Brenneman put down her legal pad and rushed outside to join the combat. Clutching a bulbous balloon in one hand, she began chasing one of her older sons amid shrieks of laughter. Just as she was about to let fly, Brenneman stepped in a hole in the ground and severely twisted her ankle. Later that afternoon at the hospital, the doctor advised her to keep off her feet. Despite the pain, Brenneman and her husband burst out laughing. Staying off her feet was going to be the one thing she could not afford to do over the next few days, when thinking on her feet was going to be her most important challenge of the trial.

A lawyer's closing argument is just that—an argument, an attempt to persuade, to convince. It is not evidence, but it is more in the nature of a summary of information, assembled in a particular order to establish the likelihood of events. In the case of a criminal trial, it is the prosecutors' job to establish that likelihood beyond a reasonable doubt. As Brenneman commenced this effort on April 21, 1992, hobbling around the courtroom with her new crutch, she knew it would be necessary to go over once again all the disparate pieces of Randy Roth's life.

"The testimony you've heard, the exhibits which have been admitted, has been substantial," she said. "They're like the pieces of a giant puzzle. But the picture before you is now clear. And it is that the defendant did indeed murder his wife, Cynthia Roth, and he did it cold-bloodedly and making it appear to have been an accident. He did it for $385,000 in insurance proceeds, her separate property, assets, and Social Security benefits.

"In this case, the evidence is overwhelming. While the defendant walked into this courtroom seven weeks ago with the presumption of innocence he was entitled to, the evidence that has been presented has proven beyond any reasonable doubt that he has committed the crimes with which he's charged."

For the next three and a half hours, Brenneman reviewed the key events in Randy's life, beginning with the marriage to Jan and ending with Randy's last illegal act, the attempt to get Social Security benefits after Cindy's death. Brenneman talked all the way to the trial's afternoon recess, endeavoring to cement all the pieces into a coherent whole. "The state," she concluded, "believes the evidence in this case is overwhelming, and the law, as applied to that evidence, should result in a verdict of guilty on all counts."

Now it would be Cody's turn.

The evidence, Cody said, simply didn't stand up to the standard of beyond a reasonable doubt. Yes, there were things that Randy said and did that might seem different from many other people. But the jury had listened to Randy on the stand for more than a week, and they should know by now that was just the way Randy was.

"There is a pattern here, that's true," Cody told the jury. "There is a pattern here of Randy Roth raising his young son Greg by himself, as a single parent himself, constantly looking for the kind of circumstance that may provide a family setting. That's about the only pattern I think you can see. And at times it's led him to have relationships with people that just simply didn't work and probably weren't going to work from the first time he considered the possibility."

Cody went on to discuss the testimony, working to point out inconsistencies, often small differences of timing or recollection. He talked for most of the rest of the day before the trial was adjourned and returned to his attack the following morning.

"Now, I suppose," he said, "if you presume guilt, you could paint every one of those pieces together as something sinister and something that indicates an intent to make certain that Cynthia Roth died. If you presume innocence, you look at that and you say, what about it actually *proves* that Randy Roth drowned his wife in the middle of the lake?

"And then what about going to the shore and acting on the shore like somebody who is not trying to cover up what they had done by acting grief-stricken, but, apparently, to try and call all the attention possible to [himself], acted in some other fashion.

"I think you know by now—and he spent a week on the stand in front of you—that in all those circumstances, Randy is Randy.

"Randy is here in part because of all the evidence that's been brought in about things that don't go directly to the death of Janis or to the death of Cynthia. He didn't react at times and places the way other people would say they think that they would.

"On the day of Cynthia Roth's death, you're talking about somebody dealing with the unique situation of going through for the second time in ten years the same occurrence, not the second murder, but a second death. . . . I don't know how I would react or anybody would react in that circumstance, whether they would do all the 'right' things or make all the 'right' moves. If you presume guilt from that, I think you'll get it. If you presume innocence, I don't see how it means anything. . . .

"Now in this country, we don't allow the police to decide who is guilty of a crime. And we don't allow the state and the prosecutor's office to decide that. We have a jury to decide that."

Cody now gave a homily about the pitfalls of circumstantial evidence, telling the jury about a blueberry pie that a farmer had presumed a puppy had eaten, based on the circumstance of finding the puppy next to an overturned, empty plate, when in fact a child had eaten the pie.

"The very next day," Cody said, "the puppy went back to the pound . . . because that, folks, is what it's like to be convicted on nothing but circumstantial evidence.

"But the state, with its presumption of guilt, has hung a cloud over Randy Roth for many months now . . . and suggested to you and everybody else that he has killed two wives and that everything about his life is representative of the idea that that's all he's made of. And it ain't there. It's just not there."

Now Brenneman had the last shot.

"This case doesn't involve a blueberry pie," she said. "And it doesn't involve a neighborhood boy who frames a small spaniel. Nobody framed Randy Roth. No witness came in here . . . and deliberately lied to you about Randy Roth.

"The defendant wanted to make sure that when he tired of the relationship he could profit from it.

"Just like, when he gets tired of an automobile, he sells it or strips it. Because he thinks of these people just like he thinks of automobiles. It's clear that's how he talks about them. They don't slip or fall, they break traction. They don't get hurt, they're 'not badly damaged.' That's the character that was revealed to you on the witness stand.

"Now, Mr. Cody has a job to do. And in doing that job he's tried to take the puzzle apart. It's my job to impress upon you the importance of putting it back together.

"Now, Cynthia Baumgartner Roth's death on July 23, 1991 was witnessed by only one person. The same person that witnessed Jan Roth's death ten years before in 1981. And Mr. Cody's argument to you is that because no one else saw the defendant kill her, you can't find him guilty.

"Let's not cover it up. That's the argument. That, just because you didn't see it, there is always going to be reasonable doubt. That's a frightening thought. Because what that means is unless the state has a confession or an eyewitness, no matter what the evidence, a person can't be found guilty. But that's not true.

"There's an old saying that if you fooled me once, shame on you. If you fooled me twice, shame on me. And that's the situation were in here today. Skamania County did an investigation and it didn't result in charges. But this isn't Skamania County. And if he fools us now, shame on us."

The fate of Randy Roth was up to the jury.

# 54 How Say You?

The following day found Brenneman and Storey back in their fifth-floor office, desultorily sifting through the rubble. Months of preparation, followed by eight weeks of intensity during the trial itself, left both of the prosecutors with a sense of having been through a hurricane. Now, as is often true in the hours after the storm, it seemed eerily quiet.

The jury had begun deliberating on the case the afternoon before, taking two hours after lunch and then calling it quits for the day. Doubtless the jury was as tired as everyone else. In the morning, they had resumed their discussions, calling almost immediately for a replay of a police videotape taken at Beacon Rock the prior December; apparently, the jury wanted to review the setting where Jan had died a decade earlier.

In the afternoon, Brenneman, Storey and their helpers worked to pack their files and stack the scores of boxes that the case had come to represent. Just after four P.M. the telephone rang. It was the bailiff in Sullivan's courtroom, calling to let them know that the verdict was in. Brenneman was shocked. "I can't believe it took so little time," she told Storey.

What did such a swift verdict mean? Brenneman was almost sure the jury would find Randy guilty, but the swiftness of a decision made her nervous. Was it possible that the prosecutors had somehow bombed, that the jury had reviewed the mountain of evidence and nevertheless decided, as Cody had implored them, that there was nothing there? Brenneman knew swift verdicts were usually a good sign for the prosecution, but still—only eight hours of deliberation after seven weeks of testimony? *We've got to get a grip here,* Brenneman thought. She and Storey headed up to the courtroom two floors above.

By the time they arrived, the word was out. The hallways were jammed with news people, along with the familiar routine of lights and cameras and microphones. Brenneman and Storey sat down, along with Peters and Mullinax. Randy was brought in as well and sat next to Cody and Muenster. The jury was called in.

"Does the jury have a verdict?"

"We do," said the foreman.

"How say you?"

"On count one, murder in the first degree, we the jury find the defendant guilty as charged."

The jury also found Randy guilty of the other two counts—theft from his homeowners insurance company, and theft from Social Security. It was a clean sweep for Brenneman, Storey and the police. Randy looked down at the floor as the verdicts were read, his face flushed. He rubbed his knuckles while the members of the jury were polled as to their individual verdicts.

Afterward, the jury was escorted out the back door of the courtroom to protect them from the news media, while Randy was taken out the front door. Again the lights flooded the hallway as photographers elbowed for position to capture the face of the man who had dominated the news for so long. At one point, a television crew tried to follow Randy and his guards into a secure elevator, precipitating a brief scuffle between the jailers and a cameraman.

Brenneman and Storey followed Randy into the hall and were mobbed by the news people, as were Cody and Muenster.

The key to the case, the prosecutors said, was that the public came forward and got involved. "If not for their willingness," Storey said, "this defendant would not have been prosecuted."

Cody looked miserable. "I don't see [murder] in the guy, and I guess I've got to know him better than anyone, certainly better than the jury." Cody was asked how he felt. He paused and grimaced. "I guess this really feels like a stillbirth—nine months of anticipation and hope down the tank."

But Muenster wasn't giving up. He was sure, he said, that Randy would be vindicated in an appeal. "He could be back here inside two years," Muenster said.

Brenneman and Storey returned to their office. In a few minutes, Sue Peters and Randy Mullinax joined them. Peters brought a bottle of champagne.

# 55 | Extreme Cruelty

On June 19, 1992, Randy was brought before Sullivan for his sentence. Brenneman and Storey had asked Sullivan to give Randy an exceptional sentence—one far longer than the normal eighteen-year minimum for first degree murder. The prosecution's recommendation of fifty-five years meant Randy would spend virtually the rest of his life in prison. The prosecutors also wanted Sullivan to bar Randy from ever marrying again without the permission of prison officials, or buying life insurance on any other person.

After hearing arguments from the prosecutors and the defense on what the sentence should be, Sullivan asked Randy if he wanted to say anything.

"No," said Randy. "I've been advised I should refrain from making a statement in view of the fact I will be pursuing an appeal."

Sullivan nodded. "All right," he said. Then he sentenced Randy to a year in prison for all the lesser theft charges.

"As to Count One," Sullivan continued, "the state of course has urged an exceptional sentence, citing several different reasons, the first being that this was a major economic offense and that there was an attempt to gain at least $300,000 or more as a result of the death.

"Certainly—perhaps sophisticated is not the best word, but certainly there was planning. [It] could well be argued . . . that the planning commenced years ago. And certainly also there was the violation of a trust situation between Mr. Roth and his wife."

But the key factor, Sullivan said, was the effect of Cindy's death on Tyson and Rylie.

"The impact on the victim's children was, I think, extreme. . . . The children were on the beach; and the event occurred . . . a mile or so out into the water. And when the boat got to shore, they observed their mother laying in the bottom of it. Also they observed the condition of her body. They observed the rather violent efforts that were made to resuscitate her, unsuccessfully. And Mr. Roth's conduct immediately following, at the hospital and when they left the hospital, I think all indicate extreme cruelty and abuse to the children, all of which was foreseeable by Mr. Roth. . . .

"I received a lot of correspondence regarding this matter," Sullivan continued. "And I suppose probably the majority of it ends up with the statement that 'Mr. Roth should be sentenced to prison for life without parole.' " The law didn't allow him to do that, he said. But there was little doubt that an exceptional sentence was justified. "And so," concluded Sullivan, "I am going to sentence Mr. Roth to a term of fifty years."

That meant, even with time off for good behavior, Randy would still have to spend at least thirty-seven years in prison—long enough to make him seventy-four when he would be released. And while Sullivan said he didn't think he had the authority to prevent Randy from ever marrying again, he could order that Randy not be allowed to marry anyone else unless the

intended new wife was completely informed about
Randy's past.

Afterward, Cody *did* file an appeal on Randy's behalf. Although Cody cited a dozen different rulings by
the court to justify the reversal of Randy's convictions, the principal issue was whether the life and
death of Janis Roth should have been admitted as
evidence. Jan's death, Cody continued to insist, was
just a prior bad act.

# EPILOGUE

In September of 1992, **Randy Roth** was imprisoned at the Washington State Penitentiary, where he joined his younger brother, Davy.

**Davy Roth,** described as an exemplary prisoner by penitentiary officials, is still scheduled for release in 1997.

**Lori Baker,** in addition to acting as the guardian for **Tyson and Rylie Baumgartner** in accordance with Cindy Baumgartner Roth's will, no longer works at Silver Lake Chapel. A separate lawsuit between Lori and Randy over Cindy's life insurance was settled, with two-thirds of the money going to Cindy's estate and the remaining third going to a trust for Greg Roth.

**Marilyn Brenneman** continues to serve as a senior deputy prosecuting attorney, still handling complex financial cases.

**Sue Peters** and **Randy Mullinax** remain detectives in the King County Police Department's Major Crimes section. Peters' next case involved a man who murdered his wife and two sons with an axe.

**Tim Brocato** left his job at the fire department and returned to work at the fiberglass factory.

**Mary Jo Phillips** remarried and had another child. Her cancer is still in remission.

**Terri McGuire** is happily married and a mother of three children. She testified for the prosecution during Randy's trial, recounting a time when Randy Roth had once saved her from drowning.

**Greg Roth** is living in another part of Washington State with his grandfather, **Gordon Roth.**

**Lizabeth Roth** still lives in the Puget Sound area. She believes both of her sons are innocent.